PRAISE FOR SUCH TROOPS AS THESE

"In his superb new book, Bevin Alexander continues to demonstrate the breadth of his historical knowledge, the keenness of his insight, and his outstanding capacity to write a compelling and engaging narrative. This is the best book on Stonewall Jackson's unique military genius and unmatched leadership published in many years. Alexander cuts through a century and a half of mythmaking about the Confederate high command to reveal not only Jackson's true genius, but to also expose the failures of Robert E. Lee and Jefferson Davis that cost the South any chance of victory."

—Colonel Jerry D. Morelock, PhD, U.S. Army (Ret.),
and editor in chief of *Armchair General*

PRAISE FOR MacARTHUR'S WAR

"Fascinating, factual, and well-documented . . . Overall, a fair portrayal of history."

—General Frederick J. Kroesen, former vice chief of staff of the
U.S. Army and commander in chief, U.S. Army Europe

"A stirring and insightful account of General Douglas MacArthur's controversial role in the Korean War that culminated . . . in one of the most dramatic incidents in American military history."

—Carlo D'Este, author of *Patton: A Genius for War*

"When President Harry Truman relieved General Douglas MacArthur of all his military commands at the height of the Korean War, it was a seminal moment in American history . . . Bevin Alexander's hard-hitting narrative captures in vivid detail the elements of that contest."

—Harry J. Middleton, founding director of the Lyndon B. Johnson
Presidential Library at the University of Texas, and author of
LBJ: The White House Years

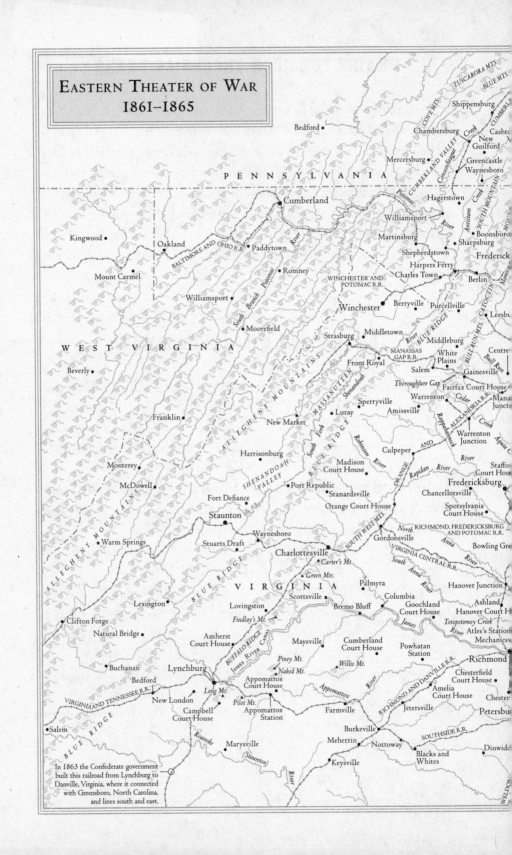

EASTERN THEATER OF WAR 1861–1865

PENNSYLVANIA

Bedford

Shippensburg

Chambersburg

Cumberland

Mercersburg

New Guilford

Greencastle

Waynesboro

Hagerstown

Williamsport

Martinsburg

Boonsboro

Sharpsburg

Shepherdstown

Frederick

Kingwood

Oakland

Paddytown

BALTIMORE AND OHIO R.R.

Harpers Ferry

Charles Town

Berlin

Mount Carmel

Romney

WINCHESTER AND POTOMAC R.R.

Williamsport

Moorefield

Winchester

Berryville

Purcellville

Leesburg

WEST VIRGINIA

Beverly

Strasburg

Middletown

Middleburg

Centre

Front Royal

MANASSAS GAP R.R.

White Plains

Salem

Gainesville

Thoroughfare Gap

Fairfax Court House

Franklin

New Market

Luray

Sperryville

Warrenton

Amissville

Warrenton Junction

Harrisonburg

Culpeper

Monterey

Madison Court House

Staffo Court Hou

Fredericksburg

McDowell

Port Republic

Stanardsville

Chancellorsville

Fort Defiance

Orange Court House

Spotsylvania Court House

Staunton

Waynesboro

RICHMOND, FREDERICKSBURG AND POTOMAC R.R.

Stuarts Draft

Gordonsville

Bowling Gr

Warm Springs

Charlottesville

VIRGINIA CENTRAL R.R.

Carter's Mt.

Green Mts.

Palmyra

Hanover Junction

VIRGINIA

Lexington

Lovingston

Scottsville

Columbia

Ashland

Bremo Bluff

Goochland Court House

Hanover Court H

Clifton Forge

Findlay's Mt.

Totopotomoy Creek

Natural Bridge

Amherst Court House

Maysville

Cumberland Court House

Powhatan Station

Atlee's Station

Mechanicsv

Buchanan

Lynchburg

Piney Mt.

Willis Mt.

Richmond

Bedford

Naked Mt.

Chesterfield Court House

New London

Appomattox Court House

Long Mt.

Pilot Mt.

Amelia Court House

Chester

VIRGINIA AND TENNESSEE R.R.

Campbell Court House

Appomattox Station

Farmville

Jetersville

RICHMOND AND DANVILLE R.R.

Petersbu

Salem

Marysville

Burkeville

Meherrin

Nottoway

SOUTHSIDE R.R.

Blacks and Whites

Dinwidd

Keysville

In 1863 the Confederate government built this railroad from Lynchburg to Danville, Virginia, where it connected with Greensboro, North Carolina, and lines south and east.

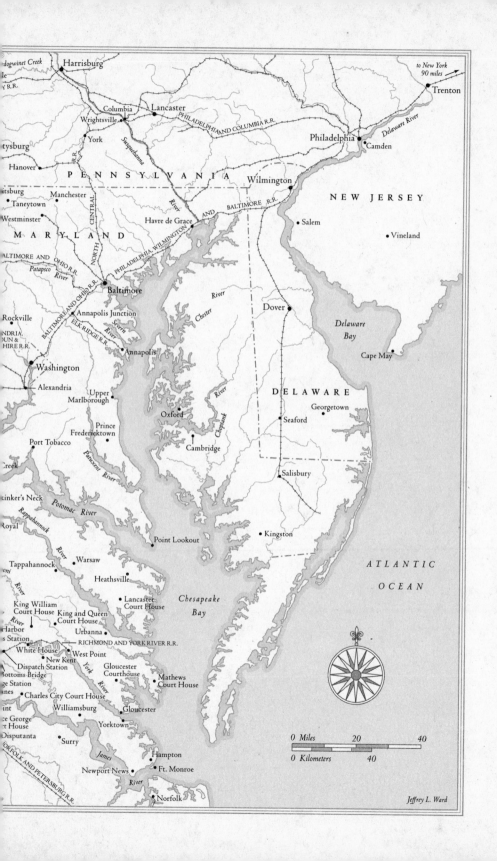

SUCH TROOPS AS THESE

The Genius and Leadership
of Confederate General
Stonewall Jackson

———•———

BEVIN ALEXANDER

BERKLEY CALIBER, NEW YORK

**BERKLEY
CALIBER**

**An imprint of Penguin Random House LLC
375 Hudson Street, New York, New York 10014**

Copyright © 2014 by Bevin Alexander.
Penguin supports copyright. Copyright fuels creativity, encourages diverse voices,
promotes free speech, and creates a vibrant culture. Thank you for buying an authorized
edition of this book and for complying with copyright laws by not reproducing, scanning, or
distributing any part of it in any form without permission. You are supporting writers and
allowing Penguin to continue to publish books for every reader.

BERKLEY CALIBER and its colophon are trademarks of Penguin Random House LLC.
For more information about the Penguin Group, visit penguin.com.

ISBN: 978-0-425-27130-8

The Library of Congress has catalogued the Berkley Caliber hardcover edition as follows:

Alexander, Bevin.
Such troops as these : the genius and leadership of Confederate General Stonewall Jackson /
Bevin Alexander.
p.   cm.
Includes bibliographical references and index.
ISBN 978-0-425-27129-2
1. Jackson, Stonewall, 1824–1863.   2. Jackson, Stonewall, 1824–1863—Military leadership.
3. Virginia—History—Civil War, 1861–1865—Campaigns.   4. United States—History—
Civil War, 1861–1865—Campaigns.   5. Command of troops—Case studies.
6. Generals—Confederate States of America—Biography.   I. Title.
E467.1.J15A43 2014
973.7'3092—dc23
[B]
2014009038

PUBLISHING HISTORY
Berkley Caliber hardcover edition / September 2014
Berkley Caliber trade paperback edition / September 2015

PRINTED IN THE UNITED STATES OF AMERICA

10   9   8   7   6   5   4   3

Cover design by Richard Hasselberger.
Interior maps by Jeffrey L. Ward.
Interior text design by Laura K. Corless.

Penguin
Random
House

CONTENTS

MAPS

ACKNOWLEDGMENTS

I am extremely grateful to Natalee Rosenstein, vice president and senior executive editor of the Berkley Publishing Group, for her splendid, insightful, and discerning support of this project. It has been a pleasure working with her and with Robin Barletta, editorial assistant at Berkley. Robin is a most remarkably sensitive, understanding, and efficient person who expedited the project most wonderfully. She corrected all my errors, removed all roadblocks, and turned the entire endeavor into an adventure.

Richard Hasselberger produced a superb cover design that conveys the content of the book most effectively. Laura K. Corless conceived a tasteful and truly beautiful design for the interior text. My longtime cartographer, Jeffrey L. Ward, drew the exceptionally accurate maps that allow the reader to follow exactly where the actions took place. Clear and comprehensible maps are mandatory for understanding military operations, and Jeffrey, in my opinion, draws the best maps in America today.

I have relied for a long time on my agent, Agnes Birnbaum, for her friendship, sage advice, and surpassing knowledge of the publishing industry, but mostly for the inspiring example she presents of a caring and considerate human being.

Finally, I am most honored that my sons Bevin Jr., Troy, and David, and my daughters-in-law, Mary and Kim, have always supported me steadfastly in my long and exhausting writing ventures.

INTRODUCTION

—◆—

Jackson's Recipes for Victory

Thomas J. (Stonewall) Jackson was a unique, incredibly complicated figure. He was committed to his Presbyterian religious faith, devoted to his second wife, so reserved that even his close friends seldom knew what he was thinking, dedicated to duty and the cause of Southern independence, and by far the greatest general ever produced by the American people.

Very early, Jackson discerned a way for the South to win the Civil War with speed and few losses. He recognized that the North, with three times the population of the South and eleven times its industry, was so sure of victory that it had sent practically all of its military forces into the South and had left the North almost entirely un-defended. The only thing the South had to do to win, Jackson saw, was to invade the eastern states of the Union, where the vast majority of Northern industry was located and where most of its population resided. Before any Union armies could be extricated from the South, Confederate troops could cut the single railway corridor connecting

Washington with Northern states, force the Abraham Lincoln administration to abandon the capital, and, by threatening the railroads, factories, farms, and mines along the great industrial corridor from Baltimore to southern Maine, compel the Northern people to give up the struggle.

A similar assault on Southern economic prosperity was precisely the strategy that Lincoln was using to conquer the South. But the Confederate president, Jefferson Davis, was a decidedly third-rate leader who possessed extremely little vision or imagination. He was committed to passive defense of the South, despite the fact that it was guaranteed to fail.[1] Davis refused to endorse Jackson's strategy, although he pressed it on Davis four times.

Once Jackson realized that Davis was never going to authorize a decisive invasion of the North, he developed another method of winning the war. He saw that two new weapons had made attacks against defended positions almost certain to fail. The first weapon was the single-shot Minié-ball rifle, with a range four times that of the old standard infantry weapon, the smoothbore musket. The second was the lightweight "Napoleon" cannon (named after Napoleon III, not the emperor) that could be rolled up to the firing line and could spew out clouds of deadly metal fragments called canister into the faces of advancing enemy troops. Jackson saw that the South could be victorious if it induced Northern armies to attack well-emplaced Confederate positions. The Union armies would inevitably be defeated, and the Confederates could swing around the flank of the demoralized Northerners and force them into retreat or surrender.

None of the other commanders on either side identified the revolutionary implications of these two weapons, however, and Jackson had an extremely difficult time trying to convince the senior Confederate commander in the East, Robert E. Lee, to follow his new system.

Jackson recognized that there is only one fundamental principle of military strategy, or the successful conduct of war. It is to attack the enemy where he is *not*. That is, to exert force where there is little or no opposition. All the other axioms of warfare can be reduced to variations on this single elementary theme. The ancient Chinese military sage Sun Tzu encapsulated the idea in a single sentence around 400 B.C.: "The way to avoid what is strong is to strike what is weak."[2] Jackson knew nothing of Sun Tzu, but he developed the same understanding on his own.

This is an extremely difficult concept to get across, however. Warfare to most people does not seem to be so simple. They view it through the lens of very different experiences. Human beings built their concept of warfare in the Stone Age. The small bands and tribes into which the human race was divided found that direct confrontation was the most likely way to deter opposing bands and tribes from encroaching on their safe havens and hunting grounds.[3] We have carried this concept of frontal challenge forward into modern times. It is deeply ingrained in the human psyche. We label persons who act otherwise as sly and shifty; we say that they blindside other people, that they stab them in the back. We revile and despise such people, while we admire people who act in a direct, straightforward manner.

Over the aeons, highly observant individuals have occasionally seen, however, that indirection is the most effective way to achieve success, in military and in other matters, and they have attacked their opponent's weakness. But these have been rare occurrences. In times of stress we usually revert to the instinctive response we learned in the Stone Age. We challenge the opponent right in front of us.

Therefore it is the extraordinary person who can avoid straight confrontation and can recognize the wisdom of Sun Tzu, who said: "All warfare is based on deception."[4] Stonewall Jackson was such an extraordinary person. And he saw clearly ways to win by going around the enemy, not confronting him headlong.

The Civil War of 1861–65 was the greatest crisis ever to befall the American Union. This war pitted the industrial North against the agricultural South. Though the population of the United States in 1860 was only 31.5 million people, less than a tenth of what it is today, 600,000 men were killed in the war, far more than in any other war in American history, including World War II.

The primary fact about the South was that it was an overwhelmingly agrarian, preindustrial society within a larger society that was rapidly industrializing. Because of the railroad, this larger industrial society was spreading its influence and power over the entire country. Until the coming of the railroads in the 1840s, North and South had been able to maintain radically different economies without great conflict because they interacted with each other largely at the peripheries.

For example, New England was developing a textile industry that used Southern cotton as its main feedstock. But, because roads were atrocious, it was easier to import cotton from the South and to export finished textiles to the South by ship rather than by land. Therefore, New England competed directly with Britain for the South's raw cotton and for the South's finished textile trade. This competition kept cotton prices high and finished product prices low. Much the same was true of iron and steel. The North produced some metal products, but it competed directly with Britain's vast iron and steel industry.

By 1860, however, the extension of the railroads had made feasible the economical shipping of Northern industrial products throughout the country. This had aroused a tremendous move in the North to establish high tariffs to protect Northern industry from the far larger and more proficient British factories. In other words, Northern industrialists wanted to create a closed American economy in which only their products would be available. And these products would cost more than British products because American industry was newer and less efficient than British industry. The South was being asked to pay to strengthen Northern industry, while at the same time it was being asked to weaken Britain, by far the greatest market for its cotton. Also, Northern textile manufacturers, with reduced competition from Britain, would have to pay less for Southern cotton. Since, therefore, a high tariff would directly damage Southern pocketbooks, Southerners were violently opposed to it—and this conflict played an important role in the division of North and South.

The key immediate dispute, however, was over the continued bondage of 3.5 million black slaves in fifteen Southern states. Only a fraction of the Southern people owned slaves. Of the 1.6 million white families in 1860, only one in four owned any slaves, and only 133,000 owned ten or more slaves, or about one family in thirteen. Only 7,000 families owned fifty or more slaves, or one family in 228.[5] The overwhelming majority of slaves were owned by an extremely small, wealthy aristocracy that possessed most of the good farmland and that dominated the South politically.

Although slavery was extremely controversial, and people North and South knew it was evil and had to be ended, it was the foundation of Southern agriculture. Cotton, produced largely on big plantations in the Deep South, constituted by far the greatest portion of the region's wealth. The Industrial Revolution had not mechanized agriculture to any substantial degree, and farmers and planters relied overwhelmingly on hand labor to produce all crops, but most especially cotton, whose fiber bolls had to be picked one at a time. Therefore, eliminating slavery in one swift process would devastate the South's economy, and, if slave owners were not compensated, would not only impoverish the elite landed aristocracy, but also the overwhelming bulk of the Southern people, white and black.

The only equitable solution was to pay the owners the value the slaves represented. But the politicians of the North were not inclined to induce the Northern people to foot most of the cost of such a transformation. This was a profoundly wrong decision, for the cost of the conflict in money alone—not to speak of the human cost and the social upheaval that it caused—was at least twice what it would have taken to purchase all of the slaves and give every freed family forty acres and a mule.[6]

The issue came to a head in the presidential election of 1860. Abolitionists, who were pushing for an immediate end of slavery and nothing for the planters, gained momentum, and an antislavery Republican, Abraham Lincoln, won the election. Southern planters feared he would force through laws demanded by the abolitionists.

No aristocracy ever voluntarily gives up its privileges. Every aristocracy is willing to bring down the entire social edifice to preserve its favored position. The British aristocrats refused to grant the American colonies any political rights. This set off the American Revolution of 1775 to 1783, causing the aristocrats to lose the greatest empire Britain ever possessed. The French aristocracy refused to offer the peasants and the merchants any rights and brought on the French Revolution of 1789, which destroyed the aristocracy but also threw French society into chaos.

The Southern aristocrats were no different from their British and French counterparts. Since they controlled the political fortunes of the Deep South, they passed secession ordinances in the seven Deep South states in late 1860 and early 1861. These acts catered to the aristocrats' economic interests, and also reflected their belief that the Constitution gave them the legal right to do so. Lincoln denied this right, and in April 1861, he called on the remaining states to quash what he called the "rebellion" of these seven states. Forced to choose between Lincoln's demand and what they believed to be morally correct and honorable, four Upper South states that had remained steadfastly loyal—North Carolina, Virginia, Tennessee, and Arkansas—refused to accept the idea of forcing their "erring sisters" back into the Union at the bayo-net's point, and seceded as well.

The entire issue of the Civil War was summarized brilliantly by an astute South Carolina woman, Mary Boykin Chesnut (1823–86), wife of a U.S. senator who became a Confederate officer. She wrote in her diary on July 8, 1862: "This war was undertaken by us to shake off the yoke of foreign invaders, so we consider our cause righteous. The Yankees, since the war has begun, have discovered it is to free the slaves they are fighting, so their cause is noble."[7]

With both sides so starkly divided regarding even what the war was all about, there was little hope of compromise. Each side was con-vinced of the justice of its cause. The war was going to be pursued to the bitter end.

This book is a very human story of Stonewall Jackson, who was caught in the vortex of this great crisis, and of how he made the judg-ments that could have won the war for the South and prevented the South from descending into catastrophe. In carrying out his mission, Jackson demonstrated a transcendent superiority over every other gen-eral he encountered. He ranks as one of the supreme military geniuses in world history. Unfortunately for the South, the Confederacy was ruled by leaders who possessed none of Jackson's vision.

CHAPTER 1

The Making of a Soldier

Thomas Jonathan Jackson was born January 21, 1824, in Clarksburg, Virginia (now West Virginia), into a family that was beset with tragedy. On March 6, 1826, when Thomas was two years old and his brother Warren was five years old, his sister Elizabeth, six years old, died of typhoid fever. Only twenty days later his father, Jonathan, an unsuccessful attorney, also died of typhoid fever. The very next day, Thomas's mother, Julia, gave birth to a daughter, who was named Laura.[1]

Julia, twenty-eight years old, was left destitute with two small boys and an infant daughter. She had to give up her home and nearly all of her resources to pay off her husband's debts. She barely supported herself and her family by moving to a donated one-room cottage, where she took in sewing and taught paying children school. Julia herself began to weaken with the first signs of tuberculosis. Realizing that her health was slipping, Julia married Blake B. Woodson, an attorney fifteen years her senior, in 1830.

The next year Woodson became clerk of court of newly created

Fayette County, in the high mountains 125 miles south of Clarksburg. The family moved to the county seat of Ansted, but Julia's health was now deteriorating badly, and she was forced to send her son Warren, now ten years old, to live with her brother, Alfred Neale, and his family in Parkersburg, on the Ohio River, and to send Thomas and Laura to live with their uncle, Cummins Jackson, twenty-nine years old, who operated a farm and two water-powered mills, one lumber, the other grist, at a place named Jackson's Mill on the West Fork River, four miles north of Weston, and eighteen miles south of Clarksburg. In December 1831 Julia died, leaving her children as orphans.

Young Thomas and Laura were distraught at losing the love and devotion of their mother. Although they were welcomed in the Jackson household, the children found no father figure and little comfort in Cummins Jackson. He was tall, strong, generous to his friends, and, at the time, successful in business. But he was also unscrupulous and was accused of taking over the estate of his father, Edward Jackson, and denying other members of the family their rightful share. He was extremely litigious and filed lawsuits for many causes—delinquent accounts, land claims, timber rights, and other complaints. His legal costs as well as his fondness for gambling, horse racing, and drinking caused a slow but steady decline in his fortunes over the years.

Young Tom Jackson learned a great deal at Jackson's Mill about farming, horses, and lumbering, but he had only one close and dear confidante, his sister Laura. They faced the world together. In 1835, however, the woman who had mostly tended the children, their step-grandmother, Elizabeth Brake Jackson, died at Jackson's Mill. Laura was sent to Parkersburg to join the Neale family, and Tom was sent to live with his aunt Polly, his father's sister, and her husband, Isaac Brake, on a farm four miles from Clarksburg. The separation from Laura was most painful to Tom, and the situation at his new home was disastrous. Isaac Brake treated Tom as an outsider, subjecting him to verbal abuse and at least one severe whipping. Tom endured the trauma for a year, then, twelve years old, he ran away to a cousin in Clarksburg. He politely asked for food and a place to stay for the night. When the cousin remonstrated with Tom to go back to Aunt Polly's, he answered: "Maybe I ought to, ma'am, but I am not going to."[2]

The next day Tom walked the eighteen miles to Jackson's Mill. Cummins Jackson was happy to take him in. But the experience of losing the companionship of Laura and the ill treatment of his uncle Isaac Brake left a profound and permanent mark on Thomas Jackson. They contributed to the extreme reticence to show his feelings and express his thoughts that characterized him as an adult.

Another fact became apparent after he returned to Jackson's Mill—he was an orphan with no economic prospects whatsoever. Cummins Jackson offered no possibilities. Tom realized that whatever he achieved he would have to do alone. He saw that his only real hope was to gain an education. For the next six years, Tom spent much of his time trying to acquire knowledge. Cummins Jackson was not interested in helping, but Tom finally prevailed on him to establish a small school at the mill for boys, taught by a young man, Robert P. Rhea, who had a better-than-average education. The school, the first Tom had ever attended, opened the floodgates of Tom's desire for knowledge.

Tom was not a great scholar, but he possessed an extraordinary attribute. He could concentrate wholly on a subject, losing sight of everything else until he had solved the problem at hand. This ability to become absorbed in a subject, to exclude all extraneous elements in order to understand fully a subject's ramifications and extent, is a mark of genius, especially military genius.[3] Nobody noticed this at the time. But when students of military leadership in later times looked back on Jackson's origins, they saw that its appearance so early marked him as possessing a brain of exceptional strength, originality, and power.

In 1837 Tom was one of six indigent children taught by a prominent

Weston citizen, Phillip Cox Jr., and in 1839 he studied for several weeks with Weston's resident scholar, Colonel Alexander Scott Withers, who formed a special attachment to Tom. Other local people encouraged Tom's interest in books by lending him volumes from their shelves. Even so, Tom's education was spotty, undirected, and incomplete.

A further element of deep sadness struck Tom in November 1841 when his brother, Warren, who was teaching in Upshur County to the east of Weston, died of tuberculosis. Now only his sister Laura in Parkersburg was left as a member of his immediate family. In January 1842 Tom reached his eighteenth birthday. He had attained almost his full height, just below six feet. He was slender and strong, with brown hair, blue-gray eyes, and a bronzed complexion from outdoor life. But his prospects were as dismal as ever.

Then, suddenly, everything changed. Samuel L. Hays, congressman for the district including Clarksburg and Weston, announced that he would shortly interview candidates for an appointment to the United States Military Academy at West Point, New York. Tom saw at once that this offered everything he was searching for.

Tom knew only that West Point had a high reputation and that it offered a college education at public expense. But, over the past quarter century, the academy had become a tremendously important factor in the development of the United States. The War of 1812 had revealed that the nation's reliance on state militias for defense was totally inadequate. The politically appointed and generally unskilled officers of the state militias were almost uniformly incompetent and incapable of leading men into battle. A few outstanding commanders emerged during the war, especially Andrew Jackson, who defeated the British at New Orleans, and Winfield Scott, who conducted excellent campaigns around Niagara Falls. But the nation could not depend on the fortuitous appearance of skilled generals after a war had begun. It needed military officers who already had been trained.

National leaders found a vehicle for change in the United States Military Academy. It had been established in 1802, but had played an insignificant role to date. Under President James Madison, the academy was reorganized and given additional support. And, in 1817, it received an inspired leader, Colonel Sylvanus Thayer. By the end of his tenure in 1833, Thayer had built a school that was producing an entirely new kind of military leader. He prevailed on the U.S. government to foot all the costs of the school and of the cadets, and for congressmen and senators to appoint cadets from their states and districts. In this fashion, Thayer created a *democratic* officers' corps drawn from the entire population of the United States. These citizen-soldiers reflected all the concepts of freedom, independence, and equality that permeated the American population.

In contrast, the military schools of Europe were largely limited to the aristocracy or the extremely well off. Their guiding philosophy was upholding the social and economic privileges of the upper classes, not, as was the driving ethos of West Point, to promote democracy. For the foreseeable future, the United States was not going to be a land of a huge professional standing army, and American officers were not going to constitute a separate, aloof social class, like the aristocratic *Junkers* who dominated the Prussian army, or the less professional but still detached gentry who held most of the places in the British army.

Under the inspiration of Colonel Thayer, West Point began producing officers who were competent and skilled, and who could adjust to and exploit the fluid, dynamic American society around them. West Point also became the top engineering school as well as one of the leading institutions of higher learning in the nation.

Four candidates emerged to take up Congressman Hays's appointment: Tom, Gibson J. Butcher, and two others, both of whom fell by the wayside. Butcher, a local acquaintance of Tom, had far better educational preparation, however, and Hays awarded the appointment to him. It was a crushing blow to Tom Jackson. He had no other plan to fall back on, and could see only gloom in his future.

But an unexpected event took place. When Gibson Butcher arrived at West Point on June 2, 1842, he found the stern atmosphere and rigid discipline not at all to his liking. Without saying anything to anybody, Butcher turned around and went back to Weston. One of Tom's friends discovered that Butcher had returned home. Tom saw a chance to take up the appointment, but West Point's term began in less than three weeks. Tom frantically rushed around Weston seeking, and getting, endorsements from leading citizens that he could present to Congressman Hays.

On a morning in mid-June 1842, Tom, clad in homespun, scuffed shoes, and a floppy wagoner's hat, all his personal possessions stuffed into a couple of saddlebags, bid farewell to Cummins Jackson, caught the eastbound stagecoach from Clarksburg, and got off at Green Valley Depot, sixteen miles east of Cumberland, Maryland, the farthest western point the Baltimore & Ohio Railroad had yet reached. Taking his first train ride, Tom arrived at Hays's office in Washington on June 17. He informed the congressman that Butcher had left the academy, and presented his letters of endorsement. Hays immediately wrote the secretary of war, John C. Spencer, recommending Tom for the place. Spencer made the appointment the next day, conditional on Tom's passing West Point's entrance exam.

Hays urged Tom to remain in Washington a few days to see the sights, but Tom was determined to get to the academy as quickly as possible. He made only a single tourist detour, climbing to the roof of the unfinished Capitol and gazing out over the city. Tom caught the northbound afternoon train, riding it all night to New York City. He made his way to the docks, and caught a Hudson River ferry, which deposited him on the boat landing at West Point on Sunday, June 19, 1842.

Tom passed his entrance exam, but he was woefully unprepared for college work. He was also woefully unprepared to mingle with the other cadets on a friendly, casual basis. He was solitary and awkward to begin with. And most of his fellow cadets were from far wealthier families and most were much more at ease in social situations than he. Tom also realized that he had to devote his mind fully to his subjects, for the academy dismissed all cadets who failed to keep up their work. As a result, Tom immediately got a reputation as an aloof, morose, silent, and unapproachable person. He accordingly made few friends at West Point. But he survived the intense discipline and work of learning to march and to obey the stern regulations of the academy, and he also survived the academic rigors of the classroom, but only after unrelenting, dogged work.

His first summary examination in January 1843 was almost his last. Of the 101 cadets in his class, he stood sixty-second in mathematics and eighty-eighth in French, but he barely passed. From then on, his academic path was upward, although at an extremely slow pace. Of the seventy-nine cadets still remaining in his class in January 1844, Tom was twenty-first in mathematics, sixty-first in French, fifty-eighth in grammar, but seventy-fourth in drawing. In subsequent evaluations, Jackson continued to rise slowly, reaching seventeenth among the fifty-nine cadets to graduate in June 1846. But he never excelled in academic studies. He also did not attain cadet rank, a mark of his unpopularity at the school. He served his senior year as a private in the ranks.

The West Point class of 1846 graduated just as the United States was entering into war with Mexico. The war was caused primarily because many Americans believed that the United States had a "manifest destiny" to expand all the way to the Pacific Ocean. Under President James K. Polk, the United States sought to acquire a huge region that Mexico possessed, all the territory from Texas west to California.

Brevet (provisional) Second Lieutenant Thomas J. Jackson had the great fortune to take part in the key campaign of the war, General Winfield Scott's drive to seize Mexico City in 1847. This was one of the most successful campaigns ever undertaken in all military history. With an army far inferior in size to the Mexican forces confronting him, Scott made an unopposed amphibious landing at Mexico's main seaport, Veracruz, marched 270 miles across the high mountains in the center of Mexico, broke through numerous barriers, and overwhelmed fiercely contested fortresses at the gates of Mexico City. Nowhere was he defeated, or even severely checked. In the last stage of his drive against the capital, Scott had fewer than a third the troops that the Mexicans had arrayed against him.

Jackson, who commanded artillery sections in a number of intense battles, had a marvelous school in which to learn about warfare. He took brilliant advantage of his opportunity, observing at first hand how direct attacks against strongly fortified and defended positions could result in enormous casualties and failure while, on the other hand, flanking movements around a defended enemy position could avoid these losses and could achieve victory at minimum cost.

In learning how to conduct warfare correctly, there is no satisfactory alternative to personal, up-front observation of battle. How troops actually maneuver and how they actually respond to challenges depends on the circumstances they encounter on the ground. Theoretical students of warfare, commanders without battle experience, and amateur armchair generals can spin out plans for wonderful movements and airy sweeps that achieve glorious imaginary victories. But the precise problems and conditions that commanders and their troops face in real combat are much different and much harder. Actual combat

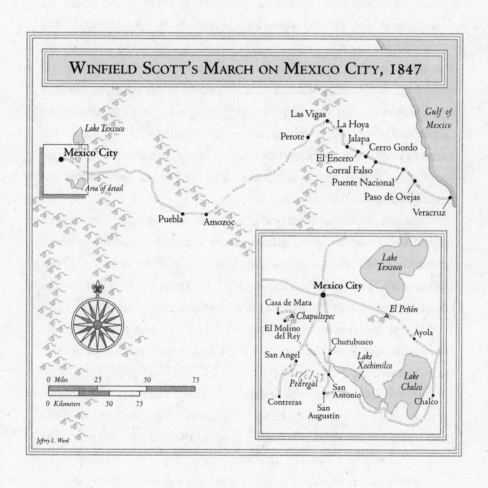

WINFIELD SCOTT'S MARCH ON MEXICO CITY, 1847

Gulf of Mexico

Las Vigas
La Hoya
Perote
Jalapa
Cerro Gordo
El Encero
Corral Falso
Puente Nacional
Paso de Ovejas
Veracruz

Lake Texcoco
Mexico City
Area of detail

Puebla
Amozoc

0 Miles   25   50   75
0 Kilometers   50   75

Lake Texcoco

Mexico City
Casa de Mata
Chapultepec
El Molino del Rey
Churubusco
San Angel
Lake Xochimilco
Pedregal
Contreras
San Antonio
San Augustín
El Peñón
Ayola
Lake Chalco
Chalco

Jeffrey L. Ward

and actual campaigns are always far more complicated than paper exercises, and they are subject to immense error or misapplication.

Beyond this, learning profound lessons by personal observation requires an individual who can actually *see* what is happening and can actually *comprehend* what is taking place. History proves conclusively that Jackson *did* see and *did* comprehend the lessons taught in the campaign to capture Mexico City, for he not only summarized his knowledge in 1862 in a talk with one of his officers, John D. Imboden,[4] he also applied the lessons in later campaigns. It became clear in later years, however, that Captain Robert E. Lee, who was exposed to the same examples in the Mexican campaign as Jackson, did *not* draw the correct conclusions, although he was on Scott's staff and played a far more prominent role than did Jackson. In later years, Lee ignored the lessons that Scott had taught.

President Polk authorized Scott's invasion of Veracruz because the Americans could achieve nothing decisive by driving into northern Mexico from Texas. In 1846 an American army under Zachary Taylor advanced to Saltillo, 150 miles south of the Texas-Mexico border, but could not cross the forbidding desert that stretched 250 miles to San Luis Potosí. Because the Mexicans possessed no navy, a good alternative was to seize Veracruz and advance over the national highway from there to the capital.

The Mexicans were well aware that the Americans intended to land at Veracruz, but they failed to reinforce the garrison of 4,400 men. And the commander, Juan Morales, showed no initiative. The 10,000 Americans came ashore on March 9, 1847, in surfboats about three miles south of the city, against no opposition. Jackson got his first lesson in defensive possibilities on this day. For the Mexicans accurately anticipated the spot the Americans were going to land. If General Morales had merely hidden cannons behind the site and had rolled them forward as the Americans approached, he could have sunk many of the surfboats and decimated any soldiers who reached the beach. But Morales did not make any attempt at defense. He waited passively for the blow to be struck, withdrawing his troops behind the walls of Veracruz. It was a simple matter, therefore, for Scott's cannons to pound the garrison into surrender on March 29, 1847.

Scott gathered supplies and moved out toward Mexico City on April 8. He wanted to get into the highlands as quickly as possible, because yellow fever was endemic in the lowlands along the gulf, and was certain to break out as the hottest months approached. Yellow fever is a deadly virus, and its spread by mosquito bites was unknown until the turn of the twentieth century.

The Mexican president and commander, Antonio López de Santa Anna, tried to stop Scott before he could reach fever-free Jalapa, 4,700 feet above sea level in the Sierra Madre Mountains, seventy-four miles inland from Veracruz. Santa Anna assembled 12,000 troops at Cerro Gordo (Fat Mountain), ten miles east of Jalapa. He placed most of his troops right on the national highway, directly barring the pass through the mountains. When General Scott approached, he saw that Santa Anna had made no provision for an envelopment of his position. While holding a few forces in the roadway to threaten the pass, Scott sent a larger force, including Jackson's artillery section, around the northern flank of the Mexican position, where it emerged on the enemy rear, completely surprising the Mexican defenders and sending them into panicked flight. The Mexican army disintegrated, and Scott marched without further ado to Jalapa, then on to Puebla, only eighty miles east of Mexico City.

Cerro Gordo was a solid object lesson for a young officer like Jackson. Scott had applied one of the oldest maxims of warfare. He made threatening moves against the main enemy force, thereby holding that force at the Cerro Gordo pass. Meanwhile, Scott delivered an indirect strike with another force on the enemy rear, throwing the entire enemy army into chaos. That Santa Anna should have anticipated this flanking move is obvious. But Scott knew that generals over the aeons have tended to build their strongest defenses at places of the most evident danger, in this case the pass at Cerro Gordo. Most generals fail to anticipate that the enemy might merely fake an assault on the obvious target, and might land his real blow elsewhere. Scott recognized that Santa Anna was such an unimaginative officer, and that he could safely strike Santa Anna's rear.

By the time Scott reached Puebla, he had lost 3,000 of his men, volunteers whose one-year enlistments were expiring. As these 3,000 men marched back to Veracruz for the voyage home, President Polk and Secretary of War William I. Marcy were creating new regiments to replace them. But this would take time, and meanwhile Scott, with only 7,000 men, was immobilized at Puebla.

The major danger that Scott was facing was so-called guerrilla attacks on his supply line back to Veracruz. These guerrillas were really largely bandits, not organized Mexican army forces. But the attacks were making it too hazardous to dispatch supply convoys to and from Veracruz without strong escorts. On June 4, 1847, therefore, Scott abandoned all stations between Veracruz and Puebla, thereby cutting his army off from the coast. With no supply line, his army would have to live off the land.

It was quite plain that Santa Anna now possessed a superb opportunity to besiege the Americans at Puebla and, by denying them food, force their surrender. But Santa Anna did not make any effort to do so. He did not even dispatch forces to prevent Americans from sending foraging expeditions into the countryside to procure food and fodder. Indeed, the Americans were left wholly at ease at Puebla. This, too, was a tremendous object lesson for young officers, for it is a monstrous military mistake to allow an enemy force to abide without danger inside one's own country. The enemy should be attacked and harassed in every way possible. Most especially, his food and fodder supply should be threatened. It is evident that Jackson, while he waited with other Americans at Puebla, learned this lesson well, for he applied it to tremendous effect in a campaign that was to come.

On July 8, 1847, Scott finally received 4,500 new troops, and on August 6 got 2,400 more. Leaving a garrison at Puebla, Scott set forth the next day on the march on Mexico City. He had 11,000 men. Santa Anna meanwhile had assembled an army of 36,000 men, but no better trained or led than the army that had bolted at Cerro Gordo. He intended to remain on the defensive, relying on the fact that Mexico City is built in the Valley of Mexico on a former Aztec island in a once-huge lake that was slowly drying. The valley floor contained six lakes, extensive marshes and low-lying fields. Mexico City could be approached only along raised roads and causeways. Santa Anna figured that his troops, placed along these narrow elevated avenues, could stop any American advance.

Confident that the Americans would approach along the national highway from the east, Santa Anna posted thirty cannons and 7,000 troops atop El Peñon, a 450-foot hill just south of the highway, and eight miles east of the capital.

When the American advance guard arrived east of El Peñon on August 12, 1847, engineer Captain Robert E. Lee, on Scott's staff, rode ahead to confirm that the Mexicans were in force there and that seizing the position would be costly, since the only approach was along the causeway with a wet marsh on either side. However, Santa Anna had already failed to anticipate a tactical movement around his massed army at Cerro Gordo, and Scott figured that he might fail to anticipate a similar strategic movement around his entire position in front of Mexico City.

Accordingly, Scott told Captain Lee to search for a different avenue of approach. Lee found one in a road seventeen miles to the south. This road ran around the southern edges of lakes Chalco and Xochimilco to the town of San Augustín, nine miles due south of Mexico City.

Scott ordered the army to swing around the lakes to San Augustín, a distance of twenty-five miles. The Americans emerged on August 18 at San Augustín. By this time Santa Anna had figured out the direction of the march and had assembled more than 20,000 men, twice the size of Scott's army, along a four-mile east-west line about six miles south of the city. Santa Anna's main defensive bastion was the village of San Antonio, a couple miles north of San Augustín and on the main avenue leading to Mexico City from the south. Santa Anna believed his forces there were safe. Directly on the east was soft, marshy ground next to Lake Xochilmilco. Directly to the west was the Pedregal, an egg-shaped lava field two and a half miles wide and a couple miles deep, reputed to be impassable by man or beast.

When American cavalry rode up the avenue toward San Antonio, they met a hail of cannon fire. Once again Scott faced a heavily armed Mexican force emplaced in a strong defensive position. But unlike Cerro Gordo, the San Antonio position could not be turned by flanking it. This called for an even wider turning movement. A strike to the east was impossible because of the lakes and the marshy ground. A strike to the west seemed just as fruitless because of the Pedregal.

But Scott told Captain Lee to see if he could find some path over this lava field. Lee located a rough trail on the southern edge that connected with a north-south road west of the lava field that ran through the village of San Angel and connected to elevated causeways that led into Mexico City. Scott set soldiers to work with pickaxes and shovels to carve out a rough road over which infantry could march and cannons and artillery caissons could roll. Scott then ordered about half of his army, including Jackson's artillery section, to advance along the trail on August 19.

Just west of the Pedregal, the Americans encountered the division of

General Gabriel Valencia, a political rival of Santa Anna, who had shifted his 5,000-man force from the main Mexican defensive position at San Angel to the village of Contreras, a couple miles south. This move was in direct disobedience of orders from Santa Anna, since it split the Mexican forces. But Valencia had visions of achieving glory by defeating the Yankees.

In the early afternoon of August 19, three American brigades, 4,500 men, including Jackson's guns and other cannons, moved between Contreras and San Angel, and cut Valencia off from the rest of the Mexican army. During the whole afternoon, the Americans endured heavy artillery fire against their positions, but they held on grimly. If the Mexicans had organized infantry assaults from San Angel in one direction and Contreras in the other, the three American brigades might have been crushed. But Santa Anna did nothing. That night Santa Anna sent Valencia an order to slip his men northward in the darkness past the Americans. But Valencia refused. On the morrow, he replied, he would smash the Americans.

During this same night, American engineers found a path that circled around Contreras, and allowed picked American units to assemble in secret to the south and to the west of Valencia's division. At dawn on August 20, the Americans attacked directly from the north at the same time as the forces hidden on the south and west struck. Valencia's division collapsed in chaos, and the survivors flew in panic in all directions.

Santa Anna immediately escaped northward, ordering the forces at San Antonio, on the east, to withdraw as well. To cover his retreat, he directed 1,500 men to hold the Franciscan convent of San Mateo on the south bank of the small Churubusco River, just north of San Antonio, and for a regiment to guard a fortified bridgehead on the south bank of the river, 300 yards to the east of the convent. The remainder of Santa Anna's forces escaped to the north side of the river.

Now, for the first time, the Americans encountered inspired defense from the Mexicans. The soldiers at the convent beat off every rush of the Americans, while cannons posted there did heavy execution. The Mexican regiment at the bridgehead threw back two American charges, but at last succumbed in hand-to-hand fighting, while the troops defending the convent finally surrendered after an American scaling party breached the walls.

The Mexicans were in turmoil, the city of Mexico virtually defenseless, and the Americans surged forward in the flush of victory. But General Scott now made a grave mistake. Santa Anna proposed a truce, and Scott fell for the ploy, thinking that Santa Anna was going to agree to peace. From August 25 to September 6, 1847, while an American State Department official got nowhere negotiating terms, Santa Anna resurrected a defense of the city. At last Scott, realizing he had been duped, resumed hostilities.

On September 8, 1847, Scott's forces attacked El Molino del Rey (King's Mill) and Casa de Mata, a group of stone buildings a thousand yards west of the castle of Chapultepec, located a couple miles west of the city of Mexico. The headlong attacks were ill-conceived and badly executed. The Americans finally drove off the Mexican defenders, but they lost a quarter of their entire force. And the possession of the buildings did nothing to help in the seizure of Chapultepec Castle. Jackson was present, but took no part in the assaults. The terrible cost and the lack of any gains, however, reinforced an abhorrence already growing in his mind to headlong assaults against heavily fortified positions.

Chapultepec, on a 200-foot hill, was the former residence of the Spanish viceroys and was now the site of the Mexican military academy. Chapultepec guarded access to both causeways leading to the city from the west. On September 12, American soldiers surged over the parapets of Chapultepec, and shot or brushed aside Mexican defenders. Six young cadets died in the melee, to be venerated in Mexican history as *los Niños Heroicos*. The Americans now rushed down the two causeways to the city itself. Jackson's cannon section provided brilliant support for this advance. For his action here and throughout the campaign, Jackson was nominated for promotion to brevet major.

In the Treaty of Guadalupe Hidalgo on February 2, 1848, the Mexicans granted the Americans what they were seeking: the territory that became the states of California, Arizona, Nevada, and Utah, and parts of New Mexico, Colorado, and Wyoming.

Jackson had learned a great deal in the Mexican War. He had seen that direct assaults on fortified positions were extremely costly in lives. He had also seen that indirect moves, either on the battlefield, or in approaching the large target of Mexico City, were far more likely to produce victory.

After the war Jackson's artillery unit returned to its permanent station in New York. At this time Jackson developed a strong religious bent that had commenced in Mexico. He also was concerned about his health, although his only real complaint was dyspepsia. New York was a stimulating city, containing a large number of educated and gifted people. But Jackson's social awkwardness and his unwillingness to express his thoughts closed off this avenue of intellectual advancement. Jackson did, at least, visit art galleries and bookstores, where he purchased a number of books, especially military history studies.

Life took a decided turn for the worse in December 1850, however, when the army transferred him to a small post in near-frontier country in central Florida, east of Tampa. Conditions were uncomfortable and unhealthy, but Jackson's main complaint was a pettifogging commander who made unreasonable demands and leveled unjustified complaints.

Jackson became increasingly aware that no bright future was likely for him in the Regular Army. The campaigns of the Mexican War had been extremely stimulating, but he was finding garrison duty in

peacetime to be dull, repetitious, full of useless regulations, and offering little scope for intellectual growth. Promotion depended wholly
on time served, not merit. Ten officers were ahead of him in his artillery regiment alone. Many of the army's best officers were leaving the
service because opportunities were far better in civilian life.

One of these departed officers was about to have a profound effect
on Jackson's life and career. In early February 1851, D. Harvey Hill,
West Point class of 1842, called on a fellow West Point alumnus, Colonel Francis Henney Smith, commandant of Virginia Military Institute, a state school modeled on West Point established eleven years
previously in Lexington, a town of 1,700 people in the southern
reaches of Virginia's Shenandoah Valley. After brilliant service in the
Mexican War, Hill had resigned from the army in 1849 to become a
professor of mathematics at Washington College, located directly
alongside the VMI campus in Lexington.

Colonel Smith presented Hill with a problem. VMI was in need of
a new natural philosophy professor who could also teach artillery tactics, and his prime candidate had unexpectedly declined the job.
Smith asked Hill to look through the army register and propose an
officer of talent and character. Hill thumbed through the pages and
his eyes fell on the listing of Thomas J. Jackson, whom Hill had known
in Mexico and for whom he had high respect. This is your man, Hill
told Colonel Smith emphatically. Smith made a quick trip to the state
capital, Richmond, to learn Jackson's reputation from John S. Carlile,
a state senator from the district around Clarksburg and Weston, Jackson's home. Carlile knew Jackson and strongly seconded Hill's recommendation.

Colonel Smith immediately wrote Jackson in Florida, asking
whether he would be a candidate. This was a bolt out of the blue, but it
offered a number of advantages. Jackson would still be in a familiar
military environment, teaching offered far more stimulus than service

in isolated military posts, and a professorship would give him substantial social status. So, having just turned twenty-seven years of age, Jackson wrote Smith that he would like to be considered. On March 28, 1851, the VMI Board of Visitors, of which Senator Carlile was a member, elected Jackson by acclamation.

Jackson was neither a great scholar nor a good teacher, and he was ill-prepared to pass on to students what VMI called "natural and experimental philosophy," which was actually a loose combination of physics, astronomy, and mechanics, plus a few other sciences. Topics included electricity, magnetics, acoustics, and optics. Jackson managed to stay just ahead of his students, but the task was hard, and he never excelled. Jackson's own personality also prevented him from achieving rapport with the cadets. A member of the VMI Board of Visitors, who met him in the fall of 1851, described him as "reserved yet polite, reticent of opinion, but fixed in the ideas he had formed." The board member said his manner was abrupt, and "a crisp but not brusque form of expression did not tend to render him popular with the young men under his charge."[5]

For this reason, Jackson acquired the reputation among cadets as being "as exact as a multiplication table and as full of things military as an arsenal." As for his teaching skills, one of Jackson's students left the following verse in the flyleaf of his textbook: "'Tis said that optics treats of light, But oh! believe it not, my lark, I've studied it with all my might, And still it's left me in the dark." Whenever Jackson occasionally made an ironic remark, he quashed its impact by adding, "Not meaning exactly what I say." This expression was a wonderful bonanza to the cadets, and it became their tag line for everything in life.[6]

Jackson developed three firm friends in Lexington: Harvey Hill, who was instrumental in Jackson's appointment to VMI; his wife, Isabella, daughter of a Presbyterian minister in North Carolina; and John Blair Lyle, a bachelor sixteen years Jackson's senior, and owner of the town's primary bookstore. Harvey and Isabella were firm Calvinists, as was Lyle. They led Jackson to become a member of the Lexington Presbyterian Church, the biggest in town with 250 members. The Presbyterian faith immediately became Jackson's home, his fortress, and his refuge. He began to see everything in terms of his faith.

In late 1852 the Reverend Dr. George Junkin, president of Washington College, and a leading Presbyterian cleric, offered his friendship to Jackson, who accepted it eagerly. The academe's wife, Julia Miller Junkin, a product of Philadelphia high society, presided over a household that included, on a regular basis, three to five Junkin children and two nephews. The oldest of the Junkin daughters was redheaded Margaret, at thirty-two years of age definitely an old maid. Maggie Junkin was inseparable from her sister, Elinor or Ellie, twenty-seven years of age, and the prettier of the two. Jackson quickly became enamored of Ellie, and early in 1853 she accepted Jackson's offer of marriage. However, after Maggie exploded in anger at the news, Ellie broke the engagement. The estrangement lasted until spring, when Ellie reached some kind of sisterly understanding with Maggie, and renewed the engagement. On August 4, 1853, the Reverend Junkin married his daughter Elinor to Thomas J. Jackson in the parlor of his home.

When the new couple departed on their honeymoon, Maggie Junkin insisted on going along, and Ellie agreed. This peculiar social group went to Philadelphia, Niagara Falls, Montreal, and Quebec, where Jackson made a point of visiting the Plains of Abraham, site of the victory of British General James Wolfe over the French in 1759 that won Canada for Britain and cost Wolfe his life. After a visit to Boston, the three returned to Lexington in late August. Jackson and Ellie, despite the bizarre arrangement, had enjoyed the honeymoon. Maggie had not. Marriage, she told a friend, "took from me my only bosom companion, and put between us a stranger."[7]

Jackson and his bride moved into a new bedroom and study added to the Junkin home, so Ellie did not break her close connection with her family. In early 1854 it became certain that Ellie was pregnant, but on February 23, 1854, tragedy struck the Junkin family. The matriarch, Julia Junkin, who was thought to be suffering only from chronic rheumatism, suddenly died. Maggie collapsed in anguish, but Ellie proclaimed God's will at work and bore the loss quietly. Another loss to Jackson came in the summer, when Harvey and Isabella Hill departed for Davidson College, a few miles north of Charlotte, North Carolina, where Harvey had accepted a professorship in mathematics.

On October 22, 1854, Ellie went into labor. She gave birth to a stillborn son but appeared to have come through the ordeal safely. An hour or so later, however, an uncontrollable hemorrhage began and she died within a very short time.

Jackson was devastated. Absolute despair coursed through his heart. Mother and child were buried in a single coffin in the Junkin family plot in Lexington Presbyterian Church Cemetery on October 24, 1854. Maggie Junkin was so stunned by grief that she could not bear to visit Ellie's grave. She left in December for an extended visit to her brother, George, in Philadelphia. Jackson went to the grave site every day for a long time. He returned paler and quieter to his work at VMI, but somehow he accepted the tragedy as God's will. In this way, he survived.

In the summer of 1856, as much to get away from sad memories of his life with Ellie as for any other reason, Jackson embarked on a journey he had wanted to take all his adult life. He departed in early July on a three-month European tour. Crossing the Atlantic on the steamship *Asia*, Jackson visited England, Scotland, Belgium, France, Germany, Switzerland, and Italy. Except for visiting the battlefield of Waterloo, Jackson paid little attention to military sites. Instead, he sought famous attractions—cathedrals, abbeys, the mountains of Scotland, the castles and vineyards of the Rhine River, the Swiss Alps,

Venice, the paintings and sculpture of Florence, the ruins of Rome, the Bay of Naples, the landscapes of France, and the beauties of Paris.

Jackson returned to Lexington a new man. He had at last assuaged his grief at the loss of Ellie. He was seeking a new life, and a new wife.

Jackson remembered a visit to Lexington in the spring of 1853 by two of Isabella Hill's sisters from Lincoln County, North Carolina— Mary Anna and Eugenia Morrison. Jackson especially remembered Anna, seven and a half years younger than he, with soft brown eyes, dark brown hair, and a sunny, quiet disposition.

One day in the autumn of 1856, Anna received a letter from Jackson, expressing happy memories of her visit to Lexington. Eugenia predicted an early visit from the major. A few days before Christmas, Jackson appeared at the farm of Anna's father, the Reverend Robert Hall Morrison, about twenty miles northwest of Charlotte. Morrison had served as Davidson College's first president, but had to retire because of a throat ailment. The visit was pleasant for all concerned. Jackson made his interest in Anna known. Anna remembered with pleasure her association with Jackson in Lexington three years previously. And Morrison and his wife, Mary, were impressed with Jackson's religious faith and his integrity. Matters proceeded on a predictable path to July 16, 1857, when Jackson and Anna were married at her home.

They set out on a honeymoon to Philadelphia, New York City, West Point, Niagara Falls, and Saratoga, New York. By the time the couple headed back south to Lexington, Anna was pregnant. On April 30, 1858, mother and baby came through the ordeal of delivery safely, but the child, a daughter, was weak and died of liver failure on May 25. Five weeks later, Anna's sister Eugenia died of typhoid fever in North Carolina. Anna took the double loss extremely hard. Jackson also suffered intense sorrow, but he bore the pain in silence, attributing the deaths to God's will.

In the face of these blows, Jackson took his wife away for a second northern trip as soon as the VMI session ended. This time they rode a steamer from Old Point Comfort at Hampton Roads, Virginia, to Cape May, New Jersey, for several days of ocean bathing. They were now talking of buying a home in Lexington. In New York City, they purchased a large number of household goods, including a piano, because, even with shipping charges, they were much cheaper there than in Lexington. In November they found the property they were looking for, a two-story brick-and-stone house with an English basement in the middle of town close to the church and to VMI.

Jackson had been smitten with Anna ever since he renewed their friendship in late 1856. But his devotion to his wife grew tremendously once they were married. Indeed, with Anna Jackson he was wholly different from the rigid, austere persona he presented to the world. In later times, Anna remarked that others "would have found it hard to believe that there could be such a transformation as he exhibited in his domestic life." She wrote: "No man could be more demonstrative, and he was almost invariably playful and cheerful and as confiding as possible. . . . We rarely ever met alone without caresses and endearing epithets." On his return from the institute, "his face would beam with happiness, and he would spend a few minutes in petting me, as he called it, and then go to his duties." Jackson opened his heart to Anna with trust and tenderness, emotions that she clearly reciprocated. Jackson's love for his wife never ceased.[8]

Thomas and Anna Jackson were wholly absorbed in their home and their hopes for the future. But their concerns, as well as the concerns of virtually all Americans, were about to be swept aside by a dispute—over slavery—that was shaking the very foundations of the American union.

This issue had endured for virtually the entire existence of the American people. In 1619 a Dutch ship arrived at Jamestown, Virginia, with a load of African slaves for sale. This was just twelve years after Jamestown was founded and a year before the first Pilgrims landed at Plymouth Rock in Massachusetts. Thenceforth, slavery was practiced in all of the colonies, but slaves were especially important in the South, which depended for its prosperity on hard labor in rice, indigo, tobacco, and cotton fields. The institution was important enough that Southern politicians insisted on its acceptance in the United States Constitution.

But slavery was dying out because it could not compete with free laborers. Slaves had to be provided for all year, whereas farm laborers had to be paid only for the limited periods, like planting and harvesttime, when their labor was required. In 1793, however, Eli Whitney invented the cotton gin. The gin easily separated cottonseeds from cotton fibers and made it feasible to grow short-staple upland cotton throughout the South. Planters opened thousands of new acres to cotton, and the impetus toward emancipation stopped. In 1791 cotton exports from the South totaled 2 million pounds. By 1811 they had risen to 80 million pounds and were growing every year. Cotton was producing tremendous wealth for the great landowners, and their avarice blocked any movement to end slavery.

But the immorality of human bondage was so self-evident that, by 1859, it had been prohibited throughout the country except in fifteen Southern states. Their economies were overwhelmingly agricultural and—since the Industrial Revolution had made few inroads into farming—they depended on heavy hand labor in hot fields to produce their crops, most especially cotton, by far the most important moneymaker.

All thinking Southerners knew that slavery had to be abolished. But people argued heatedly over how to accomplish it. Outright emancipation would impoverish the landed aristocracy that had dominated the South from the earliest colonial days. The solution, of course, was for the entire nation to assume the cost of freeing the slaves, and for the national government to pay the slave owners the value of their slaves. But avarice also ruled in the North, and few Northerners were interested in giving up some of their wealth to Southern slave owners, especially as a vociferous abolitionist movement gained strength and condemned the institution strictly on moral grounds. The abolitionists wanted the slave owners to be punished for their sins, not compensated.

Like most human conflicts, therefore, the dispute over slavery came down to a question of money. In other words, who would suffer economic losses in order to eliminate the institution? If the issue could have been restricted to the financial question, it could ultimately have been solved by some monetary compromise. But the moral question was becoming paramount in the North, and an ethical crusade that seemed to Southerners to be verging on revolution finally brought the entire dispute to a tragic and decisive head in 1859.

The instrument of this pivotal transformation was a militant abolitionist, John Brown, who, on October 16, 1859, led an attack with eighteen followers on the federal arsenal at Harpers Ferry, Virginia, on the Potomac River at the northern end of the Shenandoah Valley. Brown intended to seize the 100,000 muskets and rifles stored at the arsenal in order to arm slaves and lead a bloody slave revolt across the South. The raiders killed three townspeople, including one black man, before a contingent of U.S. Marines under army Colonel Robert E. Lee arrived from Washington. The marines stormed the fire engine house where Brown and a part of his group were barricaded. The marines killed ten of the raiders, and seized Brown and the remainder to go on trial for treason, murder, and insurrection. Brown was quickly sentenced to die. The hanging took place on December 2, 1859. Jackson and the VMI corps of cadets were present as part of the security detail. The noted Northern abolitionist Frederick Douglass had refused to join Brown's cause, saying it was a suicide mission. Not a single slave joined John Brown's cause.

The John Brown raid divided the nation as nothing previously had ever done. It aroused absolute consternation and a deep fear throughout the South, but it generated tremendous excitement in the North. The raid intensified the bad feeling that existed between the two sections of the country. More important than anything else, the raid ended any rational discussion of the subject of slavery. From now on, it became a matter of intense emotional feeling. In the North, the abolitionist movement gained steady ground. In the South, resistance to forced emancipation accelerated, giving rise to more and more legal interpretations that states had the right to leave the Union if they chose. The space in which compromise could be achieved had shrunk to an almost meaningless dimension. John Brown's raid had split the nation in half ideologically. It was a deadly blow.

In the presidential election of 1860, the dominant Democratic Party splintered into three antagonistic particles, allowing the new Republican Party with strong antislavery tendencies to sweep all the Northern states and give the presidency to Abraham Lincoln.

Between late 1860 and early 1861, the seven Deep South states seceded from the Union, but the eight remaining slave states stayed loyal. Leaders launched sincere efforts to reach some arrangement to bring the seven states back in. But Lincoln refused to budge. He would allow no compromise, not even a national referendum. Yet a popular vote undoubtedly would have approved a solution acceptable to both sides—emancipation and compensation to slave owners. In April 1861, Lincoln announced that the seceded states were in "rebellion" and he called on the remaining states to force the seven states back into the Union at the bayonet's point. Lincoln's call for troops forced the hand of four border states—Virginia, North Carolina, Tennessee, and Arkansas. They could not accept the idea of fighting the Deep South states, and they seceded as well.

The Civil War had begun. The terrible division of the nation was duplicated within Jackson's own family. His beloved sister Laura, who had married and moved to Beverly in northwestern Virginia, became a Unionist, and thus in direct conflict with her brother. Thomas's last contact with his sister was a kind letter he wrote to her on April 6, 1861, a week before Confederates bombarded Fort Sumter in the harbor of Charleston, South Carolina, the event that set off the war.[9]

CHAPTER 2

"There Stands Jackson
Like a Stone Wall"

Thomas Jackson had no crisis of conscience when the nation split apart. Anna Jackson later explained his response: "He deplored the collision most earnestly. But he believed that the constitutional rights of the states had been invaded, and he never had a doubt as to where his allegiance was due. His sword belonged to his state."[1]

On Sunday April 21, 1861, Virginia governor John Letcher ordered the Virginia Military Institute cadet corps to Richmond to teach new volunteers how to drill. Major Thomas J. Jackson led the cadets to Richmond's fairgrounds west of the city, converted into an army camp. There the young cadets did excellent service in teaching the raw recruits the rudiments of marching.

Three days before the cadets departed Lexington, Colonel Robert E. Lee, fifty-four years old, was meeting in Washington with Francis P. Blair Sr., a publisher and close friend of Abraham Lincoln. Lee, scion of a famous Virginia family, fairly tall, extremely handsome, courteous to everyone high and low, had been summoned from a post in Texas by Winfield Scott, chief of the army. Scott had conveyed his high regard for Lee to Blair, who had talked with Lincoln. When he met Lee, Blair came straight to the point: "I come to you on the part of President Lincoln to ask whether any inducement that he can offer will prevail on you to take command of the Union army?" Lee responded as candidly and as courteously as he could: "Mr. Blair, I look upon secession as anarchy. If I owned the four millions of slaves in the South I would sacrifice them all to the Union; but how can I draw my sword upon Virginia, my native state?"[2]

The day previously, Virginia had formally seceded from the Union. On April 20, Lee resigned his commission, left his estate at Arlington (in time converted by the U.S. government into Arlington National Cemetery), just across the Potomac from the capital, took the train to Richmond, and accepted Governor Letcher's appointment as commander of Virginia forces.[3]

After Virginia joined the Confederacy on May 2, President Jefferson Davis made the strategic decision to move the capital from Montgomery, Alabama, to Richmond on May 29. When he arrived, Lee became the unofficial military adviser to Davis.

Jackson did not have anything like the clout of Lee. Once he had delivered the VMI cadets to Richmond, he received an appointment as a major in the topographical engineers, or map makers. This was an incredible put-down, and would have relegated Jackson to a desk in a government building. Jackson tried to conceal his feelings in a letter to his wife, Anna. "The scene here, my darling pet, looks quite animated," he wrote. "I received your precious letter, in which you speak of coming here in the event of my remaining. I would like very much to see my sweet little face, but my darling had better remain at her own home, as my continuance here is uncertain."[4]

Jackson contacted an old friend, Jonathan M. Bennett, the state auditor. Bennett got an audience with Governor Letcher, who immediately recognized the mistake, summoned Jackson to his office on April 27, appointed him as a colonel in the Virginia volunteers, and sent him to command the post at Harpers Ferry.

When Jackson arrived at Harpers Ferry, he discovered that the 2,500 men in the Virginia militia units occupying the village were really civilians, not a viable military force. Prominent men who'd received high rank because of political favor paraded around in gaudy uniforms of their own design, followed by large staffs of equally plumed favorites. Governor Letcher, recognizing that a true crisis was at hand, and that these officers knew nothing about leading men into battle, relieved from duty all militia officers above the rank of captain.

Jackson faced a vast task in converting this amorphous mass into an effective military force. He assembled several officers from VMI and a few cadets to teach the militiamen how to drill. He also discovered Major John A. Harman, of Staunton, Virginia, who was brilliant in finding food and other needed supplies. Harman became Jackson's only quartermaster officer.

The near chaos that Jackson encountered was not limited to Harpers Ferry. Throughout the South and throughout the North similar scenes of total disorganization were being repeated endlessly. Both North and South were creating armies from scratch, and the process was painful, confused, and hectic.

Jackson wrote an upbeat letter to Anna in mid-May: "I am living in an elegant mansion. I am strengthening my position, and if attacked, shall with the blessing of that God, who has always been with me, and who I firmly believe will never forsake, repel the enemy. I am in great health, considering the great labor that devolves on me, and the loss of sleep to which I am subjected."[5]

Ordering incessant drill, Jackson began turning the militiamen at the Ferry, plus thousands more who flooded into the village, into soldiers. He also organized them into effective units. The basic structure in both the Confederate and Union armies was the regiment, divided into companies and supposedly totaling a thousand men, but usually possessing far fewer. Several regiments constituted a brigade, the principal fighting unit in both armies. The main maneuver element was the division, usually consisting of three or four brigades, plus artillery companies and cavalry units.

For more than two centuries tactics had rested on the fact that the main infantry weapon, the single-shot smoothbore musket, had a maximum effective range of less than a hundred yards. Shots beyond that range were likely to miss. To reach decisions, accordingly, regiments formed in a long line, two men deep, and advanced directly on a defending force, which also was arrayed in a line two men deep. When the assaulting force got within fifty to thirty paces of the enemy, the assaulting force stopped, leveled its muskets, and fired a massed volley. In theory, this fire staggered the enemy force, whereupon the assaulting force charged with naked bayonets, and disintegrated the force or caused it to surrender.

In practice, defending forces often gave as well as they got, and battles sometimes degenerated into repeated musket volleys, causing horrible massacres on both sides. Napoleon Bonaparte, however, improved the prospects of the assaulting force by rolling up light cannons a couple hundred yards in front of a defending force—thus beyond the range of muskets—and blasting great holes in it with canister, or clouds of metal fragments that had an effect similar to the machine gun in modern wars.

Officers had followed Napoleon's example in the Mexican War, and both Confederate and Union commanders believed these same tactics could be used to win battles in the Civil War. However, a radical change had come to pass since the Mexican conflict. In 1849, a French army officer named Claude-Étienne Minié had invented a cylindrical self-cleaning bullet with a hollow base. When fired, the bullet's base expanded to fit snugly against the grooves of a rifle, scouring the gunpowder fouling of the previous shot and allowing the rifle to fire many rounds before it had to be cleaned. The Minié ball or bullet made the single-shot rifle an effective military weapon, and rendered the smoothbore musket obsolete.

The Minié-ball rifle quadrupled the effective range of the infantry weapon to 400 yards. No one recognized the revolutionary implications of this new weapon at first, but it transformed the conditions of battle. Now a defending force could cause huge casualties in an attacking enemy force long before it could get close enough to break a defending line.

And Napoleon's practice of rolling up cannons and blasting holes in an enemy line no longer worked in offensive operations, because the effective range of the Minié-ball rifle was longer than the effective range of canister. When gunners rolled their cannons forward, enemy sharpshooters killed or wounded gunners and horses, forcing them to withdraw.

In addition, cavalry lost its principal role in battle. In previous wars, cavalry had often been decisive by breaking up enemy infantry formations in charges. But infantry now could empty the saddles of charging cavalry long before they came close enough to crack their line. Cavalry's function declined to scouting, screening movements, protecting flanks, and pursuing an already broken enemy force.

But none of these facts was apparent to commanders in the spring of 1861. They organized armies in traditional fashion, and moved toward a major collision with utterly unrealistic ideas of how the war was actually going to be fought.

Jackson remained in command at Harpers Ferry only a few weeks. On May 24, the Confederate government replaced him with one of its military stars, Joseph E. Johnston, a Virginian who had attained the rank of brigadier general in the old army. Jackson wrote Anna not to be concerned about the change in command. He also advised her not to come to Winchester to visit him, because of probable troop movements. In response, Anna closed their Lexington home and, in company with her brother, Joseph Morrison, traveled to her father's home in Lincoln County, North Carolina, until Jackson summoned her.[6]

General Johnston organized his 11,000 troops from various Southern states into four brigades. Jackson received command of the 1st Virginia Brigade, which came to have five regiments (the 2nd, 4th, 5th, 27th, and 33rd) with about 2,500 men from in or near the Shenandoah Valley. On July 3, the War Department elevated Jackson to the rank of brigadier general. Johnston's other three brigades were commanded by South Carolinian Barnard E. Bee, who graduated from West Point a year before Jackson; Francis S. Bartow, a Georgia planter and graduate of Yale; and E. Kirby Smith (West Point, 1845), from Florida.

Johnston quickly decided that Harpers Ferry, located right on the Potomac River, could easily be surrounded and was indefensible. On June 13 he got permission from the War Department to withdraw to Winchester, thirty miles south. He was opposed by Union Major General Robert Patterson, sixty-nine years old, who moved his 16,000 men in early July 1861 to Bunker Hill, a crossroads ten miles north of Winchester.

President Abraham Lincoln had sent Patterson's army into the Shenandoah Valley in fear that Johnston might otherwise burst across the Potomac and attack Washington. But Johnston's force was too small for such a purpose, and placing Patterson's army to block it was a waste. The point that was strategically critical was not the valley but was the railroad crossroads of Manassas Junction, about thirty miles southwest of Washington. Here the Orange & Alexandria Railroad joined the Manassas Gap Railroad. The Orange & Alexandria extended to Lynchburg, while the Manassas Gap stretched westward into the Shenandoah Valley. Lincoln had decided to approach Richmond through central Virginia. Possession of these two railways was essential to this movement. Railroads already were becoming vital for the survival of armies. If a line was intact, it could deliver unlimited food, ammunition, and other supplies to distant points. If the line was severed, an army had to repair the damage, move, or die.

At Lincoln's direction, Major General Irvin McDowell, his new commander of field forces, had concentrated 37,000 men around Alexandria, Virginia, with instructions to seize Manassas Junction and then move down the Orange & Alexandria.[7] Thus, here on the eve of the first significant collision between Union and Confederate troops, Lincoln had already violated one of Napoleon Bonaparte's key axioms: always concentrate maximum force at the point of decision, which in this case was Manassas Junction. Instead, by keeping Patterson in the Shenandoah Valley, he had divided his forces most dangerously.

Opposing McDowell with just 22,000 Confederate troops along Bull Run, a bold stream immediately north of Manassas, was Pierre G. T. Beauregard, a fiery Frenchman from Louisiana.[8] It soon became clear that Beauregard could spin great imaginary plans for sweeping military movements that had little chance of coming to fruition while he himself was extremely erratic and disorganized. Even so, he, along with other senior Confederates, was well aware of Napoleon's axiom to concentrate forces on the decisive battlefield. Confederate leaders began to conjure up ways to deceive Patterson long enough for Johnston's 11,000 men to slip away from the Shenandoah Valley and join Beauregard at Manassas, thereby bringing Rebel forces into closer parity with McDowell's army. In the days of single-shot infantry weapons, numbers counted for a great deal, because adding numbers was the only way to increase firepower.

Anticipating that McDowell was about to move on Bull Run, Johnston made some threatening moves against Patterson's army at Bunker Hill. Johnston's feint thoroughly intimidated Patterson. Forgetting his duty to hold Johnston in place, and fearful that Johnston might cut him off from his supplies, Patterson abruptly abandoned Bunker Hill and rushed his army northeastward to Charles Town on July 16, 1861. This put Patterson twenty miles from Winchester, and released Johnston from his vise. This was the very day that McDowell, with 32,000 men, started from Alexandria west to Bull Run, leaving 5,000 men in defensive works guarding Washington.

Johnston sent his flamboyant cavalry chief, J. E. B. (Jeb) Stuart with his 300-man 1st Virginia Cavalry Regiment toward Charles Town, causing Patterson to think Johnston was coming after him, and closing all avenues of reconnaissance to Union cavalry. On July 18, Johnston set his entire army in motion for Manassas Junction. For a full day and for much of a second, Patterson was totally unaware that Johnston had disappeared. When he did learn, it was too late. Johnston's adept moves had wiped Patterson's army from the order of battle. The army might as well have been on the shores of Tripoli for all the effect it could have had on the upcoming battle.

Thomas Jackson's 1st Virginia Brigade led the march from Winchester across Ashby's Gap in the Blue Ridge Mountains (through which U.S. Routes 17 and 50 now run). At the little village of Paris, on the eastern slopes of the Blue Ridge, twenty miles from Winchester, Jackson halted his exhausted troops for the night. When an aide reported that too few pickets had been posted, Jackson replied, "Let the poor fellows sleep. I will guard the camp myself."[9] Jackson, through the summer night, stood sentry over his sleeping men.

Next morning, Jackson's brigade marched six miles down to Piedmont Station (now Delaplane) on the Manassas Gap Railroad. There they boarded trains for Manassas Junction, thirty-four miles away. This was just the second time in history that a railroad had been used to take troops to battle. In 1859, it had been done in a brief war between France and Austria in Italy.

The trip was an absolute lark for the young soldiers of Jackson's brigade. At every stop, enthusiastic crowds swarmed around the cars, young girls in their finest dresses waved and flirted with the boys, housewives pressed sweets of every kind on them, and everybody sang rousing patriotic songs like "Dixie" and "The Bonnie Blue Flag." Such excited crowds were not going to appear again in the war. Nor were wealthy men and women in expensive carriages and picnic baskets going to follow after an army to enjoy witnessing the first and last battle to restore the Union, as happened to McDowell's army as it marched toward Bull Run. When the battle actually erupted, it was far more gruesome than anyone had foreseen, and the fire the soldiers encountered was far more deadly than ever experienced in warfare.

When Jackson arrived in Manassas, he went at once to Beauregard's headquarters at the Wilmer McLean farmhouse on a shady knoll a mile south of Bull Run.[10] He told Beauregard that Johnston's remaining three brigades were coming by rail behind him.

But these brigades were being caught up in the very first railway traffic jam in military history. The brigades reached Piedmont Station on the afternoon of July 19, but the railroad had not prepared for the inundation, and besides had few extra locomotives and cars to employ. Train crews were able to get only Francis S. Bartow's brigade to Manassas by dawn on July 20. Johnston himself arrived with Barnard E. Bee's brigade during the day of July 20. On the day of the battle, Sunday, July 21, Kirby Smith's brigade arrived at noon and marched directly to the fight.

Beauregard had done an abominable job preparing for the upcoming battle. He had placed his army in a bad position to begin with, his plan for battle relied on McDowell doing just what Beauregard wanted him to do, his system of organization was antiquated and totally unsatisfactory, and, as events were to show, his entire plan collapsed in chaos the moment events in the battle didn't go as he expected.

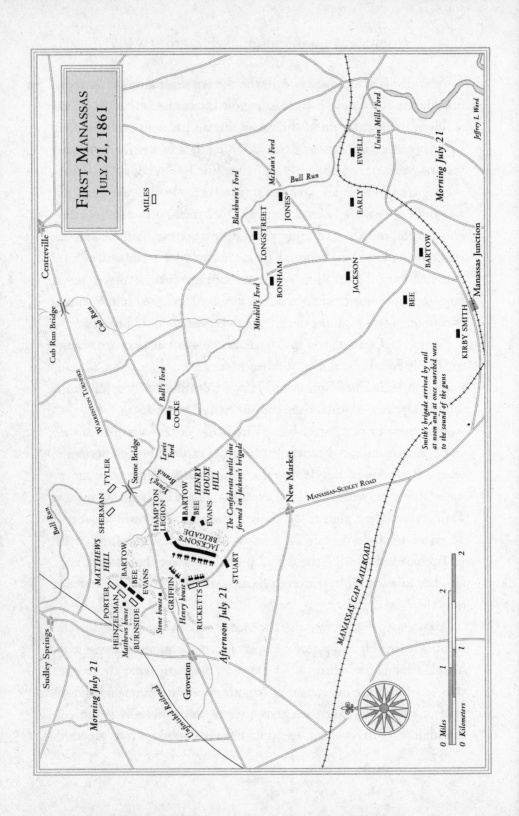

FIRST MANASSAS
JULY 21, 1861

MILES

Morning July 21

Jeffry L. Ward

EWELL

Union Mills Ford

McLean's Ford

Bull Run

EARLY

Blackburn's Ford

LONGSTREET

JONES

BARTOW

Centreville

BONHAM

JACKSON

Manassas Junction

Cub Run Bridge

Mitchell's Ford

BEE

KIRBY SMITH

Cub Run

Bull's Ford

WARRENTON TURNPIKE

COCKE

Smith's brigade arrived by rail
at noon and at once marched west
to the sound of the guns

Bull Run

Lewis Ford

TYLER

SHERMAN

Stone Bridge

Young's Branch

New Market

MANASSAS-SUDLEY ROAD

MATTHEWS HILL

PORTER

HEINZELMAN

Matthews house

BURNSIDE

Stone house

HAMPTON LEGION

BARTOW

BEE

EVANS

HENRY HOUSE HILL

JACKSON'S BRIGADE

The Confederate battle line
formed on Jackson's brigade

Sudley Springs

BARTOW

BEE

EVANS

GRIFFIN

Henry house

RICKETTS

STUART

MANASSAS GAP RAILROAD

Morning July 21

Afternoon July 21

Orange & Alexandria Railroad

Groveton

0 Miles   1   2

0 Kilometers   1   2

Beauregard had set up a line of battle that stretched for nearly seven miles along Bull Run, much too long for the troops he had available. He had placed the bulk of his forces, five brigades or about 16,000 troops, between Union Mills Ford on the extreme east to Mitchell's Ford on the west, a distance of three miles. Two other fords, Blackburn's and McLean's, were located within this stretch. Beauregard had placed most of his remaining troops, 5,000 men, in two isolated positions well to the west of the main body. One force was Philip St. George Cocke's brigade at Ball's Ford, a couple of miles west of Mitchell's Ford. The other force, located a mile west of Ball's Ford, was a two-regiment "demi-brigade" under Nathan G. (Shanks) Evans guarding the only permanent crossing of Bull Run, the Stone Bridge on the Alexandria-Warrenton Turnpike, the main north-south road in the region (present-day U.S. Route 29).

Now it might have been expected that the Union army would send a strong force down the turnpike and over the Stone Bridge, since this was the main avenue south. But Beauregard believed that McDowell would actually strike at Blackburn's Ford, four miles east of the Stone Bridge, since this was on the most direct path to Manassas Junction itself. Beauregard thus had decided that McDowell would make a headlong assault at the most obvious place. In addition, he had not even considered the possibility that McDowell might actually make a flanking attack—although Beauregard had left his eastern and western flanks completely unprotected, or, in the parlance of the time, both flanks were "floating in the air."

In keeping with his expectations, Beauregard had conceived that James Longstreet's brigade, positioned at Blackburn's Ford, would stop the attack, and that three Confederate brigades to the right or east would then cross Bull Run and swing widely around the Union army, cut its supply line, pin it against the stream, and force its surrender.

The flaws in this grandiose plan not only were that it required

McDowell's complete cooperation, but that it also required complete coordination between Longstreet's brigade and the three brigades to the east. Yet Beauregard had not given any of the three brigades any directions as to what they should do, nor had he appointed an overall commander to direct the anticipated wide sweep. Indeed, Beauregard had not even organized his army into divisions, a command structure invented by the French in the eighteenth century and used universally by Napoleon Bonaparte in all of his campaigns. Beauregard had left his army divided into individual brigades, as well as some separate regiments and independent artillery batteries. This made his command structure far too complex for him and his untrained and untested staff to handle with any degree of efficiency.

Despite Beauregard's belief, McDowell had no plan of attacking Blackburn's Ford. He intended instead to swing around the right or eastern flank of the Confederate army, because this flank was closest to Manassas Junction. However, when he arrived on the scene on July 18, he found that the country to the east was too wooded and broken with too few roads to sustain a major sweep. He thought that alternatively he might make a direct strike down the Alexandria-Warrenton Turnpike across the Stone Bridge. But, relying on only distant observation, some of his officers told him that Shanks Evans had mined the bridge and would blow it the moment Union troops tried to cross. This was untrue. Evans had only placed a few logs in the roadway, and his few six-pounder cannons were far too light to hold up any determined assault. But McDowell didn't ascertain the real situation, which a small scouting party could certainly have done. He decided not to take the chance.

His eyes turned to the western flank. His engineers found an easy ford at Sudley Springs, two miles west of the Stone Bridge. From Sudley Springs a road ran straight to Manassas, crossing the Warrenton Pike a mile behind the Stone Bridge.

In the early hours of July 21, two Union divisions set off on the circuitous march to Sudley Springs Ford, with orders to swing around behind Evans and attack him from the rear while Daniel Tyler's division made a demonstration—or feigned attack—directly down the pike toward the bridge, holding Evans in place. Once the Stone Bridge was carried, Tyler was to join the other two divisions and shatter the Confederate army by sweeping behind its left flank.

For this flanking movement to be effective, however, McDowell had to keep the main Confederate army in its defensive positions along Bull Run. This required a heavy attack to hold the Rebels in a fierce battle embrace and to prevent them from shifting troops westward to meet the move on their rear. But McDowell sent no forces to challenge St. George Cocke's brigade at Ball's Ford or the Rebel forces at Mitchell's, McLean's, and Union Mills fords to the east. He placed just one Union division under Dixon S. Miles, facing Blackburn's Ford, but told him not to launch a major attack. And his instruction to Tyler to make only a demonstration at the Stone Bridge put little pressure on Evans and allowed him to move with impunity. In these ways, McDowell fatally wounded what otherwise would have been a brilliant, unanticipated move on the left flank of the Confederate army.

When Thomas Jackson's brigade arrived on July 19, Beauregard placed it in reserve behind Mitchell's Ford. The next day, when the brigades of Bartow and Bee arrived, he stationed them in reserve behind Blackburn's Ford. Thus, on the eve of battle, the only forces with any hope of moving quickly to the west were the brigades of Jackson, Bee, and Bartow. And they were still four to five miles away from Evans at the Stone Bridge.

Beauregard, still expecting McDowell to attack Blackburn's Ford, was stunned to learn that Tyler's Union division had arrived at 6:30 A.M. on July 21 at the Stone Bridge and had begun pounding the ground behind it with artillery fire. He still had no inkling of the wider movement over Sudley Springs Ford, now developing.

Beauregard directed Bee's and Bartow's brigades to rush to Evans's assistance, and he ordered Jackson's brigade to cover the largely undefended space along Bull Run between Philip St. George Cocke's brigade and Milledge Bonham's brigade at Mitchell's Ford.

At the time, Captain Edward Porter Alexander of Georgia was on Wilcoxen Hill, six miles east of the Stone Bridge. Alexander, twenty-six years old and an 1857 graduate of West Point, had been part of a team sending messages over a distance using telescopes or field glasses to view flags or torches making dot-dash or "wig-wag" signals. Beauregard had ordered him to stay at the Wilcoxen signal station and report anything he might discover. Alexander was most unhappy with this passive assignment, but he dutifully set to work.

At 8:45 A.M. his glasses caught a flash of light beyond the Stone Bridge. He perceived at once that this was a reflection of the morning sun on a brass cannon. Alexander began an intensive field-glass survey of the area. He quickly discovered the glitter of bayonets and rifle barrels. A Union column more than half a mile long was crossing Sudley Springs Ford. It indicated at least a division of troops, probably more.

Alexander immediately flashed a message to Evans via another Rebel signal station just behind the Stone Bridge: "Look out to your left; you are turned."[11] Just about the same time, one of Evans's pickets reported the move over the ford. Alexander now informed Beauregard of the turning movement. Beauregard's planned advance over the eastern fords had now vanished. His plain duty was to order these three eastern brigades to move westward at once to contain this dire threat to the Confederate army. But Beauregard did none of this. Only one of these brigades—Jubal Early's—arrived on the west in time to be effective.

Beauregard did, however, dispatch a courier to Jackson and a 600-man battalion under Wade Hampton of South Carolina, just arrived from Richmond, with orders to go to the aid of Evans. When Jackson got the order, he immediately set his brigade in motion, sending word to Bee by courier that he was coming.

Shanks Evans displayed incredible initiative and courage. Leaving 200 men to guard the bridge, he climbed atop Matthews Hill, immediately to his west. There, a little more than a mile from Sudley Springs Ford, Evans spread out his small force to give the impression of strength and awaited the Union advance.

At 9:15 A.M. the lead brigade under Union Colonel Ambrose E. Burnside came out on an open field at the base of Matthews Hill. When two of Burnside's regiments tried to attack, they met fierce resistance from Evans's soldiers, and drew back. David Hunter, commanding the leading Union division, brought up other brigades to form a long line. As this was happening, Hunter suffered a severe neck wound, and Colonel Andrew Porter took command. As all of this was happening, the 1st Louisiana "Tigers" made a swift attack toward the Federal forces. It failed, but its surprise and ferocity delayed the Union advance, giving time for Rebel reinforcements to arrive.

Porter handled the Union attacks quite poorly. He ordered forward just one regiment at a time, 700 to 900 men, allowing Evans's soldiers to concentrate their fire wholly on it. The result was that each regiment followed a pattern of "fire and fall back" to cover.[12] This was no way to achieve a decision. If, instead, Porter had formed two brigades in a long line, he could have enveloped the small Rebel force and crushed it inside of ten minutes.

Nevertheless, rifle fire on the Confederates at the top of the hill was extremely intense. When Bee arrived with his brigade, he was astonished at the accuracy and range of the enemy fire, which was coming from a distance of well over 200 yards. He at once devised a method of avoiding this fire—ordering his men to stand up only to deliver a volley, then to fall to the ground, so enemy bullets would pass over their heads. When Bartow's brigade arrived, Bartow told his men to follow Bee's example. This kept Rebel casualties low, but it was difficult for the soldiers to reload their long-barreled rifles while lying prone. So the practice was not a permanent solution to limiting casualties from rifle fire.

The Confederates now had about 3,600 men in a long defensive line. But Porter's method of attack was doing nothing to drive them off the hill. When Samuel Peter Heintzelman, commander of the second Union division, arrived, he formed up on Porter's right. Although the Federals now had a force four times that of the Rebels, the Union divisions were so disorganized from the Rebel fire that they milled around in confusion and failed to advance.

The impasse was broken, not by Porter and Heintzelman, but by Colonel William Tecumseh Sherman, who commanded a brigade in Tyler's division on the north side of Bull Run. Since Tyler himself was not advancing on the Stone Bridge, Sherman, on his own volition, marched his brigade upstream several hundred yards and crossed Bull Run at a ford he discovered. Sherman's brigade now appeared on the right rear of the Confederates on Matthews Hill, unnerving them and causing them to retreat rapidly, a withdrawal that became increasingly disorganized. Around 11:30 A.M. they crossed the Warrenton Turnpike and onto Henry House Hill, an undulating, largely open field rising to a low plateau. The south side of the hill was bounded by the sunken road from Sudley Springs to Manassas. The modest one-story wooden house of Judith Henry was just off this road halfway between the crest and the Warrenton Pike.[13]

General McDowell, who had arrived on Matthews Hill, urged the Union troops forward, shouting, "Victory, victory! The day is ours!"[14] Only Henry House Hill remained to block a Federal sweep into the flank and rear of the Rebel army. There was no other rallying point. If Henry House Hill was lost, the Confederate army would collapse in chaos.

Beauregard's failure to make any provision for a flank attack had permitted McDowell to get well over half of his army on the Confederate left, whereas the Rebel force opposing him was not only far inferior in size, but it had now disintegrated and the men were fleeing in panic. While Evans, Bee, and Bartow were frantically trying to reorganize their forces on the lower reaches of Henry House Hill, Wade Hampton's small South Carolina battalion held the Warrenton Pike for an hour, losing a fifth of its force before also falling back in disorder.

There seemed to be nothing that could stop the Union advance. But unknown to anybody else and without orders, Thomas J. Jackson had devised a solution. As soon as he reached the crest of Henry House Hill, he saw ahead that the Confederate position on Matthews Hill had been broken, and that this hill was the only possible rallying point remaining to the Confederate army. Without hesitation he drew up his brigade on the reverse slope of the ridgeline, and told his men to lie down to avoid the heavy cannon fire that Union batteries were now spreading over the landscape. The troops could still sweep the crest of the hill if Union troops appeared and silhouetted themselves against the sky.

Shortly after he had set up his position, Captain John D. Imboden came by, leading to the rear three guns of his Staunton (Virginia) Artillery. He had been firing halfway down Henry House Hill but decided he was too exposed.

"I'll support your battery," Jackson told him. "Unlimber right here."

Imboden said he had only three rounds of ammunition left and suggested that he go to the rear to fill his caissons.

"No, not now," Jackson replied. He had to establish a new defensive line. Imboden's guns, even if silent, would give the impression of strength. Imboden pointed his guns toward the enemy. Soon afterward, the guns of the Rockbridge (Virginia) Artillery arrived, along with two pieces from Captain Philip B. Stanard's Thomas Artillery from Richmond.[15]

Jackson now had a formidable array of nine cannons along the top of Henry House Hill. His battle line stretched out for several hundred yards, but remained hidden below the crest. A small pinewood and a steep slope leading down to Bull Run protected his right, but his left or south was open. Seeing this, Jackson found Jeb Stuart and asked him to post his 1st Virginia Cavalry as a flank guard.

As Union troops assembled on and around the Warrenton Pike preparatory to assaulting the hill, Federal artillery roared in increasing volume over the heads of the soldiers as they lay in their position. A few men were killed or wounded by exploding shells, and the casualties frightened the untried soldiers. But Jackson kept them calm, riding slowly back and forth along the line. "Steady, men, steady!" he repeated over and over. "All's well."[16]

The broken regiments of Evans, Bee, and Bartow had taken cover in the ravine of Young's Branch, a tributary to Bull Run, on Jackson's right front. They had lost all cohesion. A solitary horseman rode up from Young's Branch toward Jackson's position. It was General Bee, six feet tall, black eyes, dark mustache, and long hair. He halted and asked what troops these were. A soldier pointed to Jackson.

As Bee came up to Jackson, he said, "General, they are driving us."

Jackson responded: "Sir, we will give them the bayonet!"

Jackson's resolve gave Bee renewed confidence. He wheeled his horse around and galloped back to the ravine. Bee rode into the middle of the disorganized soldiers, pointed his sword toward the crest of Henry House Hill, and shouted: "Look, men, there stands Jackson like a stone wall! Rally behind the Virginians!"[17] The response was extremely positive. Helped by Beauregard and Johnston, who had arrived on the field, the troops re-formed and moved up alongside Jackson's brigade. There they did good service, though Bee was mortally wounded during the battle.

Beauregard and Johnston were also working hard to get men and cannons from along Bull Run to bolster Jackson's line. Parts of Cocke's brigade were the first to arrive. Jubal Early's was on the march from the far eastern flank, and two regiments from Milledge Bonham's brigade from Mitchell's Ford arrived. Kirby Smith's brigade had arrived by rail at Manassas station at noon, and was marching to the sound of the guns. The Confederate position stiffened alongside Jackson. His brigade, forever after to be known as the Stonewall Brigade, had become the concentration point of the army.

Irvin McDowell still had a chance to win the battle, but he began making critical mistakes that threw his advantages to the winds. Although McDowell had about 19,000 men on the Confederate left flank, he got only 11,000 of them into action. He allowed the remainder to beg off for one reason or another. Meanwhile, Beauregard had assembled 7,000 men, but two big brigades—Jubal Early's and Kirby Smith's—were marching hard for the battle line, and would soon give the Rebels parity of force. McDowell's second great blunder was to ignore the opportunity of swinging around the left Confederate flank south of the Sudley Springs Road. This space was wide open, and Union forces could easily have moved around this flank and forced evacuation of the hill. Instead, McDowell directed his attacks directly against the massed strength of the Confederates on the summit of Henry House Hill. And he compounded this error by sending individual regiments, one at a time, into the attack, instead of assembling his brigades in a single massive assault.

One Union regiment after another gathered at the foot of the hill and advanced toward the Confederates on the crest. As soon as the heads of the soldiers appeared over the front edge of the plateau, the Rebels unleashed a curtain of fire. The Union regiment returned a volley or two, but then ran back down the hill to cover. About 3:30 P.M., realizing he was getting nowhere, McDowell ordered forward two batteries of regular army artillery, twelve rifled cannons commanded by Captains Charles Griffin and James B. Ricketts. The batteries moved to the Henry House, only 330 yards from Jackson's left flank. The aim was to employ Napoleon's system of rolling guns forward and blasting a hole in the enemy line with canister. As the two batteries moved boldly forward, two supporting New York regiments—the 11th wearing colorful Zouave attire copied from Algerians in the French army, and the 14th—took cover in the adjacent sunken Sudley Springs Road.

Shortly after they arrived, 150 horsemen of Jeb Stuart's 1st Virginia Cavalry rushed out of the woods on Jackson's left and slammed into the Zouave regiment, sabers flashing. The Zouaves did not disintegrate from the surprise onslaught, and shot down nine troopers and eighteen horses before the cavalrymen rushed back to the woods. The short action showed clearly that the day when cavalry could shatter an enemy formation with a wild charge had ended. Even so, it was a shock to the inexperienced Union soldiers, and it unnerved both New York regiments.

Soon afterward, the 33rd Virginia Regiment on Jackson's left, 400 men strong, advanced without orders directly on the massed Union guns. Captain Griffin prepared to shatter the regiment with canister, but Major William F. Barry, McDowell's artillery chief, insisted the force was the 14th New York. A moment later the 33rd Virginia proved its identity by unleashing a terrible volley that cut down forty gunners and seventy-five horses and badly wounded Ricketts. Griffin was barely able to drag away three of the guns, but nine remained abandoned, and the 33rd Virginia rushed forward to seize them.

This was the last straw for the two New York regiments, and they fled in confusion to the rear. Colonel Sherman moved his brigade up the sunken Sudley Springs Road to recover the guns, but fire from the 33rd Virginia, plus Rebel artillery rounds, broke up the attack, and Sherman was forced to back down out of range. The 33rd Virginia had lost one-third of its strength, however, and was badly exposed at the cannons. At last it withdrew to the main Rebel defensive line.

The tide was turning for the Confederacy. Kirby Smith's brigade arrived on the field and moved south of the Sudley Springs Road. This move struck the Union brigade of Oliver Howard that had finally moved up on this flank. Colonel Arnold Elzey, who took over the brigade after Smith was severely wounded, ordered a charge that staggered Howard's brigade. Shortly afterward, Jubal Early's brigade arrived, swung around to the left or south of Smith's brigade, and charged the exposed right flank of Howard's brigade. It immediately collapsed and the men fled for the rear.

Beauregard now realized the battle was won. Around 4:00 P.M. he ordered a general advance of all Confederate troops. As they surged forward, Union soldiers withdrew in panic, losing all order and cohesion. They rushed to cross the Stone Bridge and get away from the battlefield. It was a chaotic retreat, but Confederate pursuit was poor and disorganized, and the Federals largely were successful in their escape. The Union army was thoroughly defeated and humiliated, however, and the South had a great opportunity to end the war by pursuing the Union soldiers and forcing their surrender. Yet the only officer who called for a relentless chase after the fleeing Federals was Jackson, soon universally to be called Stonewall. But neither Beauregard nor Johnston carried out a pursuit with any zeal, and most of the troops got away.

George B. McClellan, who was to succeed Winfield Scott and Irvin McDowell as Union commander, gave strong evidence that the Confederacy could have won the war in a quick move. He arrived in Washington on July 26, five days after the battle. He rode around the city. "I found no preparations whatsoever for defense, not even to the extent of putting the troops in military position," he wrote. "A determined attack would doubtless have carried Arlington Heights [opposite the capital] and placed the city at the mercy of a battery of rifled guns. If the Secessionists attached any value to the possession of Washington, they committed their greatest error in not following up the victory of Bull Run."[18]

McClellan's idea that a few cannons posted on Arlington Heights and bombarding the downtown buildings could bring about the capture of Washington reveals his abysmal lack of strategic acumen. The key to Washington was the single railway corridor that connected the capital with the North, the Baltimore & Ohio Railroad. If this corridor was severed anywhere north of the city, Washington's food supply would be cut off and the Abraham Lincoln administration would be compelled to evacuate. A fugitive president and a Rebel-occupied capital would have had a devastating psychological impact on the entire North. To Britain and France, it would have signified that the insurgents were the most probable winners, and their recognition and support of the South would have become much more likely.

At any time between the battle of Manassas and the end of 1861, a modest Confederate force could have forded the Potomac west of the city, swung around to the north, and cut the B&O. The North had nothing to stop such a movement. What prevented it from happening was not the Union army, but the Confederate president, Jefferson Davis. He had decided from the beginning on a policy of passive defense of the South. He did not want to invade the North. He was convinced that the Northern people would soon tire of the war, or Britain and France would intervene to protect their vast textile industries. All the South had to do was to wait patiently, Davis believed, and victory would come.

Jefferson Davis was not a wise man, but he was a stubborn man, and he insisted on following this passive strategy.[19] It is always a mistake for a nation to depend for its fate on the actions of others. When Davis guessed wrong about the attitudes of the Northern people and the political heads of Europe, he had no other policy to fall back on.

Thus the Confederate victory at Manassas, which could easily have resulted in Southern independence, had no lasting effect—other than to convince the Northern people that their ideas of quick success and a speedy restoration of the Union were false. Their defeat revealed the vast task ahead, and they set to work to accomplish it.

At least the lull in the war gave Jackson a chance to see his beloved wife, Anna. She left her father's home in North Carolina and journeyed to Richmond. On September 8, 1861, accompanied by Captain J. Harvey White, who was going to Fairfax to visit a sick brother, Anna managed to board a crowded northbound train. She wired Jackson to meet her at Manassas Junction. He did not get the telegram until after dark. Meanwhile Anna, vainly searching the empty railroad station for her husband, saw no alternative but to reboard the train and travel with Captain White to Fairfax, where she spent the night in the railroad car because no hotel accommodations were available in the crowded town.

First thing Sunday morning, September 9, Jackson arrived in a military wagon and eagerly sought out his wife. The couple embraced ardently. They had not seen each other for five months. Jackson was able to rent a room for Anna at the home of Philip Utterback, who owned an estate a mile east of Centreville, near where Jackson's brigade was camped. Anna remained with Jackson for ten days. It was a wonderful reunion. But then orders came for the brigade to shift closer to Washington. With that, Anna stated, "I was sent back sorrowfully to North Carolina."[20]

CHAPTER 3

Jackson Shows a Way to Victory

The battle of Manassas provided a host of military lessons for both sides. The two most significant tactical ones were taught by Generals Beauregard and McDowell. Beauregard had demonstrated that his belief that the enemy will attack head-on the most obvious and most heavily defended position turned out to be wholly wrong. McDowell had demonstrated that, when the opposing side leaves both of its flanks unguarded, a general can deliver a strong force on one of these flanks and can win a decisive battle by advancing on the enemy rear.

Thus, Blackburn's Ford, where Beauregard was sure the Federals would strike, but didn't, was a minor sideshow. However, McDowell's advance on the Confederate western flank would have won the battle, and very likely the whole war, if Stonewall Jackson had not seen what was happening and placed his brigade in a position to block it.

Manassas had shown Northern strategy plainly. The North had three times the population and eleven times the industrial power of the South, and its leaders were confident that—if they only marshaled their strength—their armies could invade the South, and, by main force, beat down the South's capacity to make war. The South had to develop a strategy to counter the Northern strategy or lose the war. But Southern leaders did not address strategic questions after Manassas. Only Jackson proposed a clear program: an ardent, sustained drive after the fleeing Union army, the capture of Washington, and the ouster of the Lincoln administration.

But neither President Davis nor the senior Confederate commanders paid any attention to Jackson's admonitions. Davis's strategy scarcely deserved the name. He was waiting expectantly for the Northern people to give up the fight and grant Southern independence. Beauregard and Johnston had no alternative strategy, but they had little faith in Davis's passive approach. Although both officers talked about invading the North, there was a severe question about Beauregard's competence in light of the many errors he committed at Manassas, and Johnston made no move to cut the B&O Railroad and isolate Washington, although the Union had nothing to stop it.

There was thus an urgent need for the South to devise a true strategy to conduct the war, but President Davis and his senior generals ignored it.

At the same time, both sides also urgently needed to find some answer to the extremely bloody, unanticipated conditions soldiers had encountered in the battle of Manassas.

One of these conditions was the long range and high velocity of new rifled cannons, which tripled the reach of smoothbore guns, and could deliver rounds deep into the rear of enemy positions.[1] There was much talk that these rifled guns were going to revolutionize warfare. But they were actually making only a modest impact on the battlefield. John D. Imboden experienced their effect at Manassas. The Union battery commanders Ricketts and Griffin had twelve Parrott rifled cannons (built by Captain Robert P. Parrott at Cold Spring, New York), and two "Napoleon" twelve-pounder smoothbore howitzers. The Napoleons,

Imboden wrote, "hurt us more than all the rifles of both batteries, since the shot and shell of rifles, striking the ground at any angle over 15 or 20 degrees, almost without exception bored their way into the ground several feet and did no harm." Since all shells had time fuses, they exploded underground, not hurting the troops, but leaving the ground, Imboden wrote, "as though it had been rooted up by hogs."[2]

While the rifled cannons were affecting battle only moderately, the new long-range Minié-ball rifles were changing the entire conditions of the battlefield. General Barnard Bee discovered this the moment he arrived at the top of Matthews Hill on the day of the battle. Union rifles were scoring deadly hits on Rebels, although the Union soldiers were well over 200 yards away from the Rebels, thus more than twice the range of the old smoothbore muskets. Bee realized that the men, standing in line, as was the standard tactical practice, presented huge targets. He immediately ordered them to fall to the ground and stand up only to fire.

General Bee was fatally wounded in the battle that followed. But he had discovered an interim solution to the problem posed by the Minié ball's long range—troops had to get on the ground or behind bullet-proof barricades to avoid rifle fire. The centuries-old practice of marching men in long lines up to the enemy and exchanging fire with enemy troops, also standing in long lines in the open, was now a recipe for death and mayhem. But this lesson was not learned at Manassas.

Strangely enough, the solution had already been discovered by the Prussian army. In 1848, Prussia introduced the single-shot Dreyse "needle-gun," the first breech-loaded bolt-action rifle ever adopted for military service. The needle-gun had some problems, especially a defective gas seal, but it could fire four rounds in the time a Minié-ball rifle could fire one round, and its range was actually longer than the Minié ball's. The key advantage to the breech-loaded needle-gun, however, was that soldiers could fire and reload it while they were lying flat on the ground—an extremely slow and difficult operation for soldiers armed with the long-barreled Minié-ball rifle, which had to be reloaded at the muzzle.

Prussians armed with the needle-gun could lie on the ground hundreds of yards away from defending troops standing in formation, and cut them to pieces with aimed fire. They no longer had to follow the standard practice of marching up on the enemy in close ranks to within fifty or sixty paces and there unleashing a volley. They could also lie down and stop an enemy advancing on them in the open.

The needle-gun opened the way for entirely new infantry tactics. But it was not adopted by any other major power, including the United States. Why this happened is an object lesson in the rigid and unimaginative thinking of most military men. Geoffrey Wawro describes the bizarre reason that commanders gave for rejecting the needle-gun: soldiers could fire it *too* fast, and might use up all their ammunition before a decision could be reached. Commanders were fixated on the idea of fire *control*. They wanted to fire methodical salvos on the command of an officer. "Volley fire was always more accurate than individual fire because it was supervised," Wawro writes. "And its *moral* effect often proved decisive. Whereas individual fire merely pecked at enemy formations, salvo fire scythed them to the ground in an instant." The cries of the wounded, officers believed, caused reserve forces to retire rather than press an attack or maintain a defense.[3]

Although other armies scorned the needle-gun, Prussian soldiers lying on the ground and firing the rifle massacred Austrian forces standing in formation in the Austro-Prussian War of 1866, and achieved a quick victory. But this proof of the needle-gun's effectiveness came too late for the American Civil War.[4]

Bee had seen plainly that armies, if they were going to avoid unprecedented casualties, had to halt the traditional practice of soldiers on the defensive standing in the open in a line. It was this sight that motivated General Bee to order his men to stand up only to fire. The solution was right there in front of everybody's faces: commanders should order soldiers, as soon as they got into a defensive position, to throw up barricades that would deflect rifle and cannon fire.

But here as well, tradition, bias, and unwillingness to accept new ideas wrecked any concerted move. Building fortifications for permanent or semipermanent positions had been standard practice for centuries, but field fortifications—built quickly in fluid situations to shield temporary locations of troops on the march—were quite unusual. Although a few commanders did order men to build field fortifications, most did not.[5] The reason why is that commanders believed that soldiers behind fortifications could not form up quickly to counterattack if the enemy was repulsed. Commanders held that troops behind parapets would be reluctant to abandon them and go over to the attack. Napoleon had elevated this prejudice into doctrine in *Le Souper de Beaucaire,* a book he had written in 1793. In it he said: "He who remains behind his entrenchments is beaten; experience and theory are one on this point."[6]

But soldiers themselves—facing the unprecedented peril of the Minié ball—sought shelter at every opportunity. Union troops, for example, used the embankments of the sunken Sudley Springs Road to shield their advances on Henry House Hill at Manassas. Soldiers on their own brought about a radical reversal of policy by seeking any possible cover—fences, walls, ditches, reverse slopes of hills, even trees. By late 1862 a transformation had taken place. Wherever they had the chance, soldiers were building field fortifications the moment they got into a defensive position. These included trenches, abatis or barriers of trees and branches to slow the advance of attackers, parapets to shield against rifle and canister fire, and cleared spaces in front of breastworks to expose attackers to defenders' fire.[7]

But in the first year and a half of the war, soldiers on the defensive in fluid field operations—with a few notable exceptions—were largely ordered by their commanders to stand in the open in lines, just as they had done at Manassas, or at most to get behind existing defensive locations, like walls and embankments. And since soldiers were armed with the Minié-ball rifle, not a breech-loaded bolt-action rifle, commanders making attacks *never* were able to avoid advancing long lines of men against defended positions. As a consequence, soldiers were shot down in unparalleled numbers, and six out of seven attacks failed.

George Brinton McClellan arrived in Washington at an opportune time for himself—just after McDowell had been thoroughly defeated at Manassas. McClellan (in Thomas J. Jackson's same West Point class of 1846) had performed excellent service in the Mexican War, and, in the spring of 1861, had driven small, ill-led Confederate forces out of West Virginia. McClellan had announced his modest successes in Napoleon-like manifestos, and had thoroughly impressed Abraham Lincoln. The president put McClellan in charge of reconstituting the Union army, and, on November 1, 1861, advanced him to command all Union forces, replacing General Winfield Scott.

McClellan was an excellent organizer, and he did a superb job of turning thousands of the recruits streaming into Washington into well-drilled soldiers forming well-armed regiments. But the process was slow, and, all through the remainder of 1861, the Union army was only in the state of construction, not a viable military force.

Stonewall Jackson recognized that the North did not have an army that could contest the Army of Northern Virginia, and he became increasingly frustrated at the failure of Johnston and Beauregard to launch an invasion of Maryland.

His dissatisfaction reached a peak in mid-October 1861. He had just been promoted to major general and named to command forces in the Shenandoah Valley. Before he departed for his new job, Jackson called on Gustavus W. Smith, also just promoted to major general and placed in command of a division in the Army of Northern Virginia.

Jackson outlined to Smith a program he had been long pondering. "McClellan, with his army of recruits," Jackson said, "will not attempt to come out against us this autumn. If we remain inactive they will have greatly the advantage over us next spring. Their raw recruits will have then become an organized army, vastly superior in numbers to our own. We are ready at the present moment for active operations in the field, while they are not. We ought to invade their country now, and not wait for them to make the necessary preparations to invade ours. If the president would reinforce this army by taking troops from other points not threatened, and let us make an active campaign of invasion before winter sets in, McClellan's raw recruits could not stand against us in the field.

"Crossing the upper Potomac, occupying Baltimore, and taking possession of Maryland, we could cut off the communications of Washington, force the Federal government to abandon the capital, beat McClellan's army if it came out against us in the open country, destroy industrial establishments wherever we found them, break up the lines of interior commercial intercourse, close the coal mines, seize and, if necessary, destroy the manufactories and commerce of Philadelphia, and of other large cities within our reach; take and hold the narrow neck of country between Pittsburgh and Lake Erie; subsist mainly on the country we traverse, and making unrelenting war amidst their homes, force the people of the North to understand what it will cost them to hold the South in the Union at the bayonet's point."

Jackson asked Smith to use his influence with Johnston and Beaure-gard in favor of immediate aggressive operations. Smith responded that he had been present at a meeting in Fairfax a couple of weeks previously when the two generals had asked President Davis to find 20,000 men to raise the army to 60,000 men and to authorize their invasion of the North. Davis had rejected the proposal, giving as his excuse that he could not denude other places in the Confederacy to concentrate such a large force in northern Virginia. Neither Johnston nor Beauregard had pressed the matter further, Smith told Jackson. Consequently, he said, though he would make the proposal, he was certain nothing could be done to change Davis's mind.

When Jackson heard this, he rose, shook Smith's hand, and said, "I am sorry, very sorry." Without another word, he went to his horse and rode away.[8]

It is questionable whether Johnston and Beauregard were serious in their proposal to invade the North. Their total inaction up to this point raises the suspicion that they were merely making a pro forma proposal to cover themselves. Beauregard departed for the Western Theater in March 1862, where his poor performance soon cost him his job, and Johnston didn't mention the subject again until months later, when he gave Davis the choice of fighting the Union army in front of Richmond or invading the North. It was plain that he preferred fighting at Richmond—and so did Davis. So Johnston never made an earnest proposal to invade Maryland and seek a decision on the war.

But Jackson's proposal was completely earnest, and he was certain that it could win the war in a few weeks. There was literally nothing to stop the campaign he proposed. The north-south corridor from Baltimore to southern Maine contained most Northern industry and most of the Northern people.[9] It depended on railways running up and down this corridor. Here was the Achilles' heel of the Union. If the railways were cut anywhere along the corridor, the North could not pursue a war.

Jackson saw this vulnerability, and so did Smith. But President Davis was deeply opposed to offensive action. He fell back on his conviction that he did not have to do anything except wait patiently for the North to tire of the war. Or maybe Britain and France would intervene to protect their immense textile industries. It was a fatal and foolish belief, because the European powers did not want to get involved, and Abraham Lincoln was showing unmistakably that he intended to pursue the war to the bitter end. The South had to win the war all by itself. If Davis could not be pushed away from his passivity, the South was doomed to defeat.

Stonewall Jackson set up headquarters for his small Shenandoah Valley force at Winchester.[10] He accepted the offer of Lieutenant Colonel Lewis T. Moore to use his vacant home in Winchester as headquarters and a place to reside. Moore, wounded in the leg at Manassas, was hospitalized. In late December 1861, Jackson succumbed to his wife Anna's entreaties to join him. Friends accompanied Anna to Richmond, while a "kind-hearted but absent-minded old clergyman" traveled with her the rest of the way, though losing her trunk in the process. Anna arrived late at night at the Taylor Hotel in Winchester, where Jackson met her and swept her into his arms. He took her to the Moore house, and made arrangements for them to eat their meals at the manse of the Reverend James and Fanny Graham two doors down the street. The Reverend Graham was pastor of the Kent Street Presbyterian Church in Winchester. Anna and Jackson soon moved to the Graham house, and Anna quickly blended into Winchester society. Jackson attended an occasional function now that his wife was there.[11]

This was the only time in the war that they had an extended time together. In February 1862 she announced to Jackson that she was pregnant. By early March 1862 it was clear that campaigning would soon begin and Winchester was no place for Anna. He put her on a stagecoach for Strasburg, where she could catch a train for Richmond. Anna remembered the day well: "To the last moment he lingered at the door of the coach in which I left with bright smiles, and not a cloud upon his peaceful brow."[12]

They were not to see each other again for thirteen months. Anna went first to Hampden-Sydney College, just south of Farmville, Virginia, where two of her second cousins lived. One was the wife of Benjamin M. Smith, a theology professor at the seminary. The other was Lavinia Morrison Dabney, the wife of the Reverend Robert L. Dabney, another cleric professor. Before the end of the month Jackson drew Dabney into service as his adjutant, a post he maintained until midsummer 1862 when ill health required him to give up the post.

It was in late winter 1862 during his stay with the Grahams that Jackson pronounced one of the only two utterances he ever made openly about the conduct of war. The other occasion was to John D. Imboden (see page 107). Speaking to the Reverend Graham one evening, Jackson said: "War means fighting. The business of the soldier is to fight. Armies are not called out to dig trenches, to throw up breastworks, and live in camps, but to find the enemy, and strike him, to invade his country, and do him all possible damage in the shortest possible time." Graham, taken aback, responded: "This would involve great destruction of both life and property." Jackson nodded, then answered: "Yes, while it lasted; but such a war would of necessity be of brief continuance, and so would be an economy of prosperity and life in the end. To move swiftly, strike vigorously, and secure all the fruits of victory, is the secret of successful war."[13]

It was during this period that Jackson began to work out in his mind methods and means to win the war for the South. As Colonel G. F. R. Henderson wrote in his brilliant biography of Jackson, "Intense concentration of thought and purpose, in itself an indication of a powerful will, had distinguished Jackson from his very boyhood."[14] A distinctive pattern emerged. This pattern continued on through the campaigns that were to follow. Jackson would pace for hours in his office or outside his tent, his hands behind his back, absorbed in meditation. He would ride for hours without raising his eyes or speaking.

Henderson wrote: "It was unquestionably at such moments that he was working out his plans, step by step, forecasting the counter movements of his enemy, and providing for every emergency that might occur. And here the habit of keeping his whole faculties fixed on a single object, and of imprinting on his memory the successive processes of complicated problems, fostered by his methods of study which at West Point and Lexington must have been an inestimable advantage. Brilliant strategic maneuvers are not a matter of inspiration and of decision on the spur of the moment. The problems presented by a theater of war, with their many factors, are not to be solved except by a vigorous and sustained intellectual effort."[15]

This was the identical pattern of Napoleon Bonaparte. "If I always appear prepared," he wrote, "it is because, before entering on an undertaking, I have meditated for long and have foreseen what may occur. It is not genius which reveals to me suddenly and secretly what I should do in circumstances unexpected by others; it is thought and meditation."[16]

By early 1862, McClellan had built a military machine approaching 240,000 men, but he was unwilling to move against Johnston's Army of Northern Virginia around Centreville and Manassas. The reason he gave was that his spy service under a private detective, Allan Pinkerton, had reported that Johnston had a well-drilled, well-armed, ably led, and strongly entrenched army of 150,000 men. In fact, Johnston's army had just 40,000 men, was wretchedly equipped, very poorly drilled, and possessed few entrenchments. Though it numbered able officers among its generals, it was still badly commanded, and had only been formed into divisions as winter came on.

McClellan's claim that the Confederate army was so huge was only an excuse to cloak a crippling defect that he was trying to hide—his extreme reluctance to use his army. By late February 1862, President Lincoln and his secretary of war, Edwin McMasters Stanton, were becoming painfully aware of this failing, and were trying to figure what to do about it.

McClellan at last submitted a campaign plan to Lincoln. He proposed to transfer 150,000 men to Fort Monroe, an old post never given up by the U.S. Army at the tip of the peninsula between the York and James rivers, and from there march on Richmond, seventy miles to the northwest. This plan exploited Northern sea power, both to transfer the army by water and to supply it thereafter by ships.

Lincoln did not like the plan because he feared that Johnston would make a dash for Washington. Lincoln had an exaggerated fear for the safety of the capital, despite the fact that McClellan had constructed a solid ring of forts around the city in 1861 that could have stopped or slowed any direct assault on it. Lincoln was consumed with anxiety that Rebel forces nevertheless might rush on the city at any time and seize it. Lincoln had little strategic sense, and never understood that the way to capture Washington was to cut the rail lines leading north, not to assault the city directly.

McClellan responded that the garrisons in the forts around Washington, plus strong field forces left behind, were more than enough to protect the capital. Anyway, he said, Johnston was certain to move to the defense of Richmond the moment he discovered the Union army advancing on it.

Lincoln wasn't convinced. While he and McClellan were debating the issue, Johnston, realizing that his army was exposed so far north, began pulling it back on March 8, 1862, first to the Rappahannock River, some fifty miles south of Washington, then to the more defensible Rapidan River, a few miles farther south and just north of Orange Court House and Gordonsville.

This unexpected move placed Johnston's army in a position to reinforce Rebel forces on the peninsula east of Richmond. But the advantage of sea supply of Fort Monroe by way of Chesapeake Bay was decisive in McClellan's eyes, and he pressed Lincoln for a decision. Secretary of War Stanton wired McClellan on March 13, 1862, that the president made no objection so long as enough troops were left to protect Washington. On March 17, McClellan stood on a wharf at Alexandria and watched the first contingent of the army head down the Potomac and into Chesapeake Bay. McClellan had assembled 113 steamers, 188 schooners, and eighty-eight barges to shuttle the army 10,000 men at a time to Fort Monroe. The transfer was going to take three weeks.

But Lincoln and Stanton had lost faith in McClellan, and on March 12, 1862, they instituted an almost unbelievably ill-conceived program. Neither Lincoln nor Stanton had any training in military theory, but they decided they knew how to win the war, and they set about to do it. First, without even informing McClellan, they stripped him of his title as general in chief, and restricted him to command only of the Army of the Potomac, about to move to Fort Monroe. They then divided the Eastern Theater of war into separate departments, each one reporting directly to Lincoln and Stanton. These included the garrison guarding Washington, plus three unattached armies—a 15,000-man force under John C. Frémont in the Allegheny Mountains descending on Staunton, Virginia; a 23,000-man force under Nathaniel P. Banks, moving south up the Shenandoah Valley;[17] and a 38,000-man corps under Irvin McDowell, supposed to join McClellan, but held up around Alexandria as an extra guard for Washington. The upshot was that McClellan, who expected to have 150,000 men, was left with just over 100,000, while the bulk of the Union forces, 140,000 men, were spread across the map.

Lincoln and Stanton had learned nothing from the fateful consequences of keeping Robert Patterson's 16,000-man army in the

Shenandoah Valley when the battle of Manassas was about to be joined. They were ignorant of Napoleon's fundamental rule for victory: a commander must concentrate his maximum force at the point of decision—in this case McClellan's march on Richmond. And they had no inkling of the advice of the Prussian king Frederick the Great in the eighteenth century. "A defensive war is apt to betray us into too frequent detachments," he wrote. "Those generals who have had but little experience attempt to protect every point, while those who are better acquainted with their profession, having only the capital object in view, guard against a decisive blow, and acquiesce in smaller misfortunes to avoid greater."[18]

The Confederacy had been handed a truly amazing gift. Lincoln and Stanton had scattered an immense force over the landscape to accomplish a number of inessential tasks, and had saddled their main commander, McClellan, with a force only slightly larger than what the Confederacy could mobilize against him.

The main job of the Confederacy, besides keeping McClellan from seizing Richmond, was to find some way to prevent the scattered Union elements from joining him. Unfortunately there were only the tiniest of forces available to attempt this. Stonewall Jackson had just 4,600 men at Winchester to confront Banks, and Edward Johnson had only 2,800 men at Staunton standing in the path of Frémont. There was no significant force available to deal with McDowell if he marched directly on Richmond from the north, as was being contemplated once Washington was seen to be secure. The Confederate War Department had raised Johnston's combined force to 65,000 men by urgent reinforcements. It was searching everywhere for additional troops, but few were available.

The task seemed hopeless to most of the senior Confederate officers, and the early demise of the Confederacy appeared certain. But Stonewall Jackson felt otherwise. He saw something no one else saw—

the very scattering of the Union forces could be exploited to keep them from aiding McClellan. And this failure might just keep McClellan, already notorious in both armies for his "slows," from moving. In other words, Jackson saw the opportunity for a swift campaign that not only could neutralize all the scattered Union forces, but also could stop McClellan from attacking Richmond. If he could accomplish this, Jackson was already putting together a proposal to President Davis to transfer the entire campaign entirely out of Virginia and move it "to the banks of the Susquehanna" in Maryland and Pennsylvania.

As soon as McClellan landed his army at Fort Monroe, he reverted to form. Instead of driving straight on Richmond, he stopped to lay siege to a tiny force of 13,000 Rebels under General John B. Magruder, who had built a flimsy line across the peninsula around Yorktown. McClellan was prevented from moving on the wide, tidal James River and outflanking the line because of the Confederate ironclad *Virginia,* which generally went by its old name, the *Merrimac.* Based on Norfolk, the *Virginia* made all the wooden ships of the U.S. Navy obsolete. Even after a Union armored gunboat, the *Monitor,* had fought the Confederate ship to a draw, the *Virginia* remained a threat.[19]

McClellan could easily have smashed Magruder's line with his vastly superior force, but he settled down for a month in front of it, giving Stonewall Jackson ample time to implement his plan.

Once Johnston had pulled the Army of Northern Virginia back to the Rapidan, Jackson was too exposed at Winchester, in the northern reaches of the Shenandoah Valley. Accordingly, he withdrew southward fifteen miles up the macadamized Valley Pike (now U.S. Route 11, parallel to I-81) to Strasburg, and then to Mount Jackson, twenty-one miles farther south, hoping to pull Nathaniel P. Banks's Union army after him.

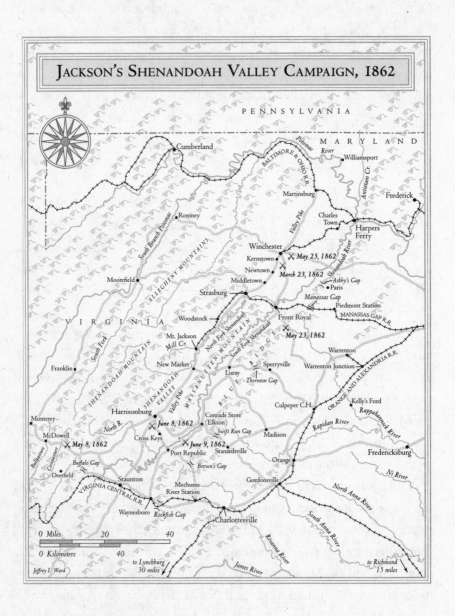

JACKSON'S SHENANDOAH VALLEY CAMPAIGN, 1862

PENNSYLVANIA

MARYLAND

Cumberland

Potomac River

Williamsport

BALTIMORE & OHIO R.R.

Frederick

Romney

Martinsburg

Antietam Cr.

South Branch Potomac

Charles Town

Harpers Ferry

ALLEGHENY MOUNTAINS

Moorefield

Winchester

Kernstown ✕ May 25, 1862

Newtown

March 23, 1862

Middletown

Shenandoah River

Ashby's Gap

Paris

VIRGINIA

Strasburg

Manassas Gap

Woodstock

Front Royal

Piedmont Station

MANASSAS GAP R.R.

North Fork Shenandoah

May 23, 1862

SHENANDOAH MOUNTAIN

South Fork

Mt. Jackson
Mill Cr.

New Market

South Fork Shenandoah

Warrenton

Sperryville

Warrenton Junction

Franklin

Luray

Thornton Gap

RIDGE

MASSANUTTEN MOUNTAIN

Valley Pike

B L U E

SHENANDOAH VALLEY

Culpeper C.H.

Kelly's Ford

ORANGE AND ALEXANDRIA R.R.

Rappahannock River

Monterey

North R.

Harrisonburg

✕ June 8, 1862

Conrads Store
(Elkton)

Swift Run Gap

Madison

Rapidan River

McDowell

✕ May 8, 1862

Cross Keys

Fredericksburg

Bullpasture

Cowpasture

Buffalo Gap

✕ June 9, 1862

Port Republic

Stanardsville

Orange

Ni River

Deerfield

Brown's Gap

Gordonsville

North Anna River

Staunton

VIRGINIA CENTRAL R.R.

Mechums
River Station

South Anna River

Waynesboro

Rockfish Gap

Charlottesville

Rivanna River

to Richmond
15 miles

0 Miles   20   40

0 Kilometers   40

to Lynchburg
30 miles

James River

Jeffrey L. Ward

But when Banks arrived at Winchester, he found out the tiny size of Jackson's force. Deciding it was of little consequence, he got permission to move the bulk of his 23,000-man army east toward Manassas. His new orders were to protect Washington and the line of the Potomac while McClellan's army completed its move to the peninsula. He then was to seize Warrenton, on the Orange & Alexandria Railroad southwest of Manassas, and reopen the Manassas Gap Railroad from Manassas to Strasburg to ensure supplies for a 9,000-man division under James Shields, which was the only Union force to remain in the Shenandoah Valley.

Jackson's daring cavalry chief, Turner Ashby, had been monitoring these Union movements. On March 21, 1862, he told Jackson incorrectly that not only had Banks's main force departed the valley, but that all of Shields's division except four regiments, or about 3,000 men, had also evacuated.

This was precisely the break Jackson had been waiting for. Jackson was well aware of Abraham Lincoln's unreasonable anxiety about the safety of Washington. He was certain that any strike that seemed to threaten the capital would evoke an excessive defensive reaction from Lincoln. Accordingly, Jackson set his little army in motion northward. Jackson's men had already dubbed themselves the "foot cavalry" because of the exceptionally fast marching Jackson was demanding of them. But the march down the Valley Pike was extreme even for them, and only 3,000 men remained in the ranks at 2:00 P.M. on Sunday, March 23, when they came up on Ashby involved in an artillery skirmish with Federals at Kernstown, four miles south of Winchester.

Ashby assured Jackson that the Union force visible on open ground to the east of the Valley Pike was only a rear guard, and that the rest of Shields's division had already left the valley. Jackson told Ashby to demonstrate with his artillery. Meanwhile, he moved the bulk of his troops and guns three miles to his left or west, up a long, low wooded hill called Sandy Ridge. He hoped to get on the flank and rear of the Union troops and evict them from their position.

But Shields's entire division of 9,000 men was hidden in woods and behind a hill north of Kernstown. Shields had been wounded, and the temporary commander, Colonel Nathan Kimball, sent a brigade onto Sandy Ridge, followed by another brigade, to stop Jackson. Realizing he was facing a much larger force than his own, Jackson ordered his last three regiments to come onto the ridge. But the Stonewall Brigade commander, Richard B. Garnett, was afraid his thin line was about to crack. Before the reinforcements could arrive, he ordered withdrawal.

The Confederate line dissolved into a crowd of skirmishers, with the regiments all mixed up. They fell back, still fighting, before the Federal troops advancing through the smoke of battle. On the Rebel extreme right a cannon firing canister at 250 yards' range drove back the Union soldiers. But in the center the guns were unable to hold their own. Union riflemen swarmed through the thickets on the hill, forcing the batteries to fall back. One Rebel six-pounder cannon was overturned. Under hot Union fire delivered at not more than fifty paces, the sergeant in charge cut loose the three remaining horses, but had to abandon the gun to the enemy.

Jackson was watching the progress of the action on the left. Suddenly he saw the lines of his old brigade falter and fall back. Galloping to the spot, he tried to restore order. Seizing a drummer boy by the shoulder, he dragged him to a rise of ground, in full view of the troops, and told him: "Beat the rally!" The drum rolled at Jackson's order. With his hand on the frightened boy's shoulder, he tried to check the flight of his defeated troops amid the storm of bullets and clouds of smoke.[20] But the Rebel fighting line had shattered into fragments. A Union officer reported: "Many of the brave Virginians lingered in the rear of their retreating comrades, loading as they slowly retired, and rallying in squads in every ravine and behind every hill—or hiding singly among the trees."[21]

But it was impossible to stay the rout. A forced retreat usually degenerates quickly into a chaotic flight, and this is what happened to Garnett's brigade. The remnants of Jackson's force fled southward, having lost 718 men to the Federals' 590. Nearly one-fourth of Jackson's infantry had fallen or been captured.

During the night of March 23, Hunter McGuire, the medical director of Jackson's army, reported to Jackson that there were not enough vehicles to carry the wounded soldiers south to safety. Jackson told McGuire to impress carriages in the neighborhood. "But that requires time," McGuire replied. "Can you stay till it has been done?" "Make yourself easy, sir," Jackson replied. "This army stays here until the last man is removed." Fortunately the work was finished before daylight.[22]

Jackson relieved Garnett of his command for retreating without orders, but the Confederate retreat had anything but a positive effect on Lincoln.[23] He put no stake in Jackson's audacity, and reasoned that he would not have attacked unless he had been strongly reinforced. Fearing an immediate descent on Washington, Lincoln ordered Banks's entire army to move back at once into the Shenandoah Valley. He also ordered Louis Blenker's 10,000-man division, scheduled to be sent to McClellan on the peninsula, to go instead to John Frémont's army, which was approaching the Shenandoah Valley from the west. Finally, he ordered Irvin McDowell's 38,000-man corps at Alexandria to remain. Secretary of War Stanton instructed McDowell: "You will consider the national capital as especially under your protection and make no movement throwing your force out of position for the discharge of this primary duty."[24]

Thus, because of the action of 3,000 Confederate soldiers under Stonewall Jackson, Banks's entire army of 23,000 men was thrown back into the valley, and 48,000 Union troops who might have been used to defeat Confederates in the main arena at Richmond were diverted to prevent an attack on Washington that never was going to come.

The effect of Jackson's strike was even more telling. McClellan, denied the reinforcement of McDowell's corps, was paralyzed. He complained bitterly to Lincoln. Exasperated, the president answered that McClellan had 100,000 men and said, "You must act."[25] But McClellan did not act. He continued to wait for McDowell. Thus Jackson's blow at Kernstown had stopped McClellan in his tracks. Johnston, President Davis, and Robert E. Lee, who had joined Davis on March 13 as his formal military adviser, had more time to work out a way to prevent disaster. Jackson was not thinking about avoiding defeat, however. He was thinking about translating Lincoln and Stanton's profound mistakes into Southern victory.

CHAPTER 4

———————

The Shenandoah Valley Campaign

As soon as it became clear that McClellan was making his major effort on the peninsula, General Johnston began moving the Army of Northern Virginia from the Rapidan River to Richmond. He left only the 8,000-man division of Richard S. Ewell in the vicinity of Culpeper to guard the Orange & Alexandria Railroad and reach out to Stonewall Jackson in the Shenandoah Valley.

On April 14, 1862, President Davis called a council of war in Richmond to discuss the crisis. Joining him were Robert E. Lee, the Confederate navy secretary George W. Randolph, General Johnston, and his two senior commanders, Gustavus W. Smith and James Longstreet. Johnston had just returned from a visit to Magruder's line at Yorktown, and he didn't like what he saw.

Johnston said the Yorktown line was untenable. It was subject to Union artillery fire on the front and the chance of an amphibious landing on the flank. Johnston (reading from a paper written by Gustavus W. Smith and approved by Johnston) asked Davis to choose between two completely contradictory courses of action. One choice was to withdraw all forces immediately to Richmond and challenge McClellan to a showdown battle at the gates of the city. The other was to leave a small force to protect Richmond, and strike with as many troops as could be gathered into Maryland and Pennsylvania. Johnston said fast-moving Confederate troops could seize Philadelphia or New York before McClellan could capture Richmond.

Johnston's whole proposal for an invasion of the North had an air of unreality about it. Striking hell-for-leather for Philadelphia and New York was not a plan, it was a fantasy. The North could be crippled by severing the Baltimore & Ohio Railroad's line just north of Washington, a much simpler and much more feasible idea. As the council of war went on, it became clear that Johnston actually entertained little interest in an invasion of the North, and what he really wanted to do was to fight McClellan at Richmond.[1] This didn't make much sense either. As things were going, fighting for Richmond would come sooner or later, but voluntarily giving up the peninsula along with Norfolk and the ironclad *Virginia* was senseless. McClellan was so slow-moving and indecisive that much might happen if he were fought every inch of the way up the peninsula.

In the end, Davis ordered Johnston to defend the Yorktown line as long as possible, and retreat to Richmond only when it became necessary. But the proposals Johnston had presented to the council of war had cast real doubt on his capacity to command the only army that could save the Confederacy.

As Nathaniel Banks's Union army returned to the Shenandoah Valley, Stonewall Jackson withdrew southward. Banks was a former governor of Massachusetts and a most uninspired general. He had been stunned by Jackson's attack at Kernstown, and, with a force now of 20,000 men, he moved only to Woodstock, thirty miles south of Winchester.

The great biographer of Jackson, English Colonel G. F. R. Henderson, wrote that "Banks, whenever his superiors wanted him to move, had invariably the best of reasons for halting. But when he was told to halt, he immediately panted to be let loose." It was said of Banks, Henderson wrote, that he had a fine career ahead of him, until Lincoln "undertook to make of him what the good Lord hadn't, a great general."[2]

At Woodstock, Banks was safe, but he and John Frémont, approaching Staunton from the Allegheny Mountains to the west with an army soon to total 25,000 men, had orders to seize the entire Shenandoah Valley and deprive the Confederacy of its well-tended fields, pastures, and orchards. They produced much of the food for the people of Virginia as well as the Confederate soldiers there. The town of Staunton was the key to the valley. The Virginia Central Railroad ran from Richmond, through Staunton, to a point near Covington. If Frémont and Banks joined at Staunton, the Confederacy would lose the valley, and Union forces could cross the Blue Ridge to Charlottesville and move on to Richmond.

From the Confederacy's point of view, the situation was dire. Jackson had raised his little army to 6,000 men by recruiting and Edward Johnson at Staunton had 2,800 men. Although President Davis and General Lee had informed Jackson that he could use Richard Ewell's 8,000-man division east of the Blue Ridge if necessary, the combined total was only a little over one-third as many troops as Banks and Frémont commanded.

Frémont was facing no opposition in West Virginia, but he still was doing a poor job reaching Staunton. He complained about supply difficulties, and had spread his force in four separate parts from Franklin northward to Romney and along the South Branch of the Potomac River. Banks had no such difficulties. The macadamized Valley Pike could bring supplies in all weathers from Winchester, which was connected by rail to Harpers Ferry and the B&O Railroad, and he could march south on this same Valley Pike to Staunton.

Although Banks had reason to be cautious, he had no idea whatsoever of the ambush that Stonewall Jackson was laying for him. Under prodding from Lincoln and Secretary of War Stanton, Banks at last moved south up the Valley Pike, ousting Jackson from Rudes Hill, an open ridge seventeen miles south of Woodstock and five miles north of New Market. On April 17, 1862, Federal troops seized New Market, forcing Jackson back to Harrisonburg, eighteen miles to the south and twenty-five miles north of Staunton.

To Banks, it seemed only a simple matter to continue pushing Jackson's much-inferior force straight on up the Valley Pike to Staunton. As Banks prepared to march on Harrisonburg, however, Stonewall Jackson made an utterly bewildering move. He completely abandoned protection of the Valley Pike, turned his little army abruptly eastward, marched eighteen miles to Conrad's Store (now Elkton), and bivouacked nearby in Elk Run Valley at the foot of Swift Run Gap in the Blue Ridge (present-day U.S. Route 33).

Despite the urgency of the situation, Jackson had time to write his wife, Anna: "I do so much want to see my darling, but fear such a privilege will not be enjoyed for some time to come." Even so, he wrote, "our gallant little army is increasing in numbers, and my prayer is that it may be an army of the living God as well as of its country."[3]

At first, Banks was delighted. He moved some of his forces on to Harrisonburg, thinking Jackson was abandoning the valley entirely and marching his little force to Richmond.

But one of his officers, Major Wilder Dwight of the 2nd Massachusetts, saw the situation more clearly. At New Market in the third week of April, Major Dwight, a former attorney in Roxbury, wrote: "Jackson was ready to run, and began to do so as soon as we began to move. But perhaps we hastened him a little. Here we are, eighty miles from our supplies, all our wagons on the road, our tents and baggage behind, our rations precarious, and following a mirage into the desert."[4]

As Banks looked more carefully at his map, he slowly realized that Jackson had used the lure of the Valley Pike to draw him into a snare, just as a spider uses light to draw moths into its web.

The map revealed the bitter truth. From Harrisonburg and Conrad's Store all the way to Front Royal, forty-five miles to the northeast, Massanutten Mountain forms a great solid mass 3,000 feet high in the midst of the Shenandoah Valley. To the east the narrow, deeply wooded Luray Valley divides Massanutten from the sharply rising Blue Ridge beyond. On the west, Massanutten drops to the broad, open Shenandoah Valley. The bold, swift South Fork of the Shenandoah River runs down Luray Valley, while the North Fork drains the main valley. The two branches join at Front Royal to run as a single stream to the Potomac at Harpers Ferry.

Banks discovered that precisely one road ran over Massanutten Mountain, from Luray on the east to New Market on the west (present-day U.S. Route 211). He realized that, if he launched his army up the Valley Pike to Staunton, Jackson could move down the Luray Valley, take the one road over Massanutten Mountain, and emerge at New Market, thereby cutting off Banks's supply line and isolating him in enemy country. Long before any Union force could rescue him, Banks would be compelled to surrender his whole army. If he divided his forces, and left a garrison at New Market while marching the rest of his army on Staunton, Jackson still might overwhelm the New Market force, still cut his supply line, and then advance on Banks's weakened force and destroy it. No, Banks saw, he had fallen into a trap. He could not budge from Harrisonburg and New Market.[5]

Unbeknownst to Banks, the move to Conrad's Store also had opened up a vast strategic opportunity to Stonewall Jackson. First, possession of Elk Run Valley guaranteed the access of Richard Ewell's division into the Shenandoah Valley. In anticipation, Jackson sent one of his young aides, Henry Kyd Douglas, across the Blue Ridge to find

Ewell somewhere near Culpeper and alert him to be prepared to move at a moment's notice.[6]

Second, Jackson had devised a plan to deal with Frémont, who at last had become a danger. His advanced brigade had reached Monterey, and was getting ready to march the thirty-five miles to Staunton.[7] But Jackson incorporated the plan to neutralize Frémont into a much vaster program—which he as yet had not divulged to Davis, Lee, or Johnston—to force McClellan to evacuate the peninsula without a decisive collision, and to take the war entirely out of Virginia.

Jackson planned to execute the first part of this plan primarily by maneuver and with only the smallest use of force. This part of his plan did not involve any of the Confederate troops under Johnston gathering to protect Richmond. Indeed, its full implementation would require only a minor proportion of this force. Jackson did not intend to *drive* McClellan out of Virginia. He intended to *pull* him out.

For the first part of his plan to work, he needed no other reinforcement than Richard Ewell's division. On April 30, he called on Ewell to move at once to Elk Run Valley, and to remain there unless Banks marched on Staunton, in which case he was to drive down the Luray Valley, cross Massanutten, and seize New Market. Jackson told his cavalry chief, Turner Ashby, merely to "feel out" the Federals toward Harrisonburg.

When Ewell arrived at Elk Run Valley, Jackson and his entire force had disappeared, no one knew where. Ewell was exasperated, but obediently kept his division there and watched Banks, who remained immobile. Jackson, in fact, had marched his little army south twelve miles to Port Republic, a place just within reach of the enemy's patrols. Then he and his army vanished. The people of Staunton, with Frémont advancing on them, were plunged into despair. On Sunday, May 3, 1862, the terrible news came that Jackson's army was crossing the Blue Ridge at Brown's Gap, southeast of Port Republic, and that the entire valley was being abandoned to the enemy.

When General Banks received the news that Jackson was in retreat, he wired Secretary Stanton he was certain that "Jackson is bound for Richmond."[8] Banks suggested that he leave the valley, cross the Blue Ridge, and clear the whole country north of Gordonsville.

But Stanton had an entirely different take on Jackson's disappearance. On April 21, Lincoln, no longer fearing Jackson, had authorized McDowell to move his corps to Fredericksburg, with the intention of his marching on to Richmond, fifty-five miles away, and reinforcing McClellan—who was still paralyzed with inaction awaiting McDowell's arrival. Jackson might be "bound for Richmond," Stanton thought. But he also might be heading to Fredericksburg to challenge McDowell head-on. Stanton wired McDowell not to move until Jackson's intentions were better known. Stanton then ordered Banks to send James Shields's 9,000-man division to McDowell as a precaution.

Thus Jackson, merely on the strength of his mysterious move over the Blue Ridge, had managed nearly to halve the size of Banks's army, stop McDowell's march on Richmond in its tracks, and keep McClellan immobilized. Much more was to come.

On May 4, Jackson emerged at Mechums River Station on the Virginia Central Railroad, nine miles west of Charlottesville. Trains were waiting, and the soldiers were sure they were headed to either Richmond or Fredericksburg. But when the trains started off, they moved *west* to Staunton. In a matter of hours, Jackson had placed his army in a position to block Frémont's advance on Staunton. And Banks could do nothing to stop it. If Jackson had marched directly on Staunton from Elk Run Valley, he would have proclaimed his intention, and Frémont and Banks could have crushed his army between them. But Jackson had moved so mysteriously that both forces had remained inactive and far apart.

Jackson joined with Edward Johnson's force and together they advanced westward to meet Frémont's lead forces, which now consisted of two brigades totaling 4,000 men under Robert C. Schenck and Robert H. Milroy, who were approaching the village of McDowell, twenty-seven miles west of Staunton.

Jackson's much superior force challenged Schenck and Milroy on May 8. The Union officers had worsened their already hopeless situation by setting up their defenses guarding the bridge at McDowell over the little Bullpasture River running through a deep hollow surrounded by high mountains. All Jackson had to do was to move on their rear, which he at once made preparations to do. But some of his soldiers had occupied steep Sitlington's Hill, overlooking the village on the east. Milroy concluded that Jackson was dragging cannons up the hill to bombard the village, a perfectly ridiculous idea. But Milroy convinced Schenck he was right, and they launched attacks straight up the mountainside at the Rebels on the summit. In this fashion, the absolutely unnecessary battle of McDowell was fought. The Union attacks all failed, but lots of men fell on both sides. At the end of the day, Schenck and Milroy realized they were trapped, and evacuated their forces during the night.

Jackson drove the Union forces far back into the Alleghenies, but wasn't interested in catching them. He was, however, determined to prevent Frémont from being able to seize Staunton, or to pose any danger to Jackson's plans. Once this task was accomplished, Jackson turned his army back into the main Shenandoah Valley and headed toward a confrontation with Banks.[9] Meanwhile, Banks had withdrawn down the valley to Strasburg, where he built formidable defensive works on the Valley Pike in anticipation of an attack by Jackson.

Jackson pulled his force onto the Valley Pike. On May 19 he pitched a tent near a stream just south of Harrisonburg. He had time for a quick letter to Anna: "How I do desire to see our country free and at peace! It appears to me that I would appreciate home more than I have ever done before. Here I am sitting in the open air, writing on my knee for want of a table."[10] The next day he marched to New Market.

While all this had been going on, McClellan at long last had broken through the frail defenses at Yorktown, and had moved to within twenty miles of Richmond. The South was forced to abandon Norfolk and to scuttle the ironclad *Virginia* because its draft was too deep to move up the James River. Union gunboats now ascended the James to Drewry's Bluff, six miles below Richmond, where Confederate batteries barred passage.

The situation was desperate for the Confederacy. Richmond was in danger. Authorities removed military stores and packed archives ready to go. In the emergency, General Johnston wired Jackson to release Ewell's division to assist in the defense of Richmond. Jackson wired back that he needed Ewell to deal with Banks. Johnston replied that Banks should be left "in his works" at Strasburg, and that Ewell should come east.[11]

Jackson had no intention of attacking Banks "in his works," but he needed Ewell's division to accomplish what he did have in mind. He telegraphed Lee: "I am of opinion that an attempt should be made to defeat Banks, but under instructions from General Johnston I do not feel at liberty to make an attack. Please answer by telegraph at once."[12] Lee responded giving Jackson authority to keep Ewell in the valley.

Banks had posted 7,400 of his men in the entrenchments at Strasburg. He placed another 1,000 to guard the wooden Manassas Gap Railroad viaduct over the Shenandoah River at Front Royal, ten miles east of Strasburg, and he located the remainder of his force back at Winchester, seventeen miles north of Strasburg.

To give Banks's spies the impression that he was massing his troops at New Market preparatory to a march directly on the defenses of Strasburg, Jackson ordered Ewell to send his Louisiana Brigade, commanded by Richard Taylor, the only son of President Zachary Taylor, from Conrad's Store around the base of Massanutten Mountain to New Market.

Taylor had been educated at West Point, Harvard, and Yale, and, before the war, had been a successful sugar planter in Louisiana. After Taylor arrived with his Louisianans, many of them French-speaking Cajuns, one of his Creole bands struck up a gay waltz, and several of the men, shockingly, danced with one another. The unmusical Presbyterian Jackson, sitting on a rail fence, stopped sucking on a lemon, watched the dancing, then said to Taylor, "Thoughtless fellows for serious work," and returned to his lemon.[13]

Jackson's soldiers were confident that they were going to march straight down the Valley Pike the next morning, May 21, and challenge Banks in a frontal battle to drive him out of his works. Jackson, as always, divulged nothing, merely telling Taylor that his brigade would take the lead and that it was heading north. Meanwhile, Jackson instructed Turner Ashby to place a solid cavalry screen in front of Strasburg to indicate to Banks that the main army was coming behind. He ordered Ashby to send other troopers to cut all communications between the Federal and the Confederate lines to prevent any spies or scouts from getting through. On May 22 the cavalry was to follow the route of the main army.

As the army moved north on the Valley Pike, Jackson rode with Taylor in the van. When they got to the northern edge of New Market, Jackson quietly turned the head of the column to the right—up the long, sloping road leading over Massanutten Mountain to Luray! While Banks was waiting confidently at Strasburg for the Rebels to come straight down the pike, they had turned completely away and were marching eastward over the one road crossing Massanutten Mountain.

The soldiers were bewildered and chattered like magpies about the possible reason. Taylor was equally baffled, but joked that Jackson must be an unconscious poet who wanted the army to enjoy the beauties of the Shenandoah Valley.

Jackson's purpose became clearer hours later when the army filed down off Massanutten into the Luray Valley, where they found Ewell's soldiers waiting. In one swift move, Jackson had concentrated all his infantry and guns. The combined army now headed straight north from Luray. The soldiers saw that a unified force of almost 17,000 men was going to fall on the Union flank, specifically on the hopelessly outnumbered garrison guarding the railroad bridge at Front Royal. And there was nothing anybody could do to stop it.

Indeed, Jackson's move was completely unanticipated by the Federal leaders. In numerous telegrams sent back and forth, they were congratulating themselves that they had handled matters well and that things were going splendidly. The Confederates had not followed up on the pursuit of Frémont in the Alleghenies. Banks felt fully secure behind his fortifications at Strasburg. McClellan was boasting of imminent success now that McDowell's corps was being promised to him. McDowell had already crossed the Rappahannock River at Fredericksburg and was beginning to move to Richmond. And Lincoln and Stanton, expecting the forthcoming fall of Richmond, were to leave for Fredericksburg the next day.

On May 23, Confederate troops stormed Front Royal, and quickly drove the Union garrison off the railroad viaduct and the bridge over the Shenandoah River. The fight was one-sided and all but a few of the 1,000 Federal soldiers were killed or fell prisoner. Jackson was now as close to Banks's rear base at Winchester as Banks himself. But Banks was stunned into complete apathy. Henderson wrote that "war is a struggle between two intellects rather than a conflict of masses."[14] Jackson fully understood this. It is most doubtful whether Banks did, however. He refused to acknowledge that Jackson's whole army had descended on his flank.

Banks was as unimaginative as Joe Johnston. When Johnston heard that Jackson wanted to challenge Banks, he assumed that Jackson intended to attack him headlong in his "works." Banks felt the same way. That's why he built them at Strasburg. But Jackson knew that an indirect approach was far more likely to ensure success. Jackson had seen in the Mexican War that the key to tactical victory was to hold the enemy in place with a strong attack or threat, and to land the telling blow on the rear or the flank. Jackson held Banks in place by sending Turner Ashby's cavalry directly against the Strasburg defenses, giving the defenders the strong impression that the whole Confederate army was descending on them. Banks was thus unsuspecting that the main assault would land on his almost undefended flank. The roundabout march to Front Royal strained the endurance of Jackson's men, but severe losses would result if he attacked Banks at Strasburg. All physical obstacles are inherently less formidable than the hazards of battle.

Despite frantic efforts by some of Banks's subordinate commanders to get Banks to order an immediate retreat, he remained in a state of disbelief until 10:00 A.M. on May 24. By then he had recovered enough to authorize withdrawal from Strasburg to Winchester. His relieved soldiers moved off fast, abandoning a mountain of supplies. Despite the delay, the Federals on the hard, macadamized Valley Pike were able to move quickly, while Jackson's forces, approaching on narrow, winding country lanes, were slower.

In the race that followed, most of Banks's infantry and guns got away on the pike to Winchester. Jackson's cavalry, however, striking along the pike at several places, seized numbers of goods wagons and the teams pulling them. Since Confederate cavalrymen had to provide their own mounts, many of Turner Ashby's young troopers led their captured horses back to their parents' farms, and were lost to the army for several days. Most of the Federal cavalry, finding the pike barred to them, had to escape by small roads westward, and were of no use in defending Winchester.

Bank's situation at Winchester was desperate. He had no more than 7,500 discouraged men, while Jackson had about 16,000 gleeful soldiers, exhilarated by success. Although the Federals, especially their guns, put up a stout defense on May 25, 1862, Jackson's troops swiftly overwhelmed them. The Confederates, rising as a single great force, descended on the Union lines. The Federal soldiers fled in panic toward the Potomac River. The Rebels captured 3,000 of them, and might have captured more, except that Turner Ashby had moved his troopers eastward without orders, and was not available to pursue the fugitives.

The liberation of Winchester created frenzy among the townspeople. Captain James Edmondson of the 27th Virginia wrote home to Lexington: "I never saw such a demonstration as was made by the citizens, the ladies especially as we passed through—every window was crowded and every door was filled with them and all enthusiastically preparing for our generals and soldiers, waving handkerchiefs and flags and others were engaged in supplying our soldiers as they passed with food and water." Jackson, in a letter to Anna the next day, wrote: "The people seemed nearly frantic with joy. Our entrance into Winchester was one of the most stirring scenes of my life. . . . Time forbids a longer letter, but it does not forbid my loving my *esposita*."[15]

The news of the rout of Banks's army created a sensation of a different sort in the North. Lincoln was afraid that Jackson would immediately cross the Potomac and advance directly on Washington. This, of course, was not going to happen, and several seasoned Union officers, including McDowell, assured Lincoln that Jackson's force, however victorious, was far too small to threaten the capital. Union forces around Washington were much larger than Jackson's army. He could not invade the North, they said, unless he was strongly reinforced.

Even so, two baleful consequences for the North sprang from

Jackson's rout of Banks and his sweep to the Potomac River. The first and by far the most significant was that Lincoln stopped permanently McDowell's march to reinforce McClellan at Richmond. McClellan was never going to have McDowell's corps. The effect was to render McClellan even more incapable of movement and decision than he already was. Jackson's victory at Winchester had spared the South a fatal blow. If McClellan had held Johnston's army east of Richmond, McDowell could have descended directly on the city and on Johnston's rear, and almost certainly forced him to surrender.

The second bad outcome for the North was that Lincoln exchanged the almost certain success of a march by McDowell on Richmond for an almost unattainable effort to bottle up Jackson in the northern end of the Shenandoah Valley and force his surrender. Lincoln looked at the Valley Pike and concluded that a Union barricade at Strasburg would close off Jackson's retreat. Accordingly, he ordered McDowell to send James Shields's division to accomplish this task, followed by another division. And he told Frémont to close off any hope of a Jackson retreat by advancing onto the Valley Pike at Harrisonburg and moving north. But Jackson had already sent parties to block the southern passes into the valley from the Alleghenies, and Frémont— one of the most incompetent generals in the Civil War—made no effort to clear the barriers. Instead, he set off on a laborious long march north to approach Strasburg directly from the west.

Jackson was not in the least perturbed by the prospect of being blocked at Strasburg. He knew that ordinary generals—and Frémont and Shields were decidedly ordinary—see a trap waiting to be sprung at every crossroads. Under the best of circumstances, such generals will move with extreme caution. Frémont and Shields were many times more cautious because they were facing an opponent who had already shown remarkable deception, and who might turn the tables and ensnare them at any moment. From such generals, Jackson knew, he had little to fear.

As a result of Jackson's actions, an amazing set of circumstances had come into play. Almost entirely by unexpected moves and surprise, not bloodbaths, Jackson, with just 17,000 men, had neutralized two Union armies and a huge corps, in all well over 75,000 men, and had thrown the commander of the North's major army of 100,000 men on the peninsula into a funk of inactivity and indecision.

Now it might be assumed that these fantastic events had revealed to the leadership of the Confederacy that they possessed in Stonewall Jackson an extraordinary commander who could bring them victory with great speed and little cost. The proper course of action was immediately to place Jackson in command of the Confederate army and give him complete freedom to use his remarkable powers to bring the war to a quick and successful conclusion. But in fact this did not happen.

It is a sad truth that intellectual brilliance does not often register on human minds at the time spectacular events take place. For example, only Jackson, and to a lesser extent Lee, recognized, before the event, the threat to Washington that overwhelming Banks's army would present to Abraham Lincoln. Joe Johnston believed that defense was the only correct policy to follow in the Shenandoah Valley. Jackson's aim was also not seen by his subordinate commanders. As G. F. R. Henderson remarked, "It was not till long after the battle of Winchester that the real purport of the operations in which they had been engaged began to dawn on them. It was not realized by Lincoln, by Stanton, or even by McClellan, for to each of them the sudden attack on Front Royal was as much of a surprise as to Banks himself."[16]

It was quite logical, then, that the leaders of the Confederacy did not see that they had been presented, in the person of Stonewall Jackson, with the means for quick and overwhelming victory. These leaders were commonplace men who held views very much like the vast majority of people. These views were determined largely by their class, training, experience, and bias. When a singular individual comes along, the response of the people in charge is never to hand over their power to the phenomenon. The almost universal response is to continue as if nothing has happened. The people in power may give the phenomenon additional resources, but they will never voluntarily relinquish their own authority and prestige to achieve their society's goals. Personal avarice and privilege always take precedence over political purposes.

Napoleon Bonaparte is a great example of this human tendency. His overwhelmingly successful campaign in Italy in 1796–97 had demonstrated to the Directory ruling France that they had been presented with a military genius of the rarest kind. Although France was beset with enemies in all directions, it never occurred to the leadership to give full authority to Bonaparte to deal with these enemies and to bring France victory. The only way Bonaparte was able to gain power was by overthrowing these leaders in a coup d'état in 1799.

In late May 1862 the whole South was ecstatic over Jackson's victories, but President Davis had drawn no conclusion that Jackson should be given greater responsibilities and a mandate to continue his dramatic moves. Davis was arrogant and overbearing, with little ingenuity and less imagination. He surrounded himself with mediocre men.[17] A British officer, Garnet Joseph Wolseley, talked with Jefferson Davis at length during a visit to Virginia in the fall of 1862. He called Davis "a third rate man, and a most unfortunate selection for the office of president." Wolseley later became a field marshal, viscount, and commander of the British army. He was the model of the "Modern Major General" in Gilbert and Sullivan's comic opera *The Pirates of Penzance* (1879), and "All Sir Garnet" became a Cockney expression for "all correct."[18] Wolseley's appraisal of Davis in 1862 has stood the test of time.

The phenomenon of Stonewall Jackson changed nothing in Jefferson Davis's mind. The brilliance of Jackson's ideas and strategy was lost on him. For Davis, the problem remained the same. McClellan's army was at the gates of Richmond, and he, as well as his military adviser, Robert E. Lee, and his army commander, Joe Johnston, could see no other choice except to smash headlong into this army and drive it away.

But sitting on a bluff and looking down at Harpers Ferry and the Potomac on May 30, 1862, Stonewall Jackson was contemplating a totally different idea. He had seen a way to win the war in weeks, as well as to remove all Union forces from Richmond and Virginia without costing a single additional Southern soldier's life.

The North was so sure of its superior strength that it had sent all of its armies into the South with the aim of beating down Southern resistance by main strength. The North had left virtually nothing to protect its factories, mines, farms, railways, and cities. Jackson saw this as a fundamental weakness. He had a plan to exploit this weakness.

Jackson awoke from a short nap to discover an old friend, Colonel Alexander R. Boteler, sitting opposite and making a sketch of him. Jackson sat up, and told Boteler to put the drawing aside. He said he had a much more important task for him. He wanted Boteler, a former congressman, to leave at once to see President Davis, a personal friend, and make the following presentation: if his command was increased to a total of 40,000 men, he would cross into Maryland, "raise the siege of Richmond and transfer this campaign from the banks of the James to those of the Susquehanna."[19]

Jackson described a campaign to defeat the North that was almost exactly the same as the plan he had asked Gustavus W. Smith to present to President Davis in October 1861 (see page 67). He planned to sweep around Washington and cut the Baltimore & Ohio Railroad north of Washington, thereby eliminating the capital's food supply. This would force the Lincoln administration to vacate the city.

Jackson then intended to move north, breaking railroads and closing factories.

The North had no forces in the interior that could possibly stop a Confederate march. Jackson told Boteler that Lincoln was certain to demand the immediate withdrawal of the Army of the Potomac to defend the North. This was the only force capable of challenging Jackson head-on. In this fashion, the main Union army would be pulled northward, and the Union campaign to seize Richmond would be ended without a battle. But it would take weeks to assemble a superior Union army in Maryland or Pennsylvania. By that time, Jackson felt, it would be too late.

Since war materials, as well as food, were being carried on the East Coast railroad corridor from southern Maine to Washington, any break along this corridor, if sustained, would bring the Northern war effort to a halt. And even if McClellan was able to get a superior army into the field in the North, Jackson was certain he could defeat it in detail. He had already proved in the Shenandoah Valley campaign that he could march rings around Union armies and could defeat detached elements of them. And McClellan was so notoriously slow that Jackson was certain he could do just as well against him. In this fashion, the South could defeat the Union army on Northern soil, and force the North to agree to Southern independence.

Although, at the moment, more than 60,000 Union soldiers were trying to cut off Jackson's retreat southward, they were scattered. Jackson was sure he could slip through the trap Lincoln was trying to set at Strasburg, and could withdraw up the Shenandoah Valley. From there, if he got the reinforcements he was requesting, he could burst through or go around any Union forces still in the valley, cross the Potomac, and have almost free rein until McClellan extricated his army from the peninsula and came to confront him.

Jackson and Boteler took the train back to Winchester, where

Jackson got together papers explaining his proposal, and Boteler set off to see Davis.

Meanwhile, Joe Johnston was sending his army into an attack on McClellan immediately east of Richmond, in a battle May 31 to June 1, known as Seven Pines in the South and Fair Oaks in the North. McClellan had posted two corps facing west just south of the Chickahominy River. Johnston planned for James Longstreet's division to strike around the northern flank of these corps, and drive them against the James River or White Oak Swamp to the south, forcing their surrender. But Johnston's implementation of his plan was atrocious. Longstreet completely missed Nine Mile Road on which he was supposed to advance, and came up instead behind D. H. Hill's division on Williamsburg Road (present-day U.S. Route 60), a couple miles south. This merely blocked the road for other Rebel forces. D. H. Hill crashed headlong into defending Federal troops on Williamsburg Road, but achieved nothing. The whole battle was a fiasco, costing the South 6,100 killed and wounded, and the North 5,700 casualties.

Johnston had proved that he was incapable of carrying out any offensive operation, but President Davis only noticed that he was inadequate. Replacing him was easy because Johnston sustained two wounds, neither fatal, but they put him out of action for six months.

It never occurred to Davis to place Stonewall Jackson in command of the Army of Northern Virginia, despite the spectacular record he had just achieved in the Shenandoah Valley. Jackson was not a member of the landed aristocracy that had ruled the South since colonial days, and that held all the high positions in the Confederacy. Davis automatically passed over Jackson and selected Robert E. Lee, who was manifestly a Southern aristocrat. Jackson was far down the social scale, and did not figure in the choice. Comparative ability had nothing to do with the decision; social caste had everything.

This was the pattern of Jefferson Davis. He had already named a friend, Lucius B. Northrup, from a prominent Charleston, South Carolina, family as commissary-general of the Confederacy. Northrup did an appalling job providing food and other supplies for the Confederate army, forcing soldiers in some cases to rely on food packages sent from their families at home. But Davis refused to remove him from his job. And on June 17, 1862, Davis appointed Braxton Bragg, another friend and member of a prominent North Carolina family, as commander of the major army in the Western Theater. Bragg was almost totally incompetent, and commenced a series of defeats for the South that ended in Union seizure of Chattanooga, Tennessee. Davis finally removed him in favor of Joseph E. Johnston early in 1864, but the damage had been done. William Tecumseh Sherman easily outgeneraled Johnston and later John Bell Hood, advanced to Atlanta, Georgia, in the spring of 1864, and on to Savannah, Georgia, in the fall. This advance was the deathblow to the Confederacy. It all could have been avoided with better leadership.

The inept British nobility selected woefully unqualified aristocrats who lost the thirteen American colonies in 1775–81. The equally incapable French aristocracy brought the entire French society down on its head in 1789. In much the same way, the Southern aristocracy was setting the stage for its own destruction and for shattering the Southern economy by blindly selecting only people from its own class, not the best men, to lead the Confederacy.

Captain Charles Blackford, a cavalry officer and member of the Southern ruling class, gave dramatic evidence of the prevailing aristocratic ethos only a little over a month after Johnston was wounded. On July 13, 1862, Blackford saw Lee and Jackson together in Richmond. Blackford wrote: "Lee was elegantly dressed in full uniform, sword and sash, spotless boots, beautiful spurs, and by far the most magnificent man I ever saw. The highest type of Cavalier class to which by blood and rearing he belongs. Jackson, on the other hand, was a typical Roundhead. He was poorly dressed, that is, he looked as though his clothes were made of good material [apparently Blackford meant that Jackson's clothes were of good material, but he still looked bad in them]. His cap was very indifferent and pulled down over one eye, much stained by weather and without insignia. His coat was closely buttoned up to his chin and had upon the collar the stars and wreath of a general. His shoulders were stooped. . . . He had a plain sword belt without sash and a sword in no respect different from that of other infantry officers that I could see. His face, in repose, is not handsome or agreeable and he would be passed by anyone without a second look." Later Blackford complained about the lack of elegance in Jackson's headquarters, and he especially disdained Jackson's sorrel horse as not being of the finest breed.[20]

While Jackson and Boteler were on the train from Harpers Ferry to Winchester, Jackson got word that James Shields's forces had driven the 12th Georgia Regiment out of Front Royal and seized the town. The Rebel regiment fled without putting up any fight at all. A courier also informed Jackson that Frémont was nearing Strasburg on the west. But Jackson was not in the least concerned. He had already ordered most of the army and the supply train—200 wagons ranging from big Conestogas to low open-sided drays—to depart Winchester on the Valley Pike. The column of men and vehicles stretched fifteen miles along the turnpike. Meanwhile, Jackson directed the only force still to the north, the Stonewall Brigade at Harpers Ferry, to move south at once. By the night of May 31, the brigade, marching hard, was well south of Winchester, while the main army was passing through Strasburg.

That evening, Jackson summoned the 12th Georgia commander, Zephanier Conner. Conner had left his regiment to fend for itself, and had raced to Winchester. "Colonel, how many men did you have killed?" Jackson asked. Conner: "None." "How many wounded?"

"None." "Colonel Conner, do you call that much of a fight?" Jackson dismissed Conner, and had him cashiered from the army for dereliction of duty.[21]

Just as Jackson expected, both Frémont and Shields acted with extreme caution. On June 1, Ewell easily held a hesitant Frémont at Cedar Creek, six miles west of Strasburg, allowing the Stonewall Brigade to get through Strasburg without incident around noon, while Shields didn't stir from Front Royal. Neither officer wanted to challenge Jackson head-on.

Ewell pulled in behind the Stonewall Brigade and headed south, Turner Ashby's cavalry bringing up the rear to form a shield against Frémont, who suddenly showed some vigor, and began pursuing the tail of the Rebel army.

Jackson had figured accurately that Shields intended to move south up the Luray Valley to Luray, cross on the one road over Massanutten, and block Jackson's passage at New Market. Accordingly, he had already sent a cavalry team straight for the two bridges over the South Fork Shenandoah at Luray. When the force Shields had sent to save the bridges arrived, only charred ruins remained, and a strong current in the river barred passage. Colonel Samuel S. Carroll, commanding the Union force, continued on to save the bridge at Conrad's Store. From there Shields could swing around the southern escarpment of Massanutten and still block Jackson's retreat at Harrisonburg. But when Carroll reached Conrad's Store on June 4, he found that Jackson's cavalry had burned this bridge as well, and the South Fork was in spate from recent heavy rains.

There was only one more bridge over the South Fork, at Port Republic, twelve miles farther south. Carroll decided on his own to press forward to seize this bridge with his team of 150 men. Jackson had taken a calculated risk and had left the Port Republic bridge intact, in hopes that Shields would be unable to beat him to it. If Jackson lost this span, Shields and Frémont could easily unite, and Jackson might be isolated west of the South Fork and cut off from the Blue Ridge in case of need. Jackson sent a small cavalry team to hold the bridge, but, if Carroll arrived before Jackson, the little Rebel band would have no chance of holding it.

Frémont exhibited much more energy in pursuit than he had ever shown in battle. Most particularly, the Federal cavalry made bold and energetic assaults that put much pressure on the Rebel rear guard. On June 2 near Woodstock, the Federal cavalry forced Ashby's horsemen and Ewell's cavalry under George H. Steuart to fall back. Some of Steuart's men broke and ran. Ashby ended the rout by forming up some infantry stragglers and stopping the charging Federals with rifle volleys.

Colonel John R. Patton, commanding the 21st Virginia, reported to Jackson about another rearguard skirmish that occurred the same day. Patton expressed regret that his men had killed three Union horsemen who had bravely charged into the regiment. After hearing his report, Jackson looked hard at Patton and asked: "Colonel, why do you say you saw those Federal soldiers fall with regret?" Patton replied that they had exhibited vigor and courage, and a natural sympathy with brave men led to the wish that their lives might have been saved. "No," Jackson replied sternly, "shoot them all. I do not want them to be brave."[22]

Jackson's tone in a letter to his wife, Anna, on June 2 was totally different: "I am again retiring before the enemy. They endeavored to get in my rear by moving on both flanks of my gallant army, but our God has been my guide and saved me from their grasp. You must not expect long letters from me in such busy times as these, but always believe that your husband never forgets his little darling."[23]

Jackson now made all speed for Port Republic, with Turner Ashby's horsemen ably protecting the army. Time after time during the retreat Ashby had exposed himself to defend the army. Near Harrisonburg, after his horse had been shot from under him, he led his supporting infantry on foot in a charge that stopped a Federal rush. In the fight a bullet struck him in the heart and he died. The whole South, Jackson especially, mourned the loss.

Shortly before reaching Port Republic, Jackson got a bare message from President Davis regretting that he could not send Jackson any more troops for his proposed offensive to the banks of the Susquehanna. Colonel Boteler's mission had failed. Jackson took the news stoically, but did not give up.

Jackson's advance force arrived at Port Republic on June 7. The bridge was still in Confederate hands. Jackson had won the race, but only by a single day. Swollen streams prevented Carroll from reaching Port Republic until the next morning.

The village of Port Republic was located just west of where North River and South River came together to form the South Fork. Over South River was a ford. Over the bolder North River was the bridge that Jackson had been so determined to preserve. So long as Jackson held this bridge, he could keep the forces of Frémont and Shields separate. This would enable him to deal first with one force, then with the other.

Leaving Ewell's division near Cross Keys, five miles northwest of Port Republic, to block Frémont, Jackson planned to strike Shields's smaller force first. This force could still block Jackson's escape route over Brown's Gap in the Blue Ridge, could capture his wagon train only a short distance below the village, and could press on to Waynesboro, sixteen miles south, and cut the Virginia Central Railroad there.

But things worked out differently. Jackson was surprised when Carroll's advance Union force unexpectedly came up on Port Republic early on June 8, scattered Jackson's cavalry vedettes, crossed the South River ford, captured part of Jackson's staff and nearly captured Jackson, and threatened the army ammunition train parked just west of the village. Jackson barely escaped over the bridge to the hill above North

River, and hurriedly pulled up artillery that pounded the Union horse-men. A quickly organized infantry assault across the bridge drove the Federals back over the South River, freeing the captives.

As this engagement was ending, the lead brigade of Shields's di-vision under Erastus B. Tyler was arriving on the other side of the South Fork, but it retired in the face of the Confederate artillery fire. Tyler had just 3,000 men, however. The rest of Shields's division was still spread out well to the north.

The same morning of June 8, Frémont, exhibiting unusual energy, came up on Ewell, who was occupying a strong position on wooded hills a mile and a half southeast of Cross Keys. Although Frémont had as many troops on hand as Ewell possessed, and many more spread out behind him, his courage vanished when he saw that the Rebels were waiting for him. Of his twenty-four regiments, Frémont sent just five regiments of Louis Blenker's division of German and other immigrants—or "Dutchmen" as the Rebels called them—against the Confederate right. There Isaac R. Trimble's brigade of Deep South troops lay on the ground on an oak-covered flat ridge. Trimble allowed the Dutchmen to advance in solid, tight lines within sixty paces. Then the Rebels abruptly rose and released a sheet of flame at the unsus-pecting soldiers. The Dutchmen staggered, attempted to rally, received another shattering volley, and fled in panic.

Trimble moved a regiment through a sheltered ravine on Blenker's left to threaten a flank attack, sending Blenker's division back for a mile in swift retreat and confusion. That was enough for Frémont. The battle of Cross Keys was over. It had cost the Federals 684 men, nearly all Dutchmen. The Confederates lost 288, mainly from artillery fire.

The next day, Jackson attacked Tyler's advanced force across the South River at Port Republic. Although he was severely outnumbered, Tyler put up a splendid defense, and Jackson had real difficulty in securing a Union artillery position on high ground by direct assault.

Once this occurred, however, Tyler's position was hopeless, and he retreated northward, where other elements of Shields's division were lined up to stop the Rebels.

That was the end of the Shenandoah Valley campaign. Jackson pulled Ewell's division over the bridge at Port Republic, then burned it to keep the two Union forces apart. He marched his army to safety in the lower cove of Brown's Gap. On June 10, Shields withdrew to Luray while Frémont retreated hastily to Harrisonburg, and, soon, all the way back to Middletown, ten miles south of Winchester. Jackson, left alone, brought his men down from the Blue Ridge on June 12, pitched camp below Port Republic, and gave his men a much-needed five-day rest.

While there, Jackson wrote a long letter to his beloved wife, who was now carrying his child. He ended the letter with this question: "Wouldn't you like to be home again?" At the same time Colonel Sam Fulkerson of the 37th Virginia concluded a letter home about Jackson: "Our men curse him for the hard marching he makes them do, but still the privates of the whole army have the most unbounded confidence in him. They say that he can take them into harder places and get them out better than any living man. . . . He is an ardent Christian."[24]

On June 13, Jackson called in Colonel Boteler again and asked him to take a letter to General Lee to explain his plan to invade the North. Jackson was highly conscious that an all-out collision was building at Richmond, and he wanted to avoid it if at all possible. There was a way to eliminate McClellan without another battle. He told Boteler, "Richmond can be relieved and the campaign transferred to Pennsylvania."[25]

Boteler gained an audience with Lee and presented Jackson's case ardently.[26] Lee answered him: "Colonel, don't you think General Jackson had better come down here first and help me to drive these troublesome people away from Richmond?" Boteler got nowhere with Lee. When Lee sent Jackson's proposal to President Davis, he wrote, "I think the sooner Jackson can move this way [toward Richmond] the better—The first object now is to defeat McClellan." Davis endorsed the letter back to Lee, saying, "Views concurred in."[27]

Thus Jackson's proposal to transform the strategy of the war had received no more than a passing nod from Lee and Davis. It was plain that Lee was planning to attack McClellan head-on at Richmond. Lee's concept of war was a polar opposite of Jackson's. Despite his extreme reticence to express his views, Jackson spoke twice of how war should be conducted. In the winter of 1862 he discussed war with the Reverend James Robert Graham in Winchester (see page 70). And sometime later in the year he also had a moment of candor with one of his officers, John D. Imboden. Jackson told Imboden: "Always mystify, mislead, and surprise the enemy, if possible, and when you strike and overcome him, never let up in the pursuit so long as your men have strength to follow, for an army routed, if hotly pursued, becomes panic-stricken, and can then be destroyed by half their number. The other rule is, never fight against heavy odds, if by any possible maneuvering you can hurl your own force on only a part, and that the weakest part, of your enemy and crush it. Such tactics will win every time, and a small army may thus destroy a large one in detail, and repeated victory will make it invincible."[28] A quarter of a century after the war, Field Marshal Viscount Wolseley wrote that these comments were "golden sentences" that "comprise some of the most essential of all the principles of war."[29]

In warfare one officer may see a situation in one way and another officer may see the same situation in a totally different way. Some persons absorb the principles of warfare, and other persons do not. In 1890 the renowned military historian Theodore Ayrault Dodge summarized the situation most succinctly: "The maxims of war are but a meaningless page to him who cannot apply them."[30]

By example, General Winfield Scott had presented fundamental maxims to Jackson, Lee, and all his other officers in the campaign to capture Mexico City in 1847, one of the most successful in history. It was evident in June 1862 in Virginia that Jackson had absorbed the lessons that Winfield Scott had taught, and that Lee had not.

This is all the more remarkable because Lieutenant Jackson had a very subordinate role in the Mexican campaign, while Captain Lee was the right-hand man of General Scott and carried out all the key missions that showed where Scott could make his decisive moves and achieve his victories.

What is more remarkable still is that the campaign that Jackson was proposing into the North in 1862 was identical in principle to the move that Winfield Scott had made before Mexico City in 1847. And Captain Lee had personally laid out the indirect route that Scott had followed. When the American army came up on the Mexican position of El Peñon east of Mexico City (see page 21), Lee reconnoitered the spot, and told Scott that it was heavily defended. Scott did not want to make a frontal assault because of the enormous casualties that would result. To avoid the formidable El Peñon barrier, he told Captain Lee to find another way to reach the Mexican capital. Lee traced a twenty-five-mile detour around the lakes southeast of Mexico City that placed the American army directly south of the city. Here Mexican defenses were inadequate, and the Americans won an overwhelming victory.

Jackson's proposal to Davis and Lee was identical in concept to Scott's move to win the war with Mexico. Instead of crashing head-long into the powerful Union defenses at Richmond, he wanted to march away from them and strike a blow in the North where there were no strong defenses. Intellectually there was no difference whatso-ever between Scott's move to avoid the strength of El Peñon and strike at weakness south of Mexico City and Jackson's proposal to avoid the strength of McClellan and strike at weakness in the Northern interior.

Based on Lee's behavior throughout the war, there is no evidence that he saw this connection. Indeed, he was soon to demonstrate that his idea of warfare was to attack the enemy headlong in his strongest and most well-defended positions. President Davis, who had even less vision than Lee, also could conceive only direct challenges, and he supported Lee.

CHAPTER 5

—◆—

The Disaster of the Seven Days

Twice in two weeks in early June 1862, Stonewall Jackson had tried to show President Davis and Robert E. Lee that a bloody, head-on collision with the Army of the Potomac at Richmond was unnecessary. He had shown that McClellan and his army could be drawn back into Maryland or Pennsylvania without a fight by threatening Northern factories, railroads, farms, and cities. Even if Confederate forces were unsuccessful in an invasion, Lincoln would demand abandonment of the attack on Richmond in order to return the Union's main field army to protect the North. Lincoln's anxiety about the protection of Washington was undisputed. Therefore, it was certain that any major move into the North would end the peninsula campaign without the loss of a single additional Southern soldier.

This outcome alone would relieve the South of the greatest danger it had faced. Many more benefits would probably accrue, most especially that of winning the war. Any contest between the slow and hesitant McClellan and the quick and bewildering Jackson would very likely result in a Southern victory. Therefore, the perils to the South of an invasion of the North were minuscule compared with the advantages.

Jefferson Davis was a man of extremely little imagination, and he was so fixated on his idea that the North would grow tired of the war and quit that he probably saw none of the opportunities that Stonewall Jackson laid out to him. Lee never acted on these opportunities, so he almost surely did not see them either. In any event, Lee had no personal interest in following Jackson's proposals. If he did endorse them and convinced Davis to go along, it would mean that Stonewall Jackson, not Lee, would lead the campaign into the North. This would diminish Lee's power and authority, and might elevate Jackson to a major political figure. Lee had grasped the reins of command quite firmly after Davis appointed him to head the Army of Northern Virginia, and he immediately began planning a campaign that would consolidate his authority as the senior Confederate officer. Consequently, it was not in Lee's interests for the South to hand power over to Stonewall Jackson to invade the North.

Lee also demonstrated in the designs he was drawing up that he had not grasped the impact of the Minié-ball rifle on the battlefield. He was planning just one indirect move against the Union army, to be followed by a series of headlong assaults against the strongest and most heavily defended Union positions. This showed that Lee had not heeded his mentor, Winfield Scott, because Scott had avoided direct attacks wherever possible and usually struck the weakest enemy positions, not the strongest.

It also showed that Lee had paid no attention to the advice of Napoleon Bonaparte, although Napoleon was regarded throughout Europe and America as a supreme master of warfare, and his teachings were studied avidly by military officers in the decades leading up to the Civil War. One extremely important piece of Napoleonic advice was especially applicable to the situation Lee faced in 1862. Napoleon wrote: "A well-established maxim of war is not to do anything which your enemy wishes—and for the single reason that he does so wish. You should therefore avoid a field of battle which he has reconnoitered and studied. You should be still more careful to avoid one which he has fortified and where he has entrenched himself. A corollary of this principle is, never to attack in front a position which admits of being turned."[1]

Lee's plans to challenge McClellan's army centered on the corps of Fitz John Porter, 30,000 men, which McClellan had posted north of the Chickahominy River and a little west of his other two corps south of the river, with 75,000 men. Porter was located there for two reasons. The first was to protect the Union army's supply base at White House, twenty miles east on the Pamunkey River. The other was to reach out to McDowell's corps, which McClellan was still hoping would approach from Fredericksburg on the north. His hope of a rescue by McDowell was vain. It was not going to happen.

Lee saw that Porter's position was exposed. His plan, therefore, was to attack Porter with superior force, drive him down the north bank of the Chickahominy, and threaten or cut McClellan's rail connection with his White House river supply base. Lee reasoned that McClellan, to protect White House, would be forced to come out of his entrenchments south of the Chickahominy and confront Lee in the open. Lee felt he had a good chance of defeating McClellan and forcing his army to retreat or surrender.

There was one glaring fact wrong with Lee's premise. Although Jeb Stuart, in a raid around McClellan's army June 12–15, had found that White House was still in operation, the Pamunkey was narrow and difficult to navigate, whereas the James was wide and deep, and, since the South had scuttled the *Virginia*, was open and much more suitable as a supply line. Therefore, McClellan was almost certainly planning to abandon White House. If it was threatened, he would immediately shift his base to Harrison's Landing on the James, the closest point where vessels could tie up safely. The landing was about eighteen miles southeast of McClellan's main position around Fair Oaks and Savage Station.

Lee knew the *Virginia* was gone. He therefore should have realized that possession of White House was no longer vital to the Union army. Porter was *no longer* protecting White House; he was shielding the main Union army south of the Chickahominy. But Lee did not recognize this, and he designed his entire campaign on a false premise.

In addition, Lee's actual battle plan was far too complicated to have any chance of success. Immediately after the battle of Port Republic, he had sent Stonewall Jackson quite openly 8,000 men under Brigadier Generals W. H. C. Whiting and Alexander R. Lawton. The aim was to deceive the Union command into thinking that Jackson was about to descend the Shenandoah Valley in another offensive sweep. But at the same time Lee told Jackson to leave all his cavalry in the valley as a decoy, and move all his infantry and guns secretly to Ashland, about eighteen miles north of Richmond. His aim was for Jackson to carry out the single indirect move he had planned. Jackson was to descend on the northern flank of Porter's corps at Hundley's Corner at the same time that Lee's main force of three divisions threatened Porter's central defensive line along Beaver Dam Creek, just east of Mechanicsville. Lee expected Jackson's arrival on Porter's flank to force Porter to abandon his position, and to retreat eastward toward White House. The aim was to avoid a bloody confrontation along Beaver Dam Creek, where Porter had built formidable defensive entrenchments.

But Lee made no provision for the two separated wings of the Rebel army to make and keep contact. This could easily have been done by placing parts of Stuart's cavalry in front of both wings to carry constant messages between the two. But Lee had not provided for any horsemen between the wings, and neither wing knew what the other was doing.

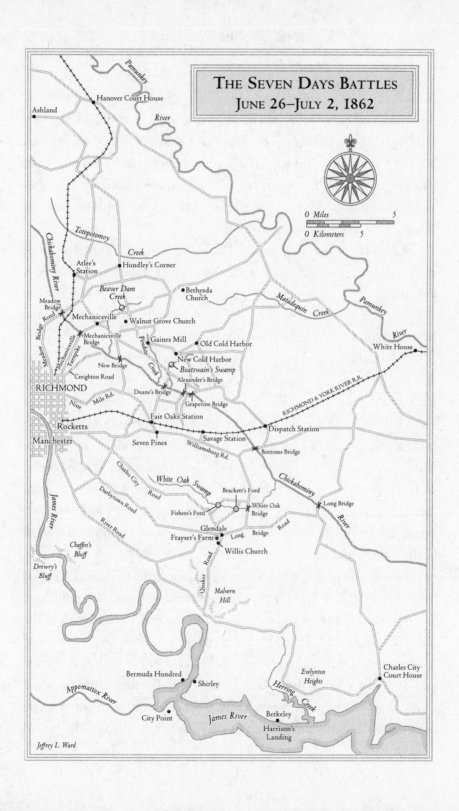

THE SEVEN DAYS BATTLES
JUNE 26–JULY 2, 1862

0 Miles 5
0 Kilometers 5

Pamunkey
River

Ashland

Hanover Court House

Chickahominy River

Totopotomoy
Creek

Atlee's
Station
Hundley's Corner

Bethesda
Church

Beaver Dam
Creek

Matadequin Creek

Pamunkey
River

Meadow
Bridge
Mechanicsville
Walnut Grove Church

Bridge Road

Meadow

Mechanicsville
Turnpike

Mechanicsville
Bridge
Gaines Mill
Old Cold Harbor

White House

New Bridge

New Cold Harbor
Boatswain's Swamp

Creighton Road
Alexander's Bridge

RICHMOND

Powhite Creek

Duane's Bridge

Grapevine Bridge

RICHMOND & YORK RIVER R.R.

Nine Mile Rd.

Fair Oaks Station

Rocketts

Dispatch Station

Manchester

Seven Pines
Savage Station

Williamsburg Rd.

Bottoms Bridge

James River

Charles City Road

White Oak Swamp

Brackett's Ford

Chickahominy

Darbytown Road

Fishers's Ford
White Oak
Bridge

Long Bridge

River Road

Glendale
Frayser's Farm
Long Bridge Road

Chaffin's
Bluff

Willis Church

Drewry's
Bluff

Quaker Road

Malvern
Hill

Appomattox River

Bermuda Hundred
Shirley

Evelynton
Heights

Charles City
Court House

Herring Creek

City Point

James River

Berkeley
Harrison's
Landing

Jeffrey L. Ward

So, before Jackson actually arrived at Hundley's Corner on June 26, 1862, A. P. Hill, commanding one of Lee's divisions, hearing nothing from Jackson, became impatient and launched a headlong assault directly against the Beaver Dam defenses. Lee immediately abandoned his plans to avoid a frontal attack, and authorized the assault, even ordering D. H. Hill, commanding a second division, to assist him. The Union soldiers threw back the assaults in a few minutes, but not before Lee had lost nearly 2,000 men.

D. H. Hill wrote afterward: "The blood shed by Southern troops there was wasted in vain, and worse than vain; for the fight had a most dispiriting effect on the troops. They could have halted at Mechanicsville until Jackson had turned the works on the creek, and all the waste of blood could have been avoided."[2]

D. H. Hill was correct. As soon as Porter got word that Jackson was on his flank, he abandoned the Beaver Dam entrenchments and withdrew during the night to Boatswain's Swamp, a stream about four and a half miles to the southeast. In doing this, Porter revealed that he had turned his corps facing *north* to protect the bridges crossing the Chickahominy, and no longer was facing *west* to protect White House. Lee completely missed this change of front, and spent the entire day of June 27 trying to drive Porter eastward, when in fact Porter had forsaken White House and was protecting the main Union army south of the Chickahominy.

The entire battle that followed, which Lee named Gaines Mill, was unnecessary. If Lee had merely reconnoitered the area, he could have ascertained that Porter was only guarding the main army south of the Chickahominy, and that the road eastward was completely open and undefended. Lee could have sent Jackson's corps, which was on the east at Old Cold Harbor, straight down to Bottoms Bridge, seven miles away. Jackson could have crossed the river and come up directly behind McClellan's entire army on Williamsburg Road. This would have cost the South scarcely any losses, and would have trapped McClellan between Lee's forces on the west and Jackson's on the east. Lee might have forced the entire Union army to surrender. But Lee made no effort whatsoever to reconnoiter. He asked himself no questions why Porter had turned his front northward instead of keeping it facing west. Instead, he ordered one frontal assault after another against the defensive works that Porter had hastily erected along Boatswain's Swamp.

"Brigade after brigade seemed almost to melt away before the concentrated fire of our artillery and infantry," Porter noted. "Yet others pressed on, followed by supports as dashing and as brave as their predecessors."[3]

Lee lost 8,000 men in a terrible bloodbath. Porter lost 4,000 men, but he was still able to pull the rest of his corps south of the Chickahominy during the night. McClellan immediately demonstrated his incapacity to conduct a battle, and began withdrawing his whole army to Harrison's Landing. Hence a bizarre situation developed. Lee, with about 70,000 men remaining (after the 10,000-man losses at Beaver Dam Creek and Boatswain's Swamp), was driving the 100,000-man Union army into swift retreat.

General Magruder allowed himself to be stopped by a single Union brigade at Savage Station, three miles east of Seven Pines, permitting the Union army to get away under cover of night. On June 30 at Glendale and nearby Frayser's Farm, Lee ordered another direct attack by the divisions of James Longstreet and A. P. Hill directly into the heart of extremely formidable Union positions. The attacks all failed, and they cost the Confederates thousands of men. Yet the whole collision was unnecessary, for McClellan was quite clearly moving toward Harrison's Landing. The Union forces at Glendale were only holding the retreat route open for the rest of the Federal army, and would be gone by the morning.

Part of the Union army fell back to Malvern Hill, a few miles north of Harrison's Landing. It was a powerful elevation, commanding the country for miles around, and extremely difficult to assault. Fitz John Porter had lined up all of the Union army's reserve artillery, along with the guns of two corps, while Union gunboats on the nearby James were on hand to deliver heavy shellfire.

Since McClellan was plainly moving to Harrison's Landing, it was quite obvious that the Union position on Malvern Hill was only a holding operation to shield the rest of the Union army until it got to the landing and the protection of the gunboats. In other words, if Lee did nothing, the Union position on Malvern Hill would be abandoned by the next day.

Lee easily could have swung part of his army around Malvern Hill to the east and seized Evelynton Heights, directly north of Harrison's Landing and completely dominating the position. Evelynton Heights was unoccupied. Confederate artillery posted there would have made Union positions at the landing untenable, and might have forced the entire army to surrender. But Lee did not see this opportunity, although his mother's home was nearby Shirley Plantation, and he knew the area well.

Instead, Lee ordered a direct onslaught against Malvern Hill on July 1, 1862. The headlong Rebel attacks all failed miserably. D. H. Hill wrote: "As each brigade emerged from the woods, from fifty to one hundred guns opened upon it, tearing great gaps in its ranks, but the heroes reeled on and were shot down by the reserves at the guns, which a few squads reached. Most of them had an open field half a mile wide to cross, under the fire of field artillery in front and the fire of heavy ordnance from the gunboats in their rear. It was not war—it was murder."[4]

The Rebel assaults appeared to the Union general Porter "as if moved by a reckless disregard of life," as the separate brigades advanced across the mostly open ground, giving clear targets one after the other, to the Union gunners.[5]

The Southern novelist John Esten Cooke wrote that "Malvern Hill was less a battle, scientifically disputed, than a bloody combat in which masses of men rushed forward and were swept away by the terrific fire of artillery concentrated on their front."[6]

The cost to the Confederacy was staggering, nearly 5,600 men killed or wounded, compared to about 2,000 Federal casualties. The next morning, Wednesday, July 2, over the field of battle the wounded and the dead were still lying. A third were corpses, a Federal officer who was there said, "but enough were alive and moving to give the field a singular crawling effect."[7]

McClellan withdrew safely to Harrison's Landing, where, protected by the gunboats and cannons he mounted on Evelynton Heights, he could not be budged. It had been an appalling introduction to the kind of direct, heedless warfare that Robert E. Lee wanted to conduct. Lee had launched five frontal assaults directly into the teeth of Union defenders. Only one of these assaults, Gaines Mill, had succeeded, and at a cost so high that to call it victory was derisory.

The only reason that Lee drove McClellan back to Harrison's Landing was that McClellan demonstrated an absolute inability to conduct a defensive battle. He had an army almost half again as strong in numbers as Lee's army, and artillery many times more numerous and deadly. Lee had utterly failed to grasp that McClellan's rear was wide open at Bottoms Bridge, and that the Union army could easily be approached in this direction. Therefore, after Lee had driven Porter across the Chickahominy, McClellan could have devised a tremendously effective defensive line along the Chickahominy and along his already existing fortified line facing Richmond south of the river. Yet he turned tail and ran on June 28, moving as fast as possible to Harrison's Landing.

Once McClellan started his retreat, all further attacks by Lee were irrelevant. All of McClellan's defensive efforts thereafter were temporary actions to allow the rest of the army to retreat. Since Lee had forfeited any chance of swinging around McClellan's army, stopping it, and forcing it to stand in open battle, McClellan had the positive advantage of a head start, and was able to get away. This flight was absolutely unmistakable by the end of June 28, and the clashes that Lee instituted along the way to Harrison's Landing, most especially the bloodbath at Malvern Hill, were unnecessary. Simple challenges, without bloody assaults, would have caused McClellan to vacate his defensive positions as soon as possible. He was going to retreat in any case. Lee should have seen this, but he didn't.

Lee lost 20,135 men in the Seven Days of the battle, one-quarter of his entire army, nearly all killed or wounded. The Union lost 9,800 men killed or wounded, and 6,000 captured. Since prisoners of war were routinely exchanged on a one-for-one basis, the real Confederate losses were twice what the Union army had sustained. The South had a population only one-third that of the North. If the South continued to challenge the North head-to-head in unnecessary battles like the Seven Days, it was heading straight to defeat and disaster.

CHAPTER 6

———◆———

Finding a Different Way to Win

Stonewall Jackson had been deeply troubled by the Seven Days. The gruesome results of Lee's tactics were even worse than he had feared, and the danger of McClellan's army had not been erased. McClellan had shown himself to be an incapable commander. But 90,000 Union soldiers were safely entrenched at Harrison's Landing, and Abraham Lincoln might appoint a really skilled commander who could achieve what McClellan had failed to accomplish: occupation of the Confederate capital and destruction of the Confederacy.

While many Confederate leaders were congratulating Lee on his victory, Jackson realized it was Pyrrhic, and the South remained in great peril. On July 7, 1862, less than a week after the end of the battle, Jackson called in Colonel Alexander Boteler one more time. He asked his old friend to approach President Davis. He told Boteler to tell Davis that invading the North was the way to bring the Northern people to their senses and to end the war. The Seven Days had shown that the South was far too weak in manpower to overwhelm the Union armies by sheer force. The proper solution was to avoid the enemy's military strength and to strike at the Northern people's property and means of livelihood, just as the North was striking at the South's property and means of livelihood.

Jackson said that McClellan's army was beaten and would pose no danger until it was reorganized and reinforced. The South should concentrate 60,000 men to march into Maryland and to threaten Washington. Boteler asked Jackson why he didn't present the idea to Lee. Jackson replied that he had done so, but that Lee had said nothing.

Boteler made another visit to President Davis. But Davis had learned nothing from the Seven Days. Once again he rejected Jackson's idea of an invasion. Once again he did not specify his real reason—that he did not want to invade the North because he believed the Northern people, on their own, would give up the fight. Instead, Davis listed a litany of excuses. McClellan might be reinforced. McClellan might cut the railroads supplying Richmond from the south. The losses of the Seven Days had been so great that the South could not undertake so dangerous an expedition as an invasion of the North.[1]

This was the fourth time that Jackson had made his plea to Davis for an invasion of the North, and this was the fourth time he had rejected it. It was plain to Jackson now that this avenue was hopeless. Davis was never going to authorize Jackson to make such a move.

The Southern aristocracy had a lock on the leadership positions of the Confederacy, and there was no chance that Davis was going to appoint Jackson to a senior military command. Jackson already had experienced this prejudice in the Mexican War. His artillery commander for a while was Captain John B. Magruder, later to direct the Confederate line at Yorktown against McClellan. Magruder was born in Tidewater Virginia and had grown up egotistical and ostentatious. He despised Jackson because, although he was a Virginian, he was not an FFV (First Families of Virginia), and did not, as did Magruder, pretend to be one and to put on airs accordingly.[2]

Lee, an integral part of the aristocracy, held the supreme position in the Eastern Theater. If he had become convinced of the validity of Jackson's proposals, he might have figured a way around Davis's objections and might have launched such an invasion under his own command. But Lee did not have the vision to carry out this kind of war. Lee was focused on defeating the Union army in battle. He had shown in the Seven Days that indirection was foreign to him.

Jackson now gave up any further effort to convince the Confederate leadership. No matter how valid his argument, it was not going to be implemented. It is a mark of his genius, however, that Jackson did not give up and quietly acquiesce to the blindness he saw at the top. Instead, he turned to another means of defeating the enemy and winning the war for the South.

The solution, he now saw, was to devise a sure way of winning battles.

Unlike Lee, Jackson had been observing closely the conduct of combat ever since First Manassas. The Seven Days especially had impressed on him that two powerful weapons were dominating battle and were proving decisive. The first of these was the Minié-ball rifle. The range and accuracy of this weapon were turning headlong assaults into mass killings. In the attacks on Boatswain's Swamp, for example, the Rebel soldiers lined up several hundred yards in advance of the Union entrenchments and launched their charges. For the entire length of their passage across a large open field, they were subjected to sheets of rifle fire. All but the last of the Rebel charges collapsed before they reached the Federal positions. In some cases one-half of the Confederate soldiers fell dead or wounded before the survivors dropped to the ground or withdrew. The Minié-ball rifle, in other words, could not be ignored.

The other weapon, the light twelve-pounder "Napoleon" cannon, had appeared numerous times in the war. But in the Seven Days it became dreadfully apparent how effective it was. This nimble gun could be rolled up quickly to the Federal defensive lines, and could spray out a deadly cloud of canister or metal fragments into the faces of the charging Rebels. Time after time, whole groups of Confederate soldiers were knocked down by a single blast. The combination of the Minié-ball rifle and the Napoleon cannon was making assaults practically impossible.

The Federal artillery and gunboat shelling had been decisive at Malvern Hill. Many of the Union guns were rifled, and their long ranges had proved effective because the battlefield was unusually large. For example, some of the rifled guns were posted on the top of the hill, more than a mile and a quarter from the Confederate positions. But most of the Union guns were lined up in front of the Union infantry a half a mile or less from the points where the Confederates launched their assaults. Many of these guns were Napoleons, and they did terrible execution.

Lee had paid no attention to the effects of these weapons, and had ordered one frontal assault after another directly into them. He had lost every one of these engagements except the one at Boatswain's Swamp. In this battle, he had lost 8,000 men. This one engagement cost nearly 80 percent as many Confederates as the entire two-day battle of Shiloh in Tennessee on April 6–7, 1862. There was an important lesson to be learned from the terrible results of the Seven Days—frontal assaults against well-prepared and resolute defenders armed with the Minié-ball rifle and Napoleon cannons were almost certain to fail, or the cost was going to be so great that the results would not be worth the victory.

Lee was not the only Civil War commander who was ordering assaults directly into the teeth of enemy resistance. McDowell had done so at First Manassas. Commanders on both sides at Shiloh had ordered a series of such attacks. Even Jackson had been obliged to order them to defeat the Union brigade at Port Republic. This was the way to achieve a decision, if no other means was present to force a defiant enemy to retreat or surrender—such as a descent on his rear. Yet the Seven Days had demonstrated that such attacks were recipes for disaster and defeat.

We don't know how long Jackson had been contemplating this dilemma. Very likely he had been thinking about it ever since First Manassas. Other commanders on both sides were thinking about it, but none had come up with any answer. Jackson, however, set up a logical set of circumstances. Outside of maneuver, the only way anyone could achieve a decision was to assault a defended position. Since this almost always resulted in defeat, the answer was to *induce* the Union forces to make these attacks, and for the Confederate soldiers to stand on the defensive. The resulting attacks would fail with huge losses and the failure would cause tremendous despair, gloom, and despondency among the repulsed Union soldiers. The Confederates could exploit this shattered morale by then launching an attack on the flank of the defeated and demoralized Union forces. They would be ripe for flight and would almost certainly collapse in chaos and disorder. In this fashion the Confederates could gain victory at a low cost.

In summary, the formula for victory under the conditions of battle in 1862 was for the Confederates to stand on the defense on a field of their choice that had at least one open flank around which they could launch a culminating sweep after they had stopped Federal attacks.[3]

How, then, to induce the Union forces to attack? There were three sure ways to make this happen. The Confederates could stand in the path of where the Union army wanted to go. They could capture or threaten some object that the North wanted to keep, like a railway line, a main supply base, or an important city. Or they could cut the

Union supply line and force the Union army to attack to reestablish its source of food, ammunition, and other goods. There was another less certain way to get an enemy commander to attack. This was to convince him that the Confederates were cowering in fear and would run the moment they were assaulted. This last method required a gullible Union commander who could easily be deceived, but it most definitely was possible.

It was not enough to develop a foolproof means of winning battles, however. Jackson had learned in his negotiations with Davis and Lee over his idea of invading the North that, no matter how correct his theory might be, it would amount to nothing if the leadership was not convinced, or, for whatever reasons, was not willing to follow it. Jackson had seen in the Seven Days that his commander, Robert E. Lee, was fixated on frontal charges. He saw that he would have to use persuasion and example to get Lee to change his mind and follow the new plan.

Jackson never spelled out his new theory of battle in so many words. However, it is certain that he had developed the concept fully by the end of the Seven Days.[4] We know this is true because he followed the theory faithfully in the campaign that was about to begin, and in all of the remaining Confederate operations in 1862.

The outcome of the Seven Days convinced Abraham Lincoln that McClellan was a defective commander. Lincoln visited McClellan personally at Harrison's Landing on July 8, 1862, and determined that the Army of the Potomac should be withdrawn from the peninsula and brought back to Washington.

Lincoln also concluded at last that he and his secretary of war, Edwin M. Stanton, knew virtually nothing about how to conduct a war. Accordingly, he brought in Henry Wager Halleck, a general who had gained some prominence in the Western Theater, and consolidated all Union forces under his direction. Lincoln also created a new

"Army of Virginia" out of various separate commands that he and Stanton had spread over the landscape. He gave command of this new army to another general from the Western Theater, John Pope.

Both new officers were quite inadequate. Halleck had graduated third in his class at West Point in 1839 and was called "Old Brains" in the army because he had written scholarly works on war. But he lacked judgment, had little strategic sense, saw dangers at every turn, and was slow, envious of the success of others, and hesitant to make decisions. Pope, an 1842 graduate of West Point, was puffed up with pride and confidence. He was incautious, ridiculed generals who thought strategy was more important than headlong fighting, and was unable to see danger until it struck him in the face.[5] But Pope was an ardent antislavery Republican, and made an excellent impression on Lincoln, Stanton, and the abolitionist congressional Committee on the Conduct of the War.[6]

It was at this point that Lincoln resolved to move the war in a revolutionary new direction. The North had suffered immense casualties in the Seven Days and in the battle of Shiloh, winning the contest but enduring 13,000 casualties to the South's 10,700. Lincoln feared that the Northern people would not continue making such terrible sacrifices, and decided that the only way to victory was to turn the war into a crusade. To do this, he had to promise to free the slaves.

Lincoln planned to issue an Emancipation Proclamation, but to apply it only to the seceded states, not to slaveholders in the four slave states (Delaware, Maryland, Kentucky, and Missouri) that had remained in the Union. On July 22, 1862, Lincoln read the proposed proclamation to his cabinet. Secretary of State William H. Seward objected. Coming on the heels of the humiliation of the Seven Days, he said, "It may be viewed as our last shriek on the retreat."[7] The proclamation, he argued, should be postponed until the Union attained a military success. Lincoln agreed, pocketed the paper, and waited for a victory.

John Pope's new army would number more than 60,000 men once it was concentrated.[8] Lincoln ordered Pope to march on Richmond from the west, by way of the Orange & Alexandria Railroad. The aim was to put Lee's army between two fires, Pope's army approaching from the west and McClellan's army at Harrison's Landing.

But Lincoln's strategy made little sense, because he also wanted McClellan to vacate Harrison's Landing as soon as possible. Halleck arrived in Washington from the west on July 23, 1862, and went to see McClellan the next day. Deferring to Lincoln, he told McClellan it was imprudent to keep two Union armies divided, with Lee between them, able to strike at one before the other could come to its aid. McClellan protested, pointing out that his army was still threatening Richmond. But Halleck had taken the measure of McClellan. He concluded that McClellan would never go on the offensive, that he didn't understand strategy, and that the army should be pulled back. On August 3, Halleck gave the order to begin withdrawal.

It quickly became plain that Pope was having a difficult time consolidating the various parts of his new army. Jackson saw an opportunity. He asked Lee to allow him to strike quickly at a part of Pope's force before the other parts could join. In this fashion, he could weaken Pope materially, and might cut his army to pieces one element at a time. But Lee, along with President Davis, was mesmerized by McClellan's army at Harrison's Landing, and would not authorize a move by Jackson northward.

It was Pope who forced Lee's hand. On July 12, 1862, some of his cavalry occupied Culpeper Court House, only twenty-seven miles north of Gordonsville. This move exposed the Virginia Central Railroad, which ran through Gordonsville and was the only rail line connecting Richmond with the Shenandoah Valley. The Confederacy could not lose this railway, and Lee immediately ordered Jackson, with the Stonewall Division and Richard Ewell's division, 12,000 men in all, to move to Gordonsville.

It took Jackson until July 16 to get his leading brigades into Gordonsville. Pope had time to beat him to this critical rail junction, but his cavalry chief, John P. Hatch, waited until he could get together a force of infantry, guns, and a wagon train before advancing. He was still some distance away when Jackson arrived and sealed off Gordonsville from anything short of a major assault.

When McClellan learned that Jackson had taken part of the Confederate army to challenge Pope, his proper response, of course, was to attack the weakened Rebel force at Richmond. But Lincoln had been right. McClellan was not going to move on his own volition.

When Jackson arrived at Gordonsville, he was eager to advance aggressively against Pope. But his force was too small. He appealed to Lee for more troops. Since Pope's menace was growing, Lee relented and sent Jackson A. P. Hill's division of 12,000 men. Hill arrived on July 29. Jackson now had a viable offensive force.

These moves alarmed Halleck, who was concerned with getting McClellan's army away from the peninsula without being attacked in transit by Lee. To distract both Jackson and Lee, Halleck told Pope to make a demonstration toward Gordonsville. In response, Pope's cavalry moved to the Robinson River, a tributary of the Rapidan, only eighteen miles north of Gordonsville.

On August 5, Federal forces reoccupied Malvern Hill and made gestures that they were about to advance on Richmond. Lee was certain this was a bluff, and he was assured of it when Captain John S. Mosby, soon to become famous as a partisan raider in northern Virginia, arrived at his headquarters. Mosby told Lee he had just been exchanged after being captured. At Fort Monroe he had heard that a 13,000-man corps under Ambrose E. Burnside, which had been lying in Hampton Roads in transports, was not docking and moving to re-inforce McClellan, as had been feared, but had lifted anchor and was moving up the Potomac to Aquia Creek, near Fredericksburg. Burn-side was going to reinforce Pope.

This was positive evidence that McClellan's army was abandoning the peninsula, confirmed by Rebel scouts who found Malvern Hill abandoned on August 7. More evidence soon came in that Federal troops were boarding transports for either Aquia Creek or Alexandria. The direct threat to Richmond was ending, and Lee could move most of his army to confront the growing danger of Pope.

Meanwhile, Pope was spinning grandiose plans for a victorious campaign in central Virginia. Given his opponent, these plans had little basis in reality. But Pope didn't know much about Jackson, and neither did Halleck. Pope informed Halleck he was about to strike out for Charlottesville, forty-five miles southwest of Culpeper. He was sure Jackson would be forced to pull back and defend this town, site of the University of Virginia and on the Virginia Central Railroad. He wired Halleck: "Within ten days, unless the enemy is heavily rein-forced from Richmond, I shall be in possession of Gordonsville and Charlottesville."[9]

This was such exciting news to Halleck that he wired Jacob D. Cox, commanding 11,000 troops at Lewisburg, West Virginia, to march eastward 130 miles across high mountains to join Pope at Charlottesville. Cox, who knew more about Jackson than either other officer, convinced Halleck that this was far too dangerous a move. There was a very serious question whether Pope would be at Char-lottesville when he arrived, he said, and he might be left alone and isolated, a perfect target for Jackson to surround and destroy. Cox's force took a roundabout journey by boat and rail to Washington, arriving far too late to play any role in the campaign.

Jackson had no intention of mounting a static defense of Charlottes-

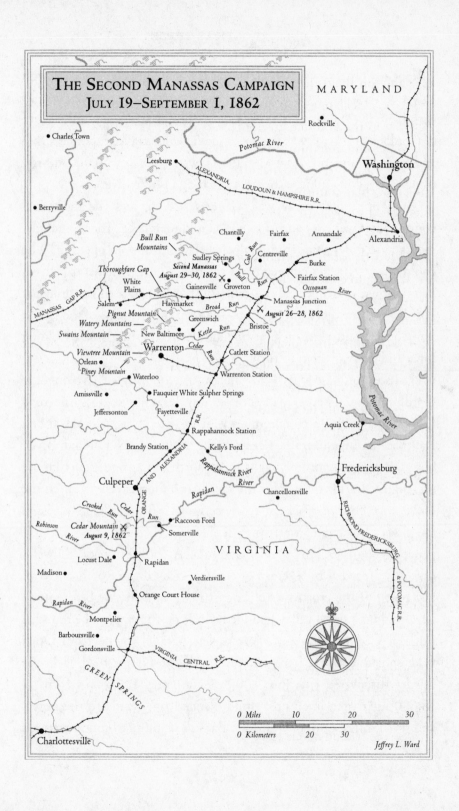

THE SECOND MANASSAS CAMPAIGN
JULY 19–SEPTEMBER 1, 1862

MARYLAND

Charles Town

Rockville

Potomac River

Leesburg

ALEXANDRIA

Washington

LOUDOUN & HAMPSHIRE R.R.

Berryville

Chantilly   Fairfax   Annandale

Alexandria

Bull Run Mountains   Sudley Springs   Centreville

Burke

Thoroughfare Gap   *Second Manassas August 29–30, 1862*   Fairfax Station

White Plains   Gainesville   Groveton   Occoquan *River*

MANASSAS GAP R.R.   Salem   Haymarket   *Broad Run*   Manassas Junction

Pignut Mountain   Greenwich   *August 26–28, 1862*

Watery Mountains   *Kettle Run*   Bristoe

Swains Mountain   New Baltimore

Viewtree Mountain   Warrenton   *Cedar Run*   Catlett Station

Orlean

Piney Mountain   Waterloo   Warrenton Station

Amissville   Fauquier White Sulpher Springs

Jeffersonton   Fayetteville

R.R.   Aquia Creek   *Potomac River*

Rappahannock Station

Brandy Station   Kelly's Ford

ORANGE AND ALEXANDRIA   *Rappahannock River*   Fredericksburg

Culpeper   *River*

Rapidan   Chancellorsville   RICHMOND FREDERICKSBURG

Crooked Run   *Cedar Run*   Raccoon Ford

Robinson   *Cedar Mountain August 9, 1862*   Somerville

River   VIRGINIA

Locust Dale   Rapidan

Madison   & POTOMAC R.R.

Rapidan River   Verdiersville

Orange Court House

Montpelier

Barboursville

Gordonsville   VIRGINIA CENTRAL R.R.

GREEN SPRINGS

0 Miles   10   20   30

0 Kilometers   20   30

Charlottesville

Jeffrey L. Ward

ville, or any other town. Rather, he was trying to lure Pope forward with a part of his army in order to trap it and destroy it. To induce Pope, he withdrew his 24,000 men to the Green Springs area a few miles south of Gordonsville. Pope was inclined to follow, but Halleck spotted a ruse and warned him off. Pope decided to wait until his 50,000 nearest troops arrived in Culpeper before launching his offensive.

But Pope's new army was widely scattered, and the individual commanders were not accustomed to rapid marching. The various elements were miles away from Culpeper. Jackson saw an opening. If he could seize Culpeper before any of the major Union elements arrived, he might use it as a central position—just as he had used the bridge at Port Republic as a central position—to keep the elements of the Union army apart, and turn on first one and then another isolated Union force and destroy them in turn.

Jackson launched his army northward on August 7 along the Gordonsville-Culpeper road (present-day U.S. Route 15). The road ran parallel to but a couple miles west of the Orange & Alexandria Railroad. Because of traffic tie-ups at the fords over the Rapidan River, however, Jackson got only eight miles north of Orange Court House on August 8. This delay, plus the fact that Union cavalry spotted the move, gave Pope another day to concentrate. But Jackson decided the risk of advancing was worth it. He launched his army for Culpeper on August 9. His lead element, Jubal A. Early's brigade of Ewell's division, preceded by a screen of cavalry, crossed the Robinson River just north of the crossroads of Locust Dale, and shortly before noon advanced up a small valley bounded a mile on the east by the rounded ridge of Cedar Mountain, more or less parallel to the road. Open fields spread to a large band of forest on the west of the road. Jackson's cavalry discovered that just 9,000 of Nathaniel P. Banks's corps of 18,600 men were lined up behind Cedar Run, a mile to the north, and seven miles south of Culpeper. Banks's inability to concentrate his force was shared by nearly all Union commanders, and this reduced their effectiveness dramatically. Banks, for example, had left 2,500 men at Winchester, and 1,000 at Front Royal, while sickness and heat kept the remainder out of ranks.

It was apparent that Banks was alone and unsupported. No other Union forces were close enough to come to his aid. Pope had managed to provide Jackson with just the isolated force he was seeking. Jackson moved to defeat Banks at once. But Banks, disregarding the fact that he was facing a Confederate army more than twice the size of his own, decided to attack. Jackson was not displeased. He told his medical director that Banks "is always ready to fight, and he generally gets whipped."[10]

Banks's attacks, though stoutly made, all failed, and Jackson swung around through the woods on the western flank of Banks's corps, and drove the remnants into flight at the end of the day. The division of James B. Ricketts, which had moved up behind Banks to form a solid defensive wall, forced Jackson to call off pursuit. But Jackson had rendered Banks's corps combat ineffective, and Pope relegated it to guard duties in the campaign about to unfold.

Jackson had also stopped a Union army twice the size of his own, and had thrown Pope on the strategic defensive. Jackson took advantage of a truce to remove the wounded from the battlefield in order to withdraw his army in the darkness of the night south to Gordonsville on August 11.

Pope, who at last had concentrated all his field forces except Jacob Cox's corps marching through West Virginia, was inclined to pursue Jackson straight to Gordonsville. But Halleck restrained him. "Beware of the snare," he warned. "Feigned retreats are 'Secesh' tactics." He forbade Pope to venture farther than the Rapidan River. Pope massed his main body on the Gordonsville-Culpeper road, well to the west of the eastern fords over the Rapidan. Aware that Jackson was based on Gordonsville, Pope was convinced that if Jackson advanced, he would come directly up the road to Culpeper. He never even considered that the Confederates might go around him. Accordingly, Pope allowed his left or eastern flank to remain woefully weak and virtually unguarded.[11]

Meanwhile, Lee was monitoring the withdrawal of McClellan's army from the peninsula. Since Jackson's position was getting perilous, he sent James Longstreet's corps to Gordonsville on August 13. The rest of the army, less a three-division garrison left at Richmond, got away on August 17. A Confederate force of 55,000 men was swiftly gathering at Gordonsville.

Jackson saw clearly that the Confederacy had only a small window of opportunity to confront Pope before the Army of the Potomac could complete its roundabout journey by water and land to reinforce Pope. Soon Pope's army would be too large to deal with. No time could be lost.

Lee himself arrived at Gordonsville on August 15, and sat down with Jackson and Longstreet. Jackson had been studying Pope's dispositions carefully, and he had already worked out a clear path to victory. He realized that his recent success over Banks at Cedar Mountain had weakened the confidence of Pope and his soldiers. Jackson saw, therefore, that the Union army was vulnerable to a sudden assault on its flank. In short, the opportunity for the Confederate army was identical to what it would have been if Pope had actually attacked along the Rapidan and had been repulsed. Pope had 50,000 men just north of the river, but he had allowed his left or eastern flank to remain virtually unguarded. It was a potentially fatal weakness. Jackson told Lee that the Confederates could sweep around Pope's left, block reinforcements coming from Aquia Creek, cut the Orange & Alexandria Railroad and Pope's supply line, and drive Pope's army against either the Rapidan or the mountains to the west. He could be forced to surrender his entire army. Pope, in his ignorance, had delivered the Confederacy the means for an overwhelming victory.

But at this juncture a strange series of facts intervened. The Confederacy possessed a military genius in Stonewall Jackson who occupied a decidedly subordinate position in the Confederate hierarchy. He was the only officer who had found ways to win the war. The military part of the Confederate hierarchy was topped by Robert E. Lee, who had recently revealed a profound lack of understanding of how to conduct successful warfare. He had, along with Davis, rejected the unequivocally feasible idea of drawing off McClellan's army without a fight by invading the North. Instead, he had lost a quarter of his entire army in headlong assaults into the very strongest parts of that army in the Seven Days.

It is doubtful whether Lee recognized Jackson's genius. A commander who does not understand the principles of warfare, which Lee clearly did not, is unlikely to appreciate the wisdom of another officer who does understand these principles. Lee had demonstrated this lack of recognition when he rebuffed the proposals Jackson had made about an invasion of the North. And in the Seven Days, Lee had asked no one's opinion and had done precisely what he wanted—advance headlong straight at the enemy.

Jackson most certainly understood that his only chance of getting his ideas accepted was to penetrate into the obtuse and unimaginative mind of Lee and to convince him that the ideas he advanced were valid. This was an extremely lonely undertaking. He had no associate who could understand what he was trying to do, and who could assist in trying to convince Lee. James Longstreet, Lee's only other senior adviser, was no help. Indeed, he was a hindrance. Longstreet was a very slow learner and, like Lee, had not grasped the deadly effects of using brute strength to defeat the Union. Power was not going to do it. The South had a third the people of the North. Some other method than sheer muscle had to be devised.

There was one additional barrier to success that Lee himself erected in the campaign about to begin: Lee had no goal whatsoever of engaging in decisive battle. He intended to *maneuver* Pope out of Virginia. He told no one of his purpose except President Davis, whom he informed at the very end of the campaign on August 30, 1862. On that date he wrote Davis: "My desire has been to avoid a general engagement, being the weaker force, and by maneuvering to relieve the portion of the country referred to [central and northern Virginia]."[12]

Lee plainly came to this decision because he wanted to avoid the kind of losses he had suffered in the Seven Days. The maneuver concept had arisen in the dynastic wars in Europe in the eighteenth century, when kings did not want to destroy their extremely expensive mercenary armies, and were generally seeking only limited goals, like small gains in territory or stopping an opponent's aggressive intent. During this period, generals normally maneuvered to cut off the enemy's access to so-called magazines, or fortresses where food and other supplies were stored. If this connection was severed, the enemy had to retreat. Wars often had few if any battles, and consisted primarily of marches on the enemy's rear. Lee saw that the same effect could be achieved by marching on the railroad that delivered supplies to Pope's army. If this line could be cut, Pope would be obliged to withdraw without a battle.

This was the only campaign in which Lee followed maneuver policy. Shortly afterward, he reverted to his previous fixation on direct attacks. Lee never explained why he had adopted the policy, or why he had then abandoned it. But the reason must have been that he realized, belatedly, that maneuver strategy has three crippling faults: it is indecisive; it inflicts little permanent harm on the enemy; and it can't force the enemy to make peace.

As the campaign opened, therefore, Jackson did not know that Lee was determined to avoid battles. So, when he recommended a course of action that could achieve victory, or, later, when he maneuvered the army, in spite of Lee's intentions, into a position where it could destroy Pope's army, he had to rely on Lee understanding what he proposed to do and acting on it. How this incredible intellectual conflict played out has gone down in history as the Second Manassas Campaign. It was surely one of the most dramatic and astonishing operations ever conducted. It pitted one officer's brain against another officer's brain. The first officer tried to show the second officer, step-by-step, how to win the war, while the second officer wanted to do nothing but push the enemy out of the country.

At the August 15 meeting, Lee accepted Jackson's plan to cross the eastern Rapidan fords, Somerville (where U.S. Route 522 now passes) and Raccoon (two miles east), and then to sweep around Pope. Jackson expected to envelop the Union army, to sever the Orange & Alexandria Railroad, and to drive Pope against the Rapidan or the mountains to the west. But Lee had no intention whatsoever of doing any of this. He didn't tell Jackson that he merely planned to force Pope to withdraw northward.

Therefore, Jackson, aiming for a decisive action against Pope, urged that the army move into position the next day, August 16, and that it strike on the early morning of August 17 so as to prevent Pope getting wind of the movement and withdrawing from the trap before it was sprung. But Lee was not concerned with speed or with laying a trap. Whenever the advance across the fords took place, Pope would withdraw. Accordingly, when Longstreet protested such an early move because he hadn't gotten his commissary organized and wanted time to bake bread, Lee agreed to delay the attack to August 18.

Lee also postponed the strike because he wanted Jeb Stuart's cavalry to move ahead of the Confederate advance and burn the railway bridge at Rappahannock Station (now Remington), twenty-five miles north, thereby cutting Pope's supply line. Jackson wasn't interested, because a movement on Pope's eastern flank would inevitably reach the railroad, and this would halt Pope's supplies just as readily as burning the railroad bridge. The cavalry strike was prevented anyway by a delay in the arrival of Fitzhugh Lee's cavalry brigade. Lee accordingly postponed the advance over the fords to the morning of August 20, because Fitz Lee's horses were worn out. Besides, he said, Richard H. Anderson's division had not arrived from Richmond, and Longstreet still hadn't baked enough biscuits.

On the night of August 17, a Union cavalry patrol crossed the Rapidan at Raccoon Ford and rode down to Verdiersville, ten miles east of Orange Court House, where Jeb Stuart and his staff were spending the night in a house. Stuart and his officers had to flee quickly. In the process Stuart was obliged to leave behind his cherished plumed hat, which the Union patrol seized. The loss of the hat vastly amused the Confederate army, because Stuart was notorious for his flamboyance and vanity.

By August 18, Pope had indeed gotten word of the planned strike across his eastern fords, and he set his troops in motion that very afternoon. By nightfall of August 19 he had them safely across the Rappahannock River.

Thus, when the Confederates rushed across the Rapidan on August 20, all they found were rear guards and a few stragglers. One of the great opportunities for a crowning Confederate victory had been lost. It was entirely the fault of Lee. Union General George H. Gordon, present during the campaign, wrote: "It was then most fortunate that Jackson was not in command of the Confederate forces on the night of the 17th of August, for the superior force of the enemy must have overwhelmed us, if we could not have escaped, and escape on that night was impossible."[13]

Jackson never made any recorded comment about the way Lee had wrecked his plan to destroy Pope's army along the Rapidan. It is certain that Jackson did not realize at the time that Lee was actively trying to avoid a collision with Pope. But Jackson knew that Lee had an aversion to indirect moves against the enemy. He had attempted just one indirect move in the Seven Days—Jackson's descent on Porter's right flank at Beaver Dam Creek on June 26, 1862. But before he had even determined that this movement had succeeded, he had abandoned it and ordered a bloody direct assault against the fortifications along the creek. All of his other operations during the Seven Days were direct and obvious. Jackson must have known, therefore, that he could not expect Lee to approve another indirect movement in advance. If he was going to use this method of winning, he had to do it on his own, and without Lee's prior approval.

CHAPTER 7

Second Manassas

When the Army of Northern Virginia rushed up to the Rappahannock River on August 20, 1862, the Rebels found John Pope's Union army arrayed solidly along it from Rappahannock Station (now Remington on U.S. Routes 15 and 29) eastward four miles to Kelly's Ford.

The Confederacy had only a short time to deal with Pope before the odds became too great to overcome. Most of McClellan's army was beginning to come ashore at Aquia Creek near Fredericksburg. Lee was afraid Halleck would order Pope's army to abandon the Rappahannock line and reinforce McClellan at Fredericksburg. Then the two combined armies might advance straight south to Richmond.

Lee sent two divisions, D. H. Hill's and Lafayette McLaws's, 17,000 men, to the North Anna River above Hanover Junction north of Richmond to stand guard. He hoped to maneuver Pope's army off the Rappahannock before having to deal with McClellan at Fredericksburg. To force Pope to withdraw northward, Lee ordered his army to move upstream to seek some ford around which it could sweep to displace Pope. But the Union army kept pace with the Confederate advance. In this way, the two armies, clashing along the way, moved their western flanks to Waterloo, thirteen miles upriver from Rappahannock Station.

Lee was still confident that Pope would withdraw if his rail connection was cut. On August 22 he approved another cavalry raid on a railroad bridge, this time at Catlett Station over Cedar Run, fourteen miles north of Rappahannock Station. Jeb Stuart's troopers struck in the midst of a raging thunderstorm that made the wooden bridge too wet to burn. Pope's headquarters was at Catlett Station, however, and Stuart found Pope's dispatch book, containing his orders.

The book revealed that Pope had not detached any of his troops to Fredericksburg after all, and that, in fact, McClellan's forces were moving to join him along the Rappahannock. The book showed that many Federal troops were already on the way. Lee had only a few days before Pope's army would be entirely too large to confront. He immediately ordered the divisions of D. H. Hill and Lafayette McLaws to reinforce him. But he could not wait until they had arrived. He had to act quickly.

Jeb Stuart had been enduring endless ribbing—from privates to generals—for having lost his beloved plumed hat to Union raiders at Verdiersville. He arrived at Jackson's headquarters at Jeffersonton on August 24, and displayed another item he had seized at Catlett Station—a beautiful blue uniform coat, inside of which was a tag with the name of its owner, "John Pope, Major General." Stuart announced he had a proposition to make. Taking a piece of paper, he wrote: "Major Genl. John Pope, Commanding, etc. General: You have my hat and plume. I have your best coat. I have the honor to propose a cartel for a fair exchange of the prisoners. Very Respectfully, J.E.B. Stuart, Maj. Genl., C.S.A." The proposed "cartel" amused Jackson immensely. The communication was sent through the lines. Nothing came of it. Perhaps it did not entertain the other party as much as it did Stuart and the Confederates.[1]

It finally was glaringly apparent to Lee that a cavalry strike on a railroad bridge was too unreliable to knock Pope's army off the Rappahannock. Something far more solid and powerful had to be employed. And it had to happen before the Union reinforcements reached Pope. Accordingly, on August 24, he called in Stonewall Jackson and told him to plant his entire corps, 23,000 men, on some point on the Orange & Alexandria Railroad, and cut Pope's supply line. After breaking the line, Jackson was to hold the Union army at bay until the rest of Lee's army could come up to rescue him.[2]

Lee merely wanted Jackson to move to a close point on the railroad and sever the line. But Jackson saw this as a chance to transform the entire campaign into a massive victory for the South. Without explaining it all to Lee, he resolved to make a strategic descent deep into the rear of the Union army. Jackson was seeking a decision in the war. Lee was seeking to evict Pope from the Rappahannock. We know the two officers had these two decidedly different ideas because they specifically explained their aims in their official reports after the end of the campaign.[3]

Both Lee and Jackson knew there was no hope in moving around Pope's eastern or left flank. The Union troops were alert in this direction and portions of McClellan's army were marching toward Pope from Fredericksburg, and might intercept any Confederate advance on this flank. But Waterloo was only a little east of the highlands known locally as the Bull Run Mountains and part of the Catoctin chain running northward into Maryland. Lee expected Jackson to move along the eastern edge of these elevations to Warrenton or vicinity, and then strike east to the railroad at Warrenton Station or Catlett Station.

But Jackson had no intention of making such a modest advance.

He called in his chief engineer, Captain J. Keith Boswell, a native of the region, and told him to chart the most covered route around Pope's right, with Manassas Junction, only twenty-seven miles from Alexandria, as the general objective. Manassas was twenty-five miles in Pope's rear. Manassas Junction was the main supply base for the Union armies in Virginia, and a Confederate force there would be a direct threat to Washington, only thirty miles to the north. The loss of his main supply base and the presence of such a huge Confederate force so close to the capital were certain to force Pope to fight a decisive battle.

Jackson assembled his three divisions around Jeffersonton, and ordered his men to cook rations for three days and to strip all vehicles from the column except ambulances and ammunition wagons. In the frantic haste, many men didn't have time to cook rations and would have to subsist on green corn and apples from fields and orchards along the way. For Jackson, there was no waiting until sufficient biscuits had been baked.

He did, however, have time to send a hurried note to his wife, Anna: "The enemy has taken a position, or rather several positions, on the Fauquier [County] side of the Rappahannock. I have only time to tell you how much I love my little pet dove."[4]

Early on the morning of August 25, Jackson's corps moved out. He was not going east of the Bull Run Mountains, he was moving west of them. He marched first to Amissville, six miles northwest, struck north across a ford on the Rappahannock River, and passed around Piney Mountain. Now behind the mountains, the men marched (on present-day Virginia Routes 688 and 647) through Orlean and north to Salem (present-day Marshall), on the Manassas Gap Railroad. It was a hard march of twenty-five miles.

Near Salem, Jackson climbed on a large rock and, taking off his hat, watched the soldiers march by. A message swept down the ranks.

"No cheering, boys. The General requests it." The soldiers passed by silently, but showed their affection by waves and swinging their caps and hats in the air. Jackson turned to his staff, his face beaming: "Who could not conquer with such troops as these?"[5]

"His men loved him," Colonel G. F. R. Henderson wrote, "not merely because he was the bravest man they had ever known, the strongest, and the most resolute, not because he had given them glory . . . but because he was one of themselves, with no interests apart from their interests; because he raised them to his own level, respecting them not merely as soldiers, but as comrades, the tried comrades of many a hard fight and weary march. . . . His congratulatory orders were conspicuous for the absence of all reference to himself; it was always 'we,' not 'I,' and he was among the first to recognize the worth of the rank and file."[6]

Early in the war, Jackson's medical officer, Hunter McGuire, was watching with Joseph E. Johnston as the 2nd Virginia Regiment marched by. McGuire said to Johnston: "If these men will not fight, you have no troops that will." Johnston replied dismissively: "I would not give one company of regulars for the whole regiment." When McGuire repeated Johnston's comment to Jackson, he replied, "Did he say that? And of those splendid men? The patriot volunteer, fighting for his country and his rights, makes the most reliable soldier on earth."[7]

Both Lee and Jackson understood this great strength of the individual citizen and they fostered leadership and initiative by subordinate officers. In Jackson's corps especially, officers and men were well aware that Jackson expected independent action and rewarded it. Jackson impressed on his officers that their first duty was to sustain their colleagues. He knew that in battle the scope of the commander is limited. Once troops are committed, it is impossible for the commander to exert further control, and he must rely on the good judgment and enterprise of his subordinates. Confederate commanders were thus served by zealous assistants, actively furthering the goals of their superiors.

Practically the opposite condition existed in the Federal army. As G. F. R. Henderson wrote, "McClellan, Pope, and Frémont, jealous of power, reduced their subordinates, with few exceptions, to the position of machines, content to obey the letter of their orders, oblivious of opportunity, and incapable of cooperation."[8] In the Federal case, subordinate commanders were taught to wait for orders. In the Confederate case, they were expected to anticipate them. In this fashion, Rebel soldiers and officers went into battle with tremendous confidence, both in themselves and in the judgment of their superiors. "The Army of the Potomac," Henderson wrote, "was an inert mass, the Army of Northern Virginia a living organism, endowed with irresistible vigor."[9]

A Union signal station atop a mountain near Waterloo discovered Jackson's movement by 8:00 A.M. on August 25, and observed its progress for fifteen miles. But Pope could not figure out what it meant, nor could any of his generals. Pope at last concluded that Jackson was heading toward the Shenandoah Valley, and that the rest of the Rebel army was probably following. But he did not send out any cavalry to ascertain whether this was correct, a monstrous failure in command responsibility.

At Salem, Jackson's troops collapsed in exhaustion, not even bothering to unroll their blankets. Long before daylight on August 26 their officers stirred them awake, and they moved off in the darkness. As usual, they had no idea where they were going. But a wild wave of excitement and enthusiasm swept through the ranks at dawn when the men realized they were marching toward the rising sun. They were moving right into the heart of enemy country. Somewhere ahead they were going to challenge some important objective that the enemy did not want to lose.

The Confederates proceeded on the road (present-day Virginia Route 55) through White Plains (now The Plains), the Bull Run Mountains, Thoroughfare Gap, Haymarket, and on toward Gainesville on the Warrenton-Alexandria Turnpike (now U.S. Route 29). Eight miles beyond that village lay Manassas Junction.

Pope did not know where Jackson's column had gone, and he told Irvin McDowell to find out. McDowell ordered his cavalry to move after Jackson, but the commander said his horses and men were broken down and he couldn't start till the morning of August 27.

During the day of August 26, Pope became convinced that the mass of the Confederate army was at or above Waterloo. What this signified, he had no idea. But, fearful that something was up, he decided to break his army away from the Rappahannock in the afternoon. Lee was observing Union movements closely, and seeing troops withdrawing, he concluded that Pope had found Jackson and was rushing back to challenge him. Pope in fact had no idea where Jackson was. He thought maybe he wasn't headed for the Shenandoah Valley after all. He had received reports that hostile troops had passed through Salem, White Plains, and Thoroughfare Gap. But he didn't connect that with Jackson's disappearance, or ask how large this force was. Worse, he didn't draw any conclusions from the news. The most he thought possible was that Jackson and Lee might attempt an attack on Warrenton, six miles northeast of Waterloo. He never conceived the possibility that Lee would dare to divide his army or that Jackson could march fifty miles in two days and place his entire corps astride Union communications.

Pope ordered three of his corps—McDowell's, Franz Sigel's, and Jesse L. Reno's of McClellan's army—to concentrate the next day, August 27, at Warrenton. He left Nathaniel P. Banks's still-shaky corps at Fayetteville (now Opal), seven miles south of Warrenton, and directed Fitz John Porter's corps of 10,000 men, just arriving, to move toward

Warrenton Station (now Calverton) on the railroad, nine miles south-east of Warrenton. Samuel P. Heintzelman's corps was already located there. Pope now had 75,000 men.[10]

Stonewall Jackson's corps arrived at Gainesville around 4:00 P.M. on August 26. Waiting for them were Jeb Stuart's cavalry. They had departed Waterloo at 2:00 A.M. and had ridden straight to the village along back ways through the Bull Run Mountains. Pope's army still remained completely unaware of their existence, despite the columns of dust the troops raised.

Now screened by Stuart's troopers, Jackson made his way not to Manassas Junction, but to Bristoe Station, four miles south. Jackson intended to break the railroad bridge over Broad Run, just a bit to the north of Bristoe. The head of the column reached Bristoe around dusk, and quickly scattered the small Federal guard. A locomotive pulling empty cars up from Warrenton Station appeared only minutes after the Rebels arrived, and they were unable to stop it before it ran through the station on north. The Rebels quickly cut the telegraph wires and tore up track. This wrecked the second and third trains bringing empties north, but the engineer of the fourth train spotted the trap and backed up to warn Pope.

The Confederates now moved up to Broad Run and broke the rail-road bridge there. Pope's supply line had been severed. Jackson's orig-inal objective had been achieved. Cutting the telegraph wires stopped Pope's direct communications with Washington until August 30. During this period, all Federal messages had to go through Falmouth, just north of Fredericksburg.[11]

The Confederate corps was exhausted, but Manassas Junction had not yet been secured. Colonel Isaac R. Trimble volunteered to lead the 21st North Carolina and the 21st Georgia, 500 men, up the tracks to secure the junction. Meanwhile, Stuart sent the 4th Virginia Cavalry around to the rear of Manassas. The Rebels quickly overcame feeble Union resistance and captured more than 300 prisoners.

Although Pope got word of the strike soon after it happened, he discounted its importance, thinking it was a small hit-and-run cavalry raid. He ordered Heintzelman at Warrenton Station to send a regiment up on a train to repair the wires and protect the railroad. The regiment soon returned with the news that a large body of infantry was at Bristoe and Broad Run, not a small group of horsemen.

By now it was 7:00 A.M. on August 27, and Pope was finally thoroughly alarmed. He sent Joseph Hooker's entire division from Warrenton Station to Bristoe to restore the situation. At 8:30 A.M. he directed most of his army to move back, not to Warrenton, but to Gainesville, twelve miles northeast. Pope had abandoned the Rappahannock line.

Meanwhile Lee, with most of the rest of the army, about 25,000 men, was on the way north as well. Lee had pulled the troops off the river on the afternoon of August 26, and set them on the same roundabout route north that Jackson had taken. He left only Richard H. Anderson's division of 6,000 men on the river. By the morning of August 27, Lee and Longstreet were well on their way toward a junction with Jackson.

The renowned English strategist Major General J. F. C. Fuller was highly critical of Lee's decision to move through Thoroughfare Gap to rendezvous with Jackson east of the Bull Run Mountains. He wrote that Lee should have struck at once for Berryville in the Shenandoah Valley, and called on Jackson, after he had destroyed the Federal supply base at Manassas, to join him by moving westward through Snicker's Gap (west of Purcellville on present-day Virginia Route 7), then advancing as a concentrated army on Harpers Ferry. From there Lee could have threatened Washington. This would have compelled Halleck and Pope to withdraw all forces from Virginia to defend the capital. Fuller's criticism of Lee is valid, since Lee's stated purpose (made to President Davis) was to avoid a battle and merely maneuver Pope out of Virginia.[12]

This solution did not occur to Lee, and his failure demonstrates his lack of strategic insight—because this would have been a far more reliable method of forcing Pope out of Virginia than Lee's only idea, to cut Pope's railroad line. Jackson, on the other hand, was not in the least interested in maneuvering Pope out of Virginia. He wanted to keep Pope's army in Virginia and destroy it. He had already worked out a means to do so. It required Lee's cooperation, so Lee's decision to join him suited him very well. And he didn't know that Lee did not want to fight a battle. Jackson's motivation in moving to Manassas Junction was to *provoke* Pope into trying to destroy his force. The whole purpose of Jackson's moves after reaching Manassas, therefore, was to deceive Pope into coming after him.

John Pope was thoroughly over his head in challenging Stonewall Jackson, but, of course, he did not know this, and kept thinking that he was making wise decisions. But the evidence was overwhelmingly against him. Only three weeks previously, he was telling Halleck confidently that he was about to evict Jackson from Charlottesville, and would soon be bringing the war to a successful close. Since that time he had been knocked off first the Rapidan and then the Rappahannock by nothing more than maneuvers designed by Jackson. Now the enemy was occupying his main supply base, and his men were running out of food. Jackson was within thirty miles of the national capital, the very city Lincoln and Secretary of War Stanton had told him it was his duty to protect.

But on the morning of August 27, 1862, a number of factors had come into alignment that offered Pope a marvelous opportunity to redeem himself. If he had examined the intelligence reports already coming to him, he could have figured out that Lee and Longstreet must be west of Thoroughfare Gap, while the mysterious infantry force at Manassas Junction had to be Jackson's corps. He also could have figured out, merely by looking at a map, that the logical junction point for these two parts of the Rebel army was Gainesville. And Pope had already directed the bulk of his army to Gainesville.

By pure happenstance, he found his army smack in the middle between the two parts of the enemy army. He was in the central position. All he had to do was to concentrate his army at Gainesville, block Thoroughfare and other passes over the Bull Run Mountains, and keep both parts of the Rebel army separate. He then could destroy one part of the army, and then destroy the other part, both with vastly superior force.

But none of this was evident to Pope. He was completely disregarding the threat of Lee and Longstreet, although they had over half of the Rebel army. He was so obsessed with the enemy force at Manassas that it wiped all other considerations from his brain. So Pope remained blissfully unaware of the opportunity that had fallen into his hands. For a general as obtuse as Pope, principles of warfare have no meaning. Instead, he spent the day of August 27 concerned mostly with getting Joe Hooker's division to Bristoe Station to deal with the Rebel infantry force there.

Meanwhile, the bulk of Jackson's corps moved up to Manassas Junction on the morning of August 27 and beheld a wonderland of stores of all kinds. Acres upon acres of goods were lying alongside the tracks and in warehouses. Every item of clothing and any sort of food, from ordinary rations to luxuries such as champagne, Rhine wine, coffee, and canned sardines, were available for the taking. As soon as Jackson loaded up all his available wagons with what supplies they could carry, he threw the entire depot open to the soldiers to take what they wanted, and could carry with them.

Halleck in Washington had no idea what the enemy force at Manassas was, but he set about trying to demolish it. His efforts were totally inadequate. First he sent down the 12th Pennsylvania Cavalry from Alexandria, which the Stonewall Brigade quickly sent flying. Soon thereafter the raw and inexperienced 1st New Jersey Brigade came from Alexandria by rail. The Union force detrained just north of the railroad bridge over Bull Run. The commander, Brigadier General George W. Taylor, had been told only to protect the bridge, but he thought he was dealing with a small Rebel force, and he decided to press on to Manassas Junction.

The New Jersey brigade ran headlong into a large part of A. P. Hill's division. Realizing that the Union force was about to be destroyed, Jackson rode forward personally and called on the Federals to surrender. He received a bullet past his ear in reply. Rebel artillery now opened on the brigade and broke it apart. More than 300 Federals surrendered, while 135 were killed or wounded, and Taylor himself died. The survivors fled in panic northward. While Fitz Lee's cavalrymen pursued fugitives all the way to Burke Station, fourteen miles from Alexandria, Rebel soldiers destroyed the bridge over Bull Run, as well as the locomotive and cars that had brought the brigade.

Jackson didn't know Pope's intentions, but he did know he couldn't remain long at Manassas Junction. All through the afternoon of August 27, Jeb Stuart's patrols sent Jackson report after report of enemy movements. A large force was marching on Bristoe from Warrenton Station; heavy columns were heading down the turnpike from Warrenton toward Gainesville. Meanwhile, a courier disguised as a countryman arrived from Lee, informing him that Lee and Longstreet were following Jackson's own track. At the same time, Jackson was sending Longstreet regular reports by courier reporting on his successful operations and his confidence that he could avoid being bottled up by the enemy.[13]

On the evening of August 27, Pope arrived at Hooker's division facing Richard Ewell's division south of Bristoe Station. He discovered for certain that Jackson's whole corps was at Manassas. Pope now drew a most remarkably wrong conclusion. He decided that Jackson's entire purpose had been merely a raid on the Union supply base. He deduced that Jackson was now trying to escape southward around Hooker's *eastern* flank, and that Hooker had stopped this effort. However, Pope knew from reports of his own troops that Lee and Longstreet had abandoned the line of the Rappahannock. Therefore, they must be moving toward Thoroughfare Gap to rescue Jackson. Consequently, it made no sense that Jackson would be attempting to flee around Hooker's eastern flank. Jackson's logical sally port was *westward* toward Gainesville and Thoroughfare Gap.

Nevertheless, Pope comprehended none of this and decided that Hooker had caught Jackson at Manassas. He saw no other choice for Jackson but to entrench himself there and await Lee's arrival. He sent out orders for all of his forces to march at once on Manassas. If his troops moved up promptly, he boasted, "We shall bag the whole crowd."[14]

So, Pope abandoned the central position between Lee and Jackson. It had offered him a potentially decisive advantage that could have won the war for the North in a couple of engagements. But Pope never knew he had even been in the central position.

During the evening, Ewell detached his forces from Hooker, withdrew north of Broad Run, and marched to join the rest of Jackson's corps at Manassas. Federal troops at Broad Run looked ahead and could see massive red flames on the horizon. Some of the Federals surmised correctly what was happening: the Rebels had set the entire Union supply base ablaze.

It was noon on August 28, 1862, when Hooker's advance guard arrived at Manassas. They encountered a burned-out wasteland. The entire cache of Federal stores had been looted in part by the Rebels, and the remainder had been consumed by fire. But Jackson and his men had disappeared, no one knew where.

Pope was completely bewildered. He had been certain that he had Jackson cornered. For four hours he had no idea what had happened to Jackson or what to do. Then at 4:00 P.M. news arrived that the rail line at Burke, just fourteen miles from Alexandria, had been cut, and that Confederates were in force between Burke and Centreville to the west. Pope now decided that the Rebels were fleeing in disorder, and he directed his whole army on Centreville, eight miles north of Manassas and just above the Bull Run battlefield of the year before.

Pope's order created a panic in the army. Troops rushed frantically toward Centreville. But when the first Union forces arrived there, they found no Confederates. The only presence of the enemy was a few Rebel horsemen who retired leisurely before the advance. The Federal soldiers collapsed in exhaustion. Where in the world was Jackson?

Then, seven miles away across Bull Run near Groveton on the Warrenton-Alexandria Turnpike, three miles northeast of Gainesville, the dull boom of cannon sounded, swelling to a continuous roar. The smoke of the gunfire was plainly visible to the soldiers at Centreville. They concluded that Jackson at last had been run to ground. Irvin McDowell's corps, coming up from Warrenton, they felt sure, had caught Jackson trying to escape and had trapped him.

But another sound intervened. Far to west, where a cleft in the blue hills marked Thoroughfare Gap in the Bull Run Mountains, the flash of distant guns lit the sky. What was this? The soldiers at Centreville didn't know. But Pope, in his haste to "bag" Jackson, had entirely forgotten Lee and Longstreet, and had made no provisions whatsoever to deal with them. But McDowell, arriving at Gainesville, was cautious enough to sense danger, and sent the 1st New Jersey Cavalry westward to Thoroughfare Gap on the morning of August 28. The horsemen found some of Longstreet's men already in possession of the pass, and they hurried back to tell McDowell. He sent James B. Ricketts's division to challenge the Rebels. It was cannon fire from this collision that the soldiers at Centreville had seen on the horizon.[15]

What the Union soldiers at Centreville thought had happened was not at all what actually had taken place. For twenty-four hours, Stonewall Jackson had been carefully drawing Pope into a noose. Jackson wanted to prove his new system of battle. To do so, he needed to entice Pope into a position where he was certain to attack Jackson head-on. Jackson was sure that the Union attacks would fail, and that the Confederates could sweep around the defeated enemy and force him into chaotic retreat or surrender. But Jackson needed a battlefield that had at least one open flank, that had an inadequate escape route for the defeated Union army, that provided an easy junction with Lee's army, and that could allow Jackson a safe place to withdraw in case, somehow, disaster struck. Beyond that, he had to find a way to induce Pope to attack. And the surest way of doing that, he saw, was to convince Pope that he was in great fear of the Union army, and was desperately hanging on, hoping he could somehow escape.

The year before, after First Manassas, Jackson had reconnoitered a place that answered all of his requirements admirably. It was an unfinished railway alongside a small elevation just above Groveton. The excavations had left deep cuts that could serve partially as defensive emplacements. The land behind the unfinished railway was fairly level and covered with trees that could hide both infantry reserves and cannons. Just to the north was Aldie Pass, which could be used as an escape route west in case everything went wrong. The Stone Bridge over which the Federals had fled at First Manassas was the only adequate crossing of Bull Run in the vicinity. Just three miles to the southwest was Gainesville, toward which Lee and Longstreet were marching. When they arrived, they would be almost exactly on the left flank of the Union army, if Pope decided to attack. All the conditions for the successful battle plan were in place at Groveton. Jackson had simply to get his corps there, and then to provoke Pope to attack him.

But Jackson had one other consideration that overrode all else. Pope had already run twice, and he was likely to run again. Jackson did not want him to flee back to Washington. He wanted to fight Pope in Virginia. He was certain he could destroy his army. So, how was he to prevent Pope from breaking and running?

Jackson had an answer to all these questions. And on the night of August 27, 1862, at Manassas Junction, he embarked on the quest. After his men had set a conflagration that was consuming the Union supply base, Jackson launched his three divisions on three separate roads. He sent A. P. Hill and his division straight to Centreville. He directed Richard Ewell's division over Bull Run at Blackburn's Ford on the old battlefield, and ordered him to watch carefully for any Union movements. He dispatched William B. Taliaferro's division directly up the Sudley Springs–Manassas road with the trains, going past Henry House Hill, scene of the battle the year before, and on until his division was hidden in the woods above Groveton, eight miles northwest of Manassas.

His positioning of Hill and Ewell north of Bull Run was to block Pope's passage if he decided to retreat back to Washington. The position of Taliaferro at Groveton also served this purpose, since it commanded the Alexandria-Warrenton Turnpike (present-day U.S. Route 29), the best retreat route for the Union army.

On the morning of August 28, neither Hill nor Ewell saw any evidence that Pope's troops were heading back to Washington, and Ewell moved his division over to Groveton to join Taliaferro. Hill remained at Centreville until 10:00 A.M. Also seeing no evidence the Federals were fleeing, he started up the Warrenton Pike to join Taliaferro and Ewell. However, one of Jackson's cavalrymen captured a Union courier carrying a message to Sigel at Gainesville to march at once to Manassas Junction. This, in fact, was part of Pope's attempt to concentrate all of his army at Manassas to "bag" Jackson. But Jackson, not believing Pope could be so foolish as to think he was still at Manassas, concluded that Pope was fleeing back to Washington by way of Manassas. Accordingly, he sent orders to Hill to block the fords of Bull Run to keep Pope from getting away.

But Hill had intercepted another Union courier ordering McDowell to prepare for battle on the Manassas plain near the junction. This showed that Pope was not fleeing, but was trying to destroy Jackson. It told Hill it was unnecessary to block the fords over Bull Run, and Hill moved at once to join the rest of the corps at Groveton.

The second captured order eased Jackson's anxiety, but during the late afternoon Jeb Stuart's horsemen reported that Pope was moving his army toward Centreville. The reason, of course, was that Pope thought he was closing in on Jackson's corps for the kill. But Jackson didn't know this, and the move reignited his fear that Pope had decided to run. One incident increased Jackson's suspicion. Colonel Bradley T. Johnson, commanding the Rebel brigade closest to Gainesville, discovered a Union column he thought was advancing on him. Actually it was John F. Reynolds's Pennsylvania division, which was still trying to get to Manassas in accordance with Pope's earlier orders. Johnson opened fire, but Reynolds's superior artillery overawed him, and he withdrew. Reynolds decided the Rebel force was only a small reconnoitering party, and he continued on toward Manassas. Jackson, however, feared that Reynolds was trying to clear the Warrenton Pike for Federal forces to march on Centreville.

Jackson resolved to stop this movement. He also wanted to bring part of Pope's force to battle to incite him to make a major attack. Accordingly, he marched Taliaferro and Ewell's divisions to a point slightly north of the turnpike and close to Gainesville. Around 5:00 P.M., Rufus King's division of McDowell's corps started down the Warrenton Pike on the way to Centreville. Near sunset it came opposite Jackson's position.

To Jackson this was confirmation of his fears. He ordered his infantry to attack, and brought forward two batteries of cannon. King's men were caught by surprise, but they quickly organized a stout defense. The so-called battle of Groveton thus developed into a bloody, stand-up fight by brigadiers who fired salvo after salvo into each other's ranks. The fight ended with darkness. It was exactly the kind of collision that Jackson wanted to avoid, but it served his purposes, for it showed Pope where he was and challenged him to battle. In the fighting both Ewell and Taliaferro were wounded, Ewell losing a leg. Command of Taliaferro's division passed to William E. Starke, and Ewell's division to Alexander R. Lawton.

The sounds of the battle caused Franz Sigel to turn his corps, and John F. Reynolds his division, back toward Groveton. Both got within a mile of King and bivouacked for the night.

During this same August 28, Lee and Longstreet arrived at Thoroughfare Gap and encountered James B. Ricketts's division, sent up by McDowell. Ricketts was thoroughly overmatched. David R. Jones's division seized the heights commanding the gap, while Cadmus M. Wilcox's division drove through Hopewell Gap, three miles north, and John Bell Hood's division crossed by a trail just north of the pass. In grave danger of being surrounded and trapped, Ricketts fled quickly back to Gainesville.

When Ricketts arrived, he encountered King, who had pulled back to Gainesville after the collision with Jackson. As King and Ricketts talked, they realized that Longstreet and his entire corps were certain to descend on Gainesville the next morning. They immediately decided that the better part of valor was for both their divisions to evacuate Gainesville at once. King left forthwith for Manassas, and Ricketts for Bristoe. They told no one of their decision, because their corps commander, McDowell, had gone off to Manassas to talk with Pope, and had gotten lost in the woods.

Pope meanwhile had drawn all the wrong conclusions about what had happened. He thought King had foiled an effort by Jackson to retreat through Thoroughfare Gap to join Longstreet, that King and Ricketts were standing fast *west* of Jackson at Gainesville, and that McDowell, in command, could fend off Longstreet long enough for Pope to bring up forces and destroy the isolated Jackson.

All Jackson's hopes had been fulfilled. Pope had been wholly deceived into thinking that Jackson was trapped between two Union forces and that he was cowering in fear. To Pope it was the perfect chance to attack Jackson headlong and destroy his entire force. To Jackson it was the opportunity to prove that his new system of defend-then-attack would bring about the utter defeat of the Federals.

Pope thus sent a message to McDowell to hold his ground at Gainesville "at all hazards and prevent the retreat of Jackson to the west." He said he believed he could crush Jackson before "Longstreet could by any possibility reach the scene of the action." Pope ordered Philip Keary's division at Centreville to advance on Jackson's left or eastern flank at dawn on August 29, to be assisted by Joseph Hooker's division and Jesse L. Reno's corps, both near Centreville. He ordered Sigel and Reynolds to attack Jackson at daylight from their present positions.[16]

It was morning before McDowell found his way out of the woods, reached Manassas, discovered what had happened, and informed Pope that his left wing had evaporated. Pope thereupon ordered McDowell with his two divisions and Fitz John Porter with his corps, 24,000 men in all, to march on Gainesville from Manassas. However, Ricketts was at Bristoe, not Manassas, and Manassas was eight miles from Gainesville, and they could not beat Longstreet to it.

Meanwhile, Jackson had made careful preparations for the expected attack. During the night he had pulled his corps up along a two-mile line behind the unfinished railway. The line was shielded on both flanks by Jeb Stuart's cavalry. A. P. Hill was on the left or east, Lawton in the middle, and Starke on the right. In front of the troops the ground was largely open, except for woods, 400 to 600 yards wide, mostly along Hill's front, but extending into Lawton's.

The short line gave Jackson three rifles to the yard and allowed him to concentrate five artillery batteries on the heights. The soldiers had to stand in double lines so each man would have space to fire his rifle. But Jackson had as many men uncommitted and hidden in the woods as he had along the line. He gave local and divisional commanders authority to call forward any and all of these reserves whenever they might need them.

Despite Pope's orders for two corps and three divisions to launch simultaneous attacks all along Jackson's front, only the commanders on the east sent in any major attacks, and then only one division at a time. The Union commanders targeted Hill's division because their troops could approach through the woods. The Union commanders along the largely open remainder of the line to the west saw that attacking the massed Rebel rifles would result in death and mayhem. They contented themselves with artillery duels with the Rebel guns.

None of the Union forces Pope ordered from Centreville arrived anywhere close to dawn. Carl Schurz's division of German immigrants—"Dutchmen" to the Rebels—of Sigel's corps was the first to launch an attack. It struck Maxcy Gregg's South Carolina brigade. As Schurz's soldiers advanced through the woods in front of the railway cut, Gregg's troops rushed into the woods, flanked the Dutchmen, split the two Federal brigades apart, and broke the division's center. The Dutchmen fell back in disorder, but rallied, and advanced once more. Again Gregg's brigade drove the Union troops out of the woods in disorder.

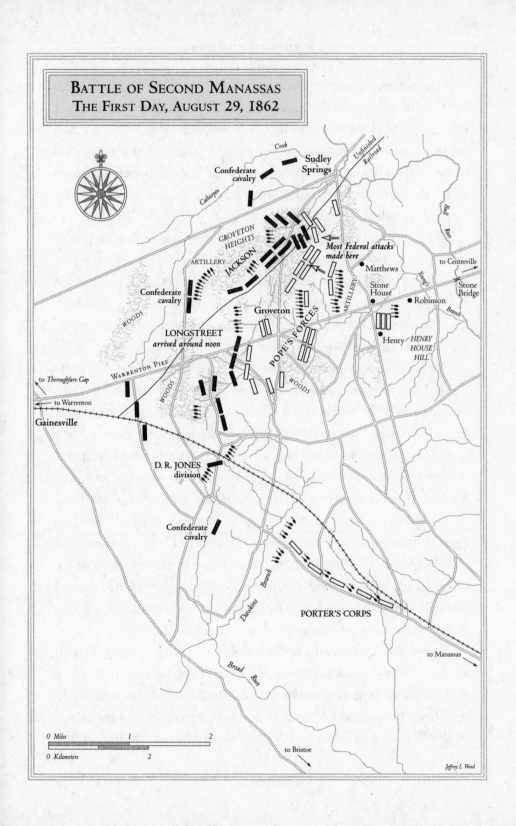

BATTLE OF SECOND MANASSAS
THE FIRST DAY, AUGUST 29, 1862

Creek

Sudley
Springs

Unfinished Railroad

Confederate
cavalry

Catharpin

Bull Run

GROVETON
HEIGHTS

Most Federal attacks
made here

ARTILLERY

JACKSON

to Centreville

Matthews

Stone
House

Stone
Bridge

Confederate
cavalry

Young's

WOODS

Groveton

Robinson

Branch

LONGSTREET
arrived around noon

POPE'S FORCES

ARTILLERY

Henry

HENRY
HOUSE
HILL

WARRENTON PIKE

WOODS

WOODS

to Thoroughfare Gap

to Warrenton

Gainesville

D. R. JONES
division

Confederate
cavalry

Dawkins Branch

PORTER'S CORPS

to Manassas

Broad Run

0 Miles		1		2

0 Kilometers		2

to Bristoe

Jeffrey L. Ward

Schurz tried again, this time reinforced by other foreign soldiers from Adolph von Steinwehr's division. These troops reached the railway cut and there a violent battle erupted. The Union soldiers made a small penetration, but two Confederate regiments crashed down on their flanks, forcing them to retreat in great disorder. Schurz's and Steinwehr's divisions pulled away at noon, riddled with losses, exhausted, and demoralized.

The fights had been bitter, but they had involved only a fraction of the Union and Confederate forces. The Union commanders, seeing the terrible odds their men were facing against a solidly emplaced enemy sending out curtains of rifle fire, were not sending their men into the inferno. Pope, however, was not satisfied, and he was preparing another series of direct assaults.

While the appalling collisions were occurring along A. P. Hill's front, Lee and Longstreet marched down from Thoroughfare Gap, arriving about 11:30 A.M. Longstreet turned east along the turnpike, and drew up on either side of it, facing approximately east and at a near right angle to Jackson's line. Pope was so absorbed with his plans to attack Jackson that he completely ignored the presence of Longstreet, with more than half of the Confederate army, on his left flank.

At about the same time, Fitz John Porter arrived at Dawkins Branch, four miles south of Gainesville, with his two divisions and King's division, 17,000 men. McDowell joined him there at noon. They heard from Federal cavalrymen that Longstreet had passed through Gainesville, and they could see dust clouds, indicating that Longstreet's whole corps was coming to the aid of Jackson.

Porter and McDowell had been delivered a chance to launch an all-out attack on Longstreet before he could get into position, using the 17,000 men already available, plus Ricketts's division of 7,000 men from Bristoe, and Nathaniel Banks's corps of 10,000 men, now at Kettle Run, just south of Bristoe. This combined force of 34,000 men was larger than Longstreet's corps of 25,000. But the idea of an assault never entered the mind of either officer. Their only thought was how to reach the rest of the Union army along the Warrenton Turnpike. They couldn't approach cross-country because the terrain was too broken. Instead, they made a remarkable decision, which proved that both officers were truly incompetent commanders. They decided that Porter would stay at Dawkins Branch, with his troops remaining in column, not battle, formation, and that McDowell would march both King's and Ricketts's divisions by roundabout roads and join Pope on the turnpike. In other words, Porter was to do *nothing,* while McDowell was to march his corps from the *flank* of the Confederate army in order to attack this army directly *in front.*

Pope was oblivious of all this, and planned two simultaneous attacks from the turnpike, one by Joseph Hooker, the other by both Philip Kearny's and Isaac I. Stevens's divisions. In what had become a pattern, Hooker selected only a single brigade, under Cuvier Grover, to make the attack, while Kearny and Stevens decided to wait until Hooker's attack had ended before mounting theirs.

Grover ordered his soldiers to load their rifles, fix bayonets, and move slowly forward until they felt the enemy's fire, then to deliver a volley. Only after they had executed these moves were they to charge and carry the position by main force, relying on the bayonet. It was an incredibly brave and utterly foolish tactic. For just one brigade of 1,500 men was trying to defeat Jackson's entire corps of 22,000 men, who were lined up waiting for them, with their cannons primed to fire.

Grover also moved against Maxcy Gregg's brigade, but reached as well to the adjacent brigade of Edward L. Thomas. The Union soldiers marched up to the railway cut, received a staggering Rebel salvo, delivered their volley, and rushed forward, driving the stunned Rebels beyond the railway line. But Confederate artillery shocked the Federals, and Rebel reserves hurried forward and broke the valiant force into pieces. The survivors fled, but left a third of their whole force dead, wounded, or captured.[17]

All day long one Federal force after another had launched a solitary attack into the teeth of Jackson's corps. All had failed. Now, around 5:00 P.M., Kearny and Stevens formed up their divisions for one last assault. Once again, they aimed their blow against Maxcy Gregg's brigade. It had already lost a third of its 1,500 men, and the soldiers were sagging with fatigue. When the Federal storm burst on Gregg once more, the South Carolinians fell back to a last-ditch stand behind the railway cut. But A. P. Hill had already primed Jubal A. Early's Virginia brigade and the 12th Georgia and the 8th Louisiana for a counterattack. They struck the Federal center with a single crushing blow. The line crumpled, the Rebels rushed through the gap they had created, and the two Federal divisions cracked. The men ran back over the railroad cut and beyond, pursued for some distance by the Confederates.

At 4:30 P.M., just as the final assault was about to begin, Pope had sent a peremptory order to Porter to attack toward Gainesville. Porter didn't get the order until 6:30 P.M. and he decided not to launch it, since Longstreet had more than twice as many men as he did.

Longstreet and Lee remained on the Union army left flank all afternoon, and Lee never ordered an attack. He allowed Jackson to absorb all the blows by Pope's troops, and he made no move to help, although Pope had placed no troops on the west, and his flank was bare. Porter's 10,000 men at Dawkins Branch were still in column formation, and far too distant to reach Longstreet if he launched his troops straight at Henry House Hill, the elevation directly above the Stone Bridge, and the key position to block the Union army from escaping. It was apparent shortly after noon that the Union army was suffering extreme loss of confidence and morale, because the assaults during the morning had failed. The Union commanders were not ordering assaults unless they were specifically directed to do so by Pope. They saw plainly, though Pope did not, that their units would be torn apart if they attacked the Confederate line. Longstreet's corps could have launched a drive at any time up to midafternoon, and it would have encountered virtually no opposition. The Rebels then would have had plenty of daylight to reach Henry House Hill.

The prospect of total victory lay directly in Lee's grasp. But he did not seize the chance. He deferred to Longstreet, who was always slow to move, and who pointed to Porter's corps at Dawkins Branch as a rationale for not advancing. But this was not a valid reason. Lee had entered the campaign not wanting to fight, and he didn't want to do so now. So Longstreet's reluctance suited him very well. Yet it was quite evident that Jackson expected Lee to swing around Pope's flank the very first moment that he could put his troops in assault formation. Jackson was holding the Federal army in a fierce battle embrace, and the opportunity was absolutely obvious. But Lee did not move.

English General Sir Frederick Maurice was highly critical of Lee for his failure to see and exploit his opportunity. "While Pope was bringing his corps up piecemeal to attack Jackson, Longstreet stood stretched well beyond the Federal left, ready to strike a deadly blow," he wrote. Maurice compared Jackson's situation with that of the Duke of Wellington at Waterloo in 1815. Jackson, Maurice wrote, was like Wellington, who absorbed Napoleon's attacks all day, waiting for the Prussian army to strike the French flank and throw the French army into disordered defeat and chaos. But Lee refused to take the role of the Prussian army and administer the coup de grâce against the Union army.[18]

Thus, at the end of the day on August 29, 1862, Stonewall Jackson's system of stopping Union attacks and demoralizing the attackers had succeeded brilliantly. But the second part of Jackson's system, a Confederate sweep around the flank of the defeated enemy army, had not taken place because Lee had refused to carry it out. It was a dismal failure. The Confederacy could easily have achieved the crowning victory that Jackson had planned for and had set in motion. He had shown a way for the South to win the war. A couple of victories like that would have proved to the North that continuing the effort was not worth the cost.

The next day, Saturday, August 30, 1862, was extremely strange on almost all counts. It started with Robert E. Lee making no plans to do anything. For Lee, Jackson's repulse of Pope was victory enough. But this was a pitiful gain compared to the tremendous efforts the Confederates had made during this entire campaign—not to speak of the opportunity for total victory that Lee had squandered. Pope had lost 6,000 men to Jackson's 1,500 men, yet this had not materially weakened the Northern war effort. The North could easily replace its losses. To force the Lincoln administration to end the war, the South had to destroy a Northern army, not merely achieve a modest battlefield decision in its favor.

Jackson never commented on the outcome of the battle on August 29. But Lee's total failure to understand that Jackson had maneuvered Pope into a position where his entire army could have been lost must have weighed heavily on his thoughts.

But then, amazingly, Pope gave the Confederates another chance to destroy his army. He had fallen for one of the oldest ruses in warfare. At the end of the day on the twenty-ninth, Jackson had pulled all his troops back into the woods behind the railway line to give them a much-needed rest, and also to mystify the Federals. Pope discovered the Rebels' absence on the morning of August 30, and immediately concluded that Jackson had fled during the night and that he had won the battle!

He wired Halleck to this effect: "The enemy was driven from the field, which we now occupy. . . . The news just reaches me from the front that the enemy is retiring toward the mountains; I go forward at once to see."[19] This was a total falsehood. There was no actual evidence that Jackson was fleeing, and Pope had not occupied an inch of Jackson's position. Pope had assembled 60,000 of his 75,000 men, yet Stonewall Jackson, with just 22,000 men, had shattered all of Pope's attacks. The results were eminent proof that Jackson's system was working, and equal proof that Pope was incapable of facing reality.

Pope now made a series of astonishingly bad decisions. First, at 5:00 A.M., he ordered Porter at Dawkins Branch to move his corps over to the Warrenton Pike. This removed the only Union force posing any possible threat to Longstreet's corps. Now Pope's western flank was totally bare. He then gave tactical control of the day to McDowell, who was as incapable of reading battlefield situations as Pope himself.

Pope and McDowell agreed that Porter's corps, once it arrived, would move west on the Warrenton Pike, and swing around the right flank of the "fleeing" Jackson, while Ricketts's division would move around the left or eastern flank of Jackson near Sudley Springs with the same aim. The decision to send Ricketts around Jackson's left flank made some sense if Jackson, in fact, was fleeing. But the decision to send Porter around Jackson's right flank simply ignored the fact that Longstreet was emplaced precisely at this location with more than half the Rebel army. Moreover, Pope had finally recognized Longstreet's existence late on August 29 by ordering Porter to attack him from Dawkins Branch.

The Federal commanders arrived at this ridiculous conclusion because Pope was convinced that Jackson was fleeing. Therefore, Longstreet must be pulling away as well. But Pope had no evidence that Jackson had actually departed other than the absence of Rebel soldiers along the railway cut, and nothing whatsoever to indicate that Longstreet had gone anywhere. The Federal commanders demonstrated on this day one of Napoleon Bonaparte's most important maxims: "The general ignorant of his enemy's strength and dispositions is ignorant of his trade."[20]

The advance westward along the turnpike did not, in fact, take place because Porter finally exhibited a bit of judgment. When he arrived he told McDowell that this flank attack should not be attempted until the actual strength, or the lack of it, of Jackson's front had been tested. If this proved that Jackson really was fleeing, then the flank advance would make sense and should be launched. McDowell acknowledged the logic of this argument, and Pope backed him.

But this meant that the Union army had to mount another major frontal assault against the very lines that had blocked the Federal army the day before. Porter began organizing a second attack. It was aimed a bit to the west of where the Union attacks had gone in the day before. Porter lined up 20,000 troops behind the belt of trees that had sheltered the Federal attacks on August 29. On the extreme right, Ricketts's division was to move along Bull Run toward Sudley Springs and around the eastern flank of Jackson. Not much opposition was expected there. On the right was John P. Hatch's division and on the left were two brigades of George W. Morell's division, now commanded by Daniel Butterfield, because Morell had gone off with one of his brigades to Centreville by mistake. This was a career-ending blunder for Morell. In reserve behind these two assault divisions were George Sykes's division and Franz Sigel's corps. Half of Pope's army remained behind in column formation. The two assault divisions represented only a 30 percent superiority of force against that portion of Jackson's line it was assaulting. Pope and McDowell had learned nothing from the attacks of the day before.

Hatch planned to advance through the woods that extended to the railroad, and aim mainly at the left sector of Ewell's division (now under Alexander R. Lawton). In front of Butterfield the woods were only a quarter of a mile deep and beyond them stretched about half a

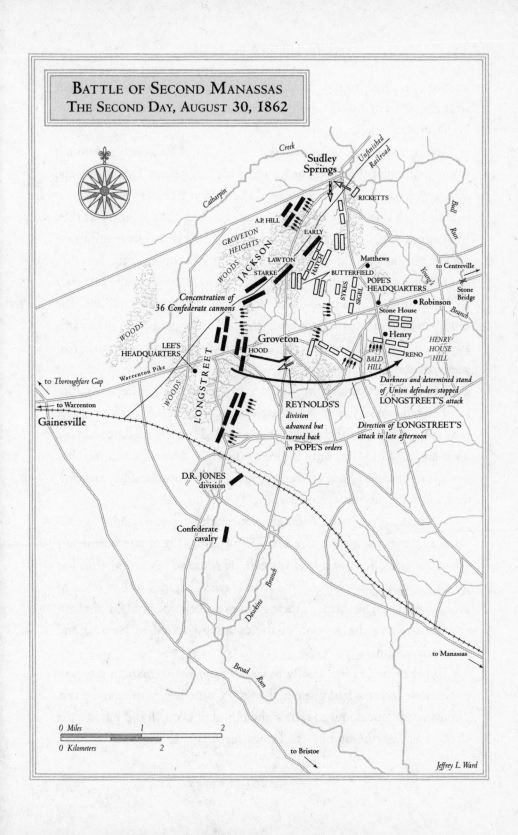

BATTLE OF SECOND MANASSAS
THE SECOND DAY, AUGUST 30, 1862

Catharpin Creek

Sudley Springs

Unfinished Railroad

Bull Run

RICKETTS

A.P. HILL

GROVETON HEIGHTS

WOODS

EARLY

JACKSON

LAWTON

HATCH

STARKE

Matthews

BUTTERFIELD

to Centreville

POPE'S HEADQUARTERS

SYKES

SIGEL

Stone Bridge

Concentration of 36 Confederate cannons

Young's Branch

Robinson

Stone House

WOODS

LEE'S HEADQUARTERS

Groveton

Henry

HENRY HOUSE HILL

HOOD

RENO

LONGSTREET

BALD HILL

to Thoroughfare Gap

Warrenton Pike

WOODS

Darkness and determined stand of Union defenders stopped LONGSTREET'S attack

to Warrenton

Gainesville

REYNOLDS'S division advanced but turned back on POPE'S orders

Direction of LONGSTREET'S attack in late afternoon

D.R. JONES division

Confederate cavalry

Dawkins Branch

to Manassas

Broad Run

0 Miles   1   2

0 Kilometers   2

to Bristoe

Jeffrey L. Ward

mile of open fields to the railroad line. His intention was to fall farther west on parts of Ewell's division and on Taliaferro's division (under William R. Starke).

The situation the Federals faced on August 30 was actually much worse than what they had encountered the day before. By moving the attack westward, Porter had opened the Union troops to terrible enfilade fire—that is, fire coming at the *side* of the Union infantry as they were advancing. The Confederates had mounted thirty-six cannons on a quarter-mile-long eminence just north of the turnpike at the juncture of Jackson's and Longstreet's lines. These guns faced generally east over the open fields in front of the center and right of Jackson's line. The only barrier they encountered was the belt of trees about 1,300 yards away in front of Jackson's left wing. These were the woods that had sheltered the Federal attacks on August 29. West of these woods, the guns could direct devastating enfilade fire against any Federal assault.

The renowned Confederate artilleryman Porter Alexander wrote that "a battery established where it can enfilade others need not trouble itself about aim. It has only to fire in the right direction and the shot finds something to hurt wherever it falls. No troops, infantry or artillery, can long submit to enfilade fire."[21]

It was plain that the Federals were making preparations for another massive assault on Jackson. Despite this, Lee made no preparations for any offensive move. Instead, he revealed his actual aim. For on this morning he wrote President Davis: "My desire has been to avoid a general engagement, being the weaker force, and by maneuvering to relieve the portion of the country referred to [central and northern Virginia]."[22]

Thus Lee had failed wholly to understand the tremendous opportunity that Jackson had presented to the Confederacy the day before. Today, with Pope about to repeat the blunder, Lee still did not see the chance that was being offered. Longstreet likewise remained as blind as Lee, because he made no overtures to Lee to prepare to strike Pope's flank. It was unconscionable. Lee and Longstreet should have drawn up assault forces in anticipation. The moment the Federal lines advanced against Jackson, Lee and Longstreet should have launched their forces straight for Henry House Hill. The Union army was wholly absorbed in the attacks, and Longstreet's men would have had plenty of time to seize the hill before darkness fell. From there they could have sealed off the Stone Bridge. Instead, Lee and Longstreet made no preparations whatsoever. Both officers simply watched the drama unfold, and had no intention of taking part themselves.

At 3:00 P.M. the Federal forces advanced. General Pope, standing on a knoll near the Stone House on the Warrenton Pike, believed he was on the verge of victory. He thought Jackson's main force was gone, that the skirmishers he saw in front of him would quickly run away, and that he would soon be sweeping westward in heavy columns toward Thoroughfare Gap. Suddenly Pope's hopes collapsed. Loud and clear above the roar of the artillery, the sound of Confederate bugles rang out, and, on the ridge above the railway line, long lines of infantry streamed forward from the woods and ran down to the embankment. "The effect," said one officer who witnessed the event, "was not unlike flushing a covey of quail."[23]

Instead of a small rear guard, which Pope thought he could quickly crush, Stonewall Jackson's entire corps was standing defiantly on the railway line.

Pope, shocked at what he saw, immediately eliminated the one small impediment Longstreet might have faced in an advance around Pope's flank. He ordered back Reynolds's division, which he had sent westward along the south side of the Warrenton Pike around 1:00 P.M. He was oblivious of the danger to his left flank to the last.

Ricketts's division moving around Jackson's far-eastern flank toward Sudley Springs ran into a hornet's nest of Jeb Stuart's cavalry, and saw beyond much of A. P. Hill's division arrayed in battle formation with canister-loaded guns pushed forward. There was no way around Jackson's flank, and Ricketts immediately withdrew.

Hatch's division on the right had an easy time advancing through the woods, and struck mainly Ewell's left sector, held by the brigades of Marcellus Douglass and Jubal A. Early. Here the fighting was fierce, but the Rebels repulsed the Federals, though Hatch's onset was so powerful that the Confederates restored the line only by sending Dorsey Pender's North Carolina brigade charging into the melee.

Butterfield's men had altogether a worse time. The first of four lines of Butterfield's division emerged from the woods and received heavy fire, but moved resolutely on across the open fields to the unfinished railroad. There some of Ewell's men and Taliaferro's division (under Starke) were waiting. Here the fighting became some of the wildest and bloodiest in the entire war. The brigades of Leroy A. Stafford and Bradley Johnson held their positions tenaciously. To their right the Federals pushed back the first line of the Stonewall Brigade, but the commander, Colonel W. S. H. Baylor, led the second line forward and drove Butterfield's men back, though Baylor died at the head of his men.

In front of Stafford and Johnson the battle raged for twenty to thirty minutes with unbelievable fury. There was no thought of retreat by either side. The Federals made assault after assault against the railway line, but the Rebels stopped every one. Some of the Confederates ran out of ammunition and grabbed replacements from dead bodies, or snatched up rocks and threw them at the enemy. General Johnson reported: "I saw a Federal flag hold its position for half an hour within ten yards of a flag of one of the [Confederate] regiments in the cut, and go down six or eight times, and after the fight one hundred dead were lying twenty yards from the cut, some of them within two feet of it."[24]

The thirty-six Confederate guns on the elevation on the flank had been unable to direct heavy fire quickly enough to damage Butterfield's first line as it moved across the open space. As the battle raged along the railway cut, however, the Rebel guns concentrated on the woods from which the succeeding lines of Butterfield's division were coming and on the fields over which they were passing to reach the railway. In this fashion, Butterfield's division, largely exposed in the open, was riddled with terrifyingly effective enfilade fire. The deadly barrage actually reached all the way across to strike Hatch's division hidden in the woods. Porter described it graphically: "The enfilading artillery, combined with the direct infantry fire, almost annihilated line after line, as each was about to crown the embankment [at the railroad]."[25]

It was plain that not only had all the Union assaults failed with terrible losses, but that the Union army itself was disintegrating from the crisis. By now it was 4:15 P.M., and at last both Lee and Longstreet recognized the fact. Casting aside his resolve to stand on the defensive, Lee finally ordered a general attack. Longstreet had already anticipated the order, and had summoned his troops to charge. But as Porter Alexander remarked, Longstreet's forces had not been previously assembled for an attack, and it took a long time to organize the pursuit.[26]

The Federal army's greatest asset now was time. John Bell Hood's division led the Confederate advance on Henry House Hill, but the delay required to form the men in assault formation meant that Federal forces got to it before Hood and stopped him as night was falling. If Longstreet's corps had already been lined up in battle formation and ready to move, and if the flanking attack had been launched an hour earlier, Hood could have seized Henry House Hill in plenty of time, and could have blocked Federal retreat over the Stone Bridge.

As it was, most of the Union soldiers evacuated across the bridge, though a few fled over Bull Run fords to the north. But thousands of Union troops surrendered. Pope's surviving forces formed a shaky line just beyond Bull Run around part of William B. Franklin's corps, which had marched from Alexandria late in the afternoon.

The next day, August 31, Jackson crossed Sudley Springs Ford and marched northwest to the Little River Turnpike (now U.S. Route 50) in an attempt to turn the Federal right flank and evict Pope from Centreville. The following day he struck the Federal flank guard at Ox Hill, about three miles east of Chantilly, and fought a hard battle in driving rain. The Federals lost two division commanders, Isaac I. Stevens and Philip Kearny, both shot down.

The fight at Ox Hill was enough for Pope. He withdrew into the Washington defenses. Lincoln relieved Pope, and sent him out west to fight Indians. He also relieved McDowell, who never held another field command. With no other officer to choose, Lincoln reinstated George B. McClellan.

The whole summer campaign cost the South 9,100 men, almost all killed or wounded. This was only marginally smaller than the cost to the North: 10,200 killed or wounded, and 7,000 captured, who were all exchanged.[27]

What almost certainly could have been the destruction of a Union army became merely a defeat of that army. Jackson had shown step-by-step how the South could have won the war in one or two engagements. But Lee had not understood, and had not followed through. The greatest chance of the South for victory since First Manassas had been wasted by Lee at Second Manassas.

CHAPTER 8

❖

Calamity in Maryland

Robert E. Lee had gone into the summer campaign of 1862 intending only to maneuver John Pope out of Virginia. He had been forced into a battle at Second Manassas by Stonewall Jackson. Even then, he refused to draw in Longstreet's corps until the very end of two days of dreadful, solitary defense against the Union army endured entirely by Jackson. Because of this, Lee had turned the total victory that Jackson had prepared for into a modest battlefield advantage, and the vast bulk of the Federal army was able to pull away to safety.

Now Lee decided to invade Maryland, but he intended to follow the same nonaggressive policy of avoiding battle there. He got President Davis's authorization by saying that, once the Southern army had established itself on Northern soil, the Confederate government should propose peace based on recognition of Southern independence. Lee did not intend to inflict any damage on the Northern economy, but the fact that the Southern army was in a position where it *might* inflict injury, would, in Lee's eyes, "prove to the country [the North] that the responsibility for continuance of the war does not rest upon us, but that the party in power in the United States elect to prosecute it for purposes of their own."[1]

There was no indication that the mere presence of a Confederate army in the North would set off a groundswell of opposition to the war. Also, relying on *others* to accomplish one's own goals is an unreliable and generally unproductive policy. Furthermore, Abraham Lincoln and the Radical Republicans in Congress were determined to put down what they called the "rebellion," and Lincoln was moving to proclaim an end of slavery in the seceded states. Lincoln was waiting for a Northern victory to announce this publicly. This would turn the war into a crusade, and would eliminate practically all organized opposition to the war. Intimations of this plan were already rife, because the astute South Carolinian Mary Chesnut wrote about it in her diary on July 8, 1862.[2] All of this should have been plain to Robert E. Lee. But it wasn't.

The Northern war policy was precisely the opposite of the pacific persuasion that Lee was proposing. The North was invading the South along every available avenue, and was inflicting the utmost damage on everything within reach. John Pope had threatened to treat mothers as traitors if they wrote their sons in the Confederate army. The Federal government had seized Lee's 1,100-acre estate at Arlington, and Union troops had absconded with the furniture and displayed in New York relics of George Washington stolen from the mansion. They had even demolished the Winchester home of James M. Mason, the Confederate representative to Britain.[3]

The North had imposed an iron blockade on all Southern ports, virtually cutting off trade with Europe except by a few blockade runners. Since the South possessed only one-eleventh the industry of the North, it could not produce anywhere close to the amount of war goods required. The North's blockade was designed to choke the Southern economy and hurt the Southern people to the maximum extent possible. There could scarcely be a more vindictive policy of pain and suffering than what the North was attempting to impose.

The results of Northern actions were great privation for the Southern people and for the Confederate army. The army, in fact, depended to a large extent on goods captured from the Union army. Old muskets were exchanged for new rifles, small-bore cannons for powerful rifled guns, tattered blankets for good overcoats. The Union armies supplied the Rebels with tents, medicines, ambulances, and ammunition wagons. Even the vehicles at Confederate headquarters bore the initials *U.S.* Many Rebel soldiers were partially clad in Union uniforms, and the Confederates, like their Union counterparts, complained about the poor quality of boots supplied by Northern contractors.[4]

But the provisioning of the Confederate armies was still woefully inadequate, and it was the women at home who kept the armies in action. Mothers, wives, and daughters pulled thousands of long-disused spinning wheels out of Southern lumber rooms, re-erected old handlooms, created homespun, and dyed it with boiled walnut shells plus vinegar to produce butternut-colored clothing for the soldiers. It was the work of these dedicated women that kept the Confederate armies reasonably well clothed and provided with blankets. And because President Davis refused to remove an old crony, Lucius B. Northrup, as commissary-general, although he was incompetent, the Confederate food supply system was highly inefficient. Accordingly, the folks at home increasingly were called upon to send food to their sons and husbands in the armies.

Given the unlimited damage that the North was trying to inflict on the South, it is astonishing that Lee would even consider a policy of inoffensive coaxing of the North. Although President Davis continued in his nonproductive policy of passive defense of the South, it was self-evident by September 1862 that only force was going to achieve any results with Lincoln and his administration.

The exact situation the South faced was summarized brilliantly by Henderson. He wrote: "A nation endures with comparative equanimity defeat beyond its own borders. Pride and prestige may suffer, but a high-spirited people will seldom be brought to the point of making terms unless its army is annihilated in the heart of its own country, unless the capital is occupied, and the hideous sufferings of war are brought directly home to the mass of the population. A single victory on Northern soil, within easy reach of Washington, was far more likely to bring about the independence of the South than even a succession of victories in Virginia. It was time, then, for a strategic counterstroke on a larger scale than had hitherto been attempted."[5]

Henderson's appraisal reflected precisely the viewpoint of Stonewall Jackson. Unlike Lee, who was seeking to *convince* the Northern people to grant the South independence, Jackson sought to inflict so much injury on the Northern economy that accepting Southern independence would be less painful to the Northern people than enduring further damage.

Lee went into Maryland believing that a Confederate army could maintain itself in the North without a military victory. But Lee quickly abandoned the idea that mere threats would gain Southern independence. He decided to make one demonstration of actual Confederate power to impress the North. On September 7, 1862, Lee told Brigadier General John G. Walker, commanding a small three-brigade division, that his goal was to break the long railroad bridge over the Susquehanna River at Harrisburg, Pennsylvania. This, Lee said, would disrupt Union communications with the West. "After that," he told Walker, "I can turn my attention to Philadelphia, Baltimore, or Washington, as may seem best for our interests."[6] This last comment indicates that Lee did not have any strategy but only hoped to exploit opportunities as they might arise.

To embark on an invasion of the North with the entire Army of

Northern Virginia, and then to seek *only* to break the railway bridge at Harrisburg, was an incredibly inconsequential goal. Such an act would not affect the North in any substantial way. Even connections with the West would not be interrupted, for railways still ran along the south shores of the Great Lakes. Besides, the vast bulk of Northern industry was located along the eastern railroad corridor from Baltimore to southern Maine. That's where the heart of the North's war-making capacity lay. Breaking a single bridge in the interior would appear merely as an act of vandalism.

Moreover, the goal was unattainable. There was no chance that Abraham Lincoln would allow a Confederate army to roam around the North unmolested for any length of time, particularly since congressional elections were going to be held in a few weeks. Lincoln was intensely aware of the consequences of an election defeat, and would demand that the Union army challenge the Southern army at the very first opportunity.

Lee must have realized how wrong he was a few days after he launched the army across the Potomac River to Frederick, Maryland, on September 3, 1862. He still planned to move westward, but he altered his goal. He now intended to *attack* the Union army.

We don't know the exact date that Lee changed his mind, but it must have occurred shortly after he talked with General Walker. We know this because he told the historian William Allan in an interview in Lexington, Virginia, on February 15, 1868, that, after he got his whole army together in the vicinity of Hagerstown, Maryland, he "*intended then to attack McClellan* [Lee's own emphasis], hoping the best results from the state of my troops and those of the enemy."[7]

In other words, Lee abandoned the passive policy that he had adopted in the summer campaign of 1862, and reverted to the aggressive policy of frontal attacks that he had followed in the Seven Days. He had failed to comprehend the policy of defend-then-attack that

Stonewall Jackson had tried to teach him at Second Manassas. As events were to show, Lee was unable to carry out his aggressive policy in Maryland, but his intention is indisputable.

Frederick is forty miles northwest of Washington, and about fifty miles west of Baltimore. McClellan got the news of the advance from his new chief of cavalry, Brigadier General Alfred Pleasonton, and shifted his headquarters to Rockville, Maryland, just northwest of Washington, on September 7. He had a field army of 85,000 men. Another 72,000 men remained in the Washington defenses under Nathaniel P. Banks. McClellan commenced a slow, hesitant advance on Frederick.

The day after the Rebels arrived at Frederick was a Sunday, and Jackson, as was his practice whenever possible, went to church, attending the services at the German Reformed Church. The pastor prayed for the president of the United States. Afterward, he got credit for much courage for offering the prayer in the presence of Stonewall Jackson. Actually, Jackson did what he usually did at church: he fell asleep shortly after he sat down in the pew, and probably didn't hear the prayer. However, as his aide, Henry Kyd Douglas, noted, he would doubtless have felt the same as Richard Ewell did the next year at Carlisle, Pennsylvania. Asked if he would permit the usual prayer for President Lincoln, Ewell replied: "Certainly, I'm sure he needs it."[8]

At Frederick, Lee held a conference with Stonewall Jackson and James Longstreet. There he outlined his plan to move westward over South Mountain, the extension into Maryland of the Blue Ridge Mountains of Virginia. The only direct account we have of this meeting comes from the Reverend Robert Lewis Dabney, a close friend of Jackson, who wrote a book on Jackson published in 1866. Dabney recounted that Lee's first design was to withdraw the army into western Maryland "for the purpose of threatening Pennsylvania, and fighting McClellan upon ground of his own choosing."[9] So Lee

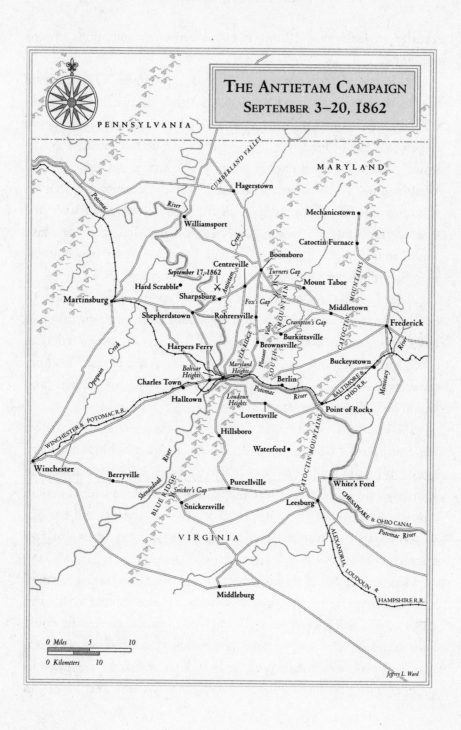

THE ANTIETAM CAMPAIGN
SEPTEMBER 3–20, 1862

PENNSYLVANIA

MARYLAND

Potomac

River

CUMBERLAND VALLEY

Hagerstown

Williamsport

Mechanicstown

Catoctin Furnace

Boonsboro

Centreville

September 17, 1862

Turners Gap

Mount Tabor

Hard Scrabble

Sharpsburg

Antietam

Fox's Gap

Middletown

Martinsburg

Shepherdstown

Rohrersville

Crampton's Gap

Frederick

CATOCTIN MOUNTAINS

River

SOUTH MOUNTAIN

Burkittsville

Harpers Ferry

ELK RIDGE

Pleasant Valley

Brownsville

Buckeystown

Opequon Creek

Bolivar Heights

Maryland Heights

Berlin

Charles Town

Loudoun Heights

Potomac River

Point of Rocks

BALTIMORE & OHIO R.R.

Monocacy

Halltown

Lovettsville

WINCHESTER & POTOMAC R.R.

Hillsboro

Waterford

CATOCTIN MOUNTAINS

Winchester

Berryville

Purcellville

White's Ford

CHESAPEAKE & OHIO CANAL

Shenandoah River

BLUE RIDGE

Snicker's Gap

Leesburg

Potomac River

Snickersville

ALEXANDRIA, LOUDOUN &

VIRGINIA

Middleburg

HAMPSHIRE R.R.

0 Miles   5   10

0 Kilometers   10

Jeffrey L. Ward

revealed to Jackson and Longstreet his aggressive intentions toward the Union army.

Jackson opposed the move westward, and proposed "to concentrate the whole army in a good position, and fight McClellan as he advanced."[10] In other words, Jackson wanted to confront the Federals somewhere east of Frederick. The situation was perfect for such a challenge. Abraham Lincoln was extremely sensitive about the safety of Washington. He had already proved in previous campaigns that he would require the Union army at all times to be located between the Confederate army and Washington. Accordingly, McClellan's first task would be to protect the national capital. But in doing so, he would expose Baltimore and Philadelphia.

Therefore, all the Confederates had to do was to move east of Frederick some miles and stop. There they would be threatening all three cities. If McClellan continued to guard Washington, the Confederates could break the railroad just south of Baltimore, and cut Washington's food supply. McClellan could not allow this to happen, and would be compelled to attack Lee.

The exact preconditions of Second Manassas would be repeated: the South could occupy some defensible elevation, with at least one open flank, and wait until McClellan attacked. Like Pope at Second Manassas, he would lose. Once he had failed, the Confederates could swing around his defeated army and force it into retreat and perhaps surrender. In this way the South could win the war in one or two engagements.

George McClellan was not much of a general, but he saw the peril with absolute clarity. In his official report on the campaign, filed in August 1863, McClellan wrote: "One battle lost and almost all would have been lost. Lee's army might have marched as it pleased on Washington, Baltimore, Philadelphia, or New York. It could have levied its supplies from a fertile and undevastated country, extorted tribute from wealthy and populous cities, and nowhere east of the Alleghenies was there another organized force to avert its march."[11]

Jackson wanted to apply the method he had employed at Second Manassas. But Lee had reverted to his fixation on frontal attacks. The South was caught on the horns of a dilemma of its own making. It was habituated to appointing only members of the aristocracy to high positions. The occupant of the top military position, Lee, did not understand strategy. The Confederate government was incapable of removing Lee and replacing him with Jackson. But if Lee remained, the South was bound to lose.

Lee rejected Jackson's plan to stand east of Frederick. There is no record that he even examined its merits. Dabney only says the plan to move west, "being preferred by the commander in chief, was adopted."[12] Thus for a third time in less than a month Stonewall Jackson offered Lee a way to destroy the Union army, and for a third time Lee refused.

Lee's resolve to move west of South Mountain created a problem: Halleck had insisted on keeping two Union garrisons in the Confederate rear—2,500 men at Martinsburg and 10,000 at Harpers Ferry. Lee wanted to capture them. Longstreet and Jackson objected, because returning to seize them would be a serious diversion of strength. Lee, however, said they might interfere with Confederate supplies coming up through the Shenandoah Valley. But food was much more plentiful in unpillaged Maryland than it was in ravished Virginia. So this was not a valid reason. Lee always looked for immediate, achievable gains, and found it virtually impossible to see longer-term dangers and implications. The immediate gain from capturing the Harpers Ferry and Martinsburg garrisons outweighed in his mind the dangers.

Jackson never commented on Lee's directives in Maryland, but he was surely deeply disappointed that Lee had rejected his proposal to stand east of Frederick. But once a decision was made, Jackson loyally supported his commander, and sought to carry out his wishes. The time would come, he hoped, when he might convince Lee to make a decisive stand. Jackson also may have reasoned that McClellan was so slow that he could capture both Union posts and get back into Maryland before McClellan would even see, much less exploit, the opportunity.

On September 9, Lee summoned Jackson and Longstreet to his tent and announced that he was going to divide the army into four parts. Beginning the next day, September 10, three of these parts, under Jackson, were to descend on Martinsburg and Harpers Ferry. The fourth, under Longstreet, was to move west from Frederick and to halt at Boonsboro, at the western foot of South Mountain. Once the two Union outposts had been seized, the entire army would reunite in Maryland, and Lee would then consider ways to attack McClellan.

The Confederate army was in extremely poor physical shape when it invaded Maryland. Because of the immense shortage of shoes, many men had been marching barefoot through much of the summer campaign. Now many feet could no longer stand the strain of rough roads and long miles. Large numbers of men also had to rely on corn on the cob and unripe apples, and were weakened accordingly.

Among Jackson's troops going through Leesburg, Virginia, on the way to Frederick, Lieutenant Robert Healy, marching with the 55th Virginia, encountered an old lady with upraised hands. With tears in her eyes, she exclaimed, "The Lord bless your dirty ragged souls!" Lieutenant Healy commented: "I don't think we were any dirtier than the rest, but it was our luck to get the blessing."[13]

Mary Bedinger Mitchell, who lived at Shepherdstown, Virginia, on the Potomac, wrote: "I saw the troops march past us every summer for four years. . . . There were always stragglers, of course, but never before or after did I see anything comparable to the demoralized state of the Confederates at this time. Never were want and exhaustion more visibly put before my eyes, and that they could march and fight at all seemed incredible."[14]

Accordingly, the Rebel army was rapidly falling to 45,000 men, half the size of the Union army advancing against it. Nevertheless, the men who stayed with the army were cheerful, enthusiastic, and supremely confident of themselves and of their leaders. A young Maryland boy, Leighton Parks, saw them march by. "They were the dirtiest men I ever saw, a most ragged, lean and hungry set of wolves," he wrote. "Yet there was a dash about them that the Northern men lacked. They rode like circus riders. Many of them were from the far South and spoke a dialect I could scarcely understand. They were profane beyond belief and talked incessantly."[15]

Longstreet, moving to Boonsboro, had 20,000 men, while the three parts of the force under Jackson had 25,000 men. McClellan thus could descend with at least twice the strength on any part of the divided Rebel army. However, McClellan's extreme deliberation and Jackson's extreme speed were known factors. The odds were greatly in favor of Jackson's seizing Martinsburg and the Ferry and getting back into Maryland before McClellan could stir himself to strike any of the exposed Confederate forces.

Instructions (Special Orders no. 191) for the army movement went out to the commanders on September 9. They called on Jackson with three divisions, 12,000 men, to march the next morning on a long arc to Martinsburg and to drive the Federal garrison toward Harpers Ferry. Meanwhile, Lafayette McLaws, with 9,000 men, was to descend on Maryland Heights, the dominating elevation across the Potomac just north of the Ferry, thus keeping the Union garrison from escaping across the river. At the same time, John G. Walker, with his division of 4,000 men, was to cross back into Virginia, march up the south bank of the Potomac, and seize Loudoun Heights, directly east of Harpers

Ferry where the Shenandoah River debouches into the Potomac. With Jackson coming up just behind Bolivar Heights, the high ground southwest of the Ferry, the Union garrison would be wholly surrounded.

While Longstreet's corps marched west to Boonsboro, Jeb Stuart's cavalry remained east of the Catoctin Mountains to observe Federal troop movements.

Jackson moved with his normal speed. Passing through Middletown, a few miles east of South Mountain, two very pretty young women, with ribbons of red, white, and blue in their hair, rushed out of their homes carrying small Union flags. With much laughter they waved the flags defiantly in the face of Jackson as he passed on his horse. Jackson bowed to the girls, raised his hat, and turning with a quiet smile to his staff, said, "We evidently have no friends in this town."[16]

Jackson's troops crossed the Potomac at Williamsport on September 11, spread out to intercept the Union forces at Martinsburg, and forced them to flee straight to Harpers Ferry. Jackson's men occupied Martinsburg on the morning of September 12. The Reverend Mr. Dabney, who was given to effusive and high-flown speech, wrote: "General Jackson was received with an uncontrollable outburst of enthusiasm. The females, especially, to whom his purity and domestic virtues made him as dear as his lofty chivalry, crowded around him with their affectionate greetings, while the foremost besieged him for some little souvenir. Blushing with embarrassment, he said: 'Really, ladies, this is the first time I was ever surrounded by the enemy,' and disengaged himself from them." But he didn't get away until the ladies had cut and carried off nearly all the buttons on his coat.[17] Jackson's force moved on toward the Ferry, arriving in the rear of Bolivar Heights at midday on September 13. Jackson's men had marched sixty miles in three and a half days. Generals McLaws and Walker, who had much less far to march, were still not in position.

General Walker, already on the Potomac, took until September 13 to march fourteen miles to Loudoun Heights, which he found unoccupied. The next morning he got five long-range Parrott rifled guns on the heights, ready to help reduce the town.

McLaws passed over Brownsville Gap in South Mountain, ten miles southwest of Frederick, on September 11, and advanced down the narrow Pleasant Valley between South Mountain and Elk Ridge, whose southern eminence is Maryland Heights. Learning there was a strong force defending the heights, McLaws sent two brigades along the crest of Elk Ridge, scattered a green New York regiment on September 13, and seized the heights. The next morning McLaws's men cut a road through the woods and dragged up four guns.

As the three parts of the Confederate army marched off on September 10 to capture Harpers Ferry, Lee got a message that an enemy force was approaching from Chambersburg, Pennsylvania, to the north. This turned out to be a false report, but Lee sent Longstreet with two divisions to Hagerstown to stand guard. Lee himself went along. This left only D. H. Hill's division at Boonsboro. It had the task of defending Turner's Gap at South Mountain on the Frederick-Boonsboro Turnpike.

On Saturday morning, September 13, most of McClellan's army arrived at Frederick, three days after the Rebels had departed. The 27th Indiana bivouacked in a meadow previously occupied by D. H. Hill's division. Corporal Barton W. Mitchell noticed, among things left behind, a bulky envelope. In it, wrapped around three cigars, was a sheet of paper entitled "Army of Northern Virginia, Special Orders No. 191," addressed to General D. H. Hill, ending "By command of Gen. R.E. Lee" and signed "R.H. Chilton, Assist. Adj.-Gen." Mitchell had discovered a copy of the order describing in detail the scattering of the Rebel army.

Within minutes Corporal Mitchell's discovery had been verified as authentic and it was presented to McClellan as he was receiving a deputation of Frederick citizens. McClellan turned aside, read the message, became elated, and shouted, "Now I know what to do!"[18]

One of the citizens was a Southern sympathizer who saw that McClellan had received important news relating to Confederate movements. He rode west, found Jeb Stuart around South Mountain, and told him the story. Stuart sent word to Lee at Hagerstown and to D. H. Hill at Boonsboro. Thus, on the night of September 13, the Confederates knew that McClellan had accurate information regarding the locations of the Rebel army. As a precaution, Hill sent Alfred H. Colquitt's brigade up to Turner's Gap to stand guard.

Hill got two copies of the orders by mistake, and it is virtually certain that he left one of them on the field at Frederick.[19]

McClellan had been handed a splendid opportunity to destroy the Southern army. He already had 65,000 men at Frederick, and could easily overwhelm the 30,000 men he believed Longstreet had at Boonsboro, just thirteen miles distant. In fact only D. H. Hill was at Boonsboro with 5,000 men. McClellan had 20,000 additional men under General William B. Franklin only twenty miles from Maryland Heights. Franklin could march on the rear of McLaws, break the siege of Harpers Ferry, and force McLaws, isolated on the north side of the Potomac, to surrender his whole force.

Alternatively, McClellan could send a small decoy force to Turner's Gap to hold Longstreet, and move with most of his troops through Crampton's Gap of South Mountain five miles south. In this way, he could rescue the Harpers Ferry garrison and eliminate McLaws's force. Jackson and Walker, on the south side of the Potomac, would have great difficulty in getting back across the river to join Lee. McClellan then could turn on Longstreet and Lee and destroy the whole force.

But McClellan waited an incredible eighteen hours after receiving accurate information as to the positions of the Confederate army before he made the first move. When he did move, he sent Ambrose E. Burnside's 30,000-man right wing up to Turner's Gap to confront Longstreet head-on, and Franklin's 20,000-man left wing to break through Crampton's Gap into Pleasant Valley onto the rear of McLaws.

Because of McClellan's delay, Lee had just enough time to warn McLaws that Federals were marching on his rear, to notify Jackson to conclude the siege of the Ferry, to tell D. H. Hill to defend Turner's Gap, and to instruct Longstreet to march at daybreak on September 14 to the aid of Hill. By the morning of September 14 the Confederates were fully alert to the danger, but by no means in position to stop a determined Federal attack at Turner's Gap. Longstreet could not possibly arrive until midafternoon.

Franklin reached Crampton's Gap at noon on September 14, and encountered the pitifully small Rebel force that McLaws had been able to get up to the gap—400 cavalry and infantry arrayed behind a stone wall at the eastern foot of the pass. Instead of rushing the pass at once and overwhelming the Confederate force, Franklin foolishly deployed an entire division, with his second division pulled up in reserve. It looked for a while that 400 Rebels had stopped the entire left wing of the Union army. But some Federal officers got exasperated with Franklin's timidity, and ordered a charge. The thin Rebel line collapsed at once, and the men fled up the pass. This scared McLaws's 1,600 reserves into flight as well. All the Confederates fell back into Pleasant Valley in confusion, losing several hundred men killed and wounded, as well as 400 prisoners. Franklin could have easily driven the Confederates away, and marched on Maryland Heights. But he thought getting through the pass was enough for one day, and put his whole force into bivouac. His third division joined the other two divisions during the night.

Meanwhile, McLaws moved up what troops he had available, making just 5,000 men all told, to form a fragile defensive line across

Pleasant Valley. When Franklin confronted this line on the morning of September 15, he decided that an attack would be suicidal, and he did nothing. Franklin somehow had estimated that the Confederate force was fully as large as his own.

At Turner's Gap on September 14, D. H. Hill was slow to respond to the danger. He realized that the Federals could reach the gap by three routes—up the main road; by way of Fox's Gap, a mile south, and along the Mount Tabor Church Road, approaching the gap from the northeast through a deep gorge. At the start of the day, he had only Colquitt's brigade to defend the main road. He found, however, that Jacob D. Cox's Union division had advanced up an old road and was already in Fox's Gap. Samuel Garland's 1,000-man North Carolina brigade was just arriving, and Hill sent it to regain the pass. But Union troops above the pass sent plunging fire down on the Rebel brigade, and it collapsed. Garland was killed, and 200 men surrendered. The remainder fled to the west side of the mountain, and was of no use all day.

Cox, however, didn't realize he had actually captured the gap, and withdrew, waiting for the rest of Jesse Reno's corps to come up.

At first Hill had nothing to defend the Mount Tabor Church Road, but Joseph Hooker, assigned to attack along this road, didn't get his forces into position until late in the day. This allowed Hill time to bring Robert E. Rodes's 1,200-man Alabama brigade into place to hold off Hooker.

Since Reno's corps soon came up to threaten Fox's Gap, Hill sent down two more of his brigades and two of Longstreet's brigades that arrived in the afternoon. But Reno's troops threw them all into confusion. Only at the end of the day was John Bell Hood's two-brigade division able to charge through the disordered Rebels and push the Federals back to the edge of the pass as darkness fell. Reno himself was mortally wounded.

The Rebels had doggedly held on to Turner's Gap throughout the day, but as night fell Union troops gained commanding heights north of the pass. From that position, they could shatter Confederate forces the next morning. It was plain, therefore, that the Rebels had to abandon South Mountain during the night. The battle of South Mountain cost the Federals about 2,300 men, mostly killed and wounded. The Confederates lost about 1,000 killed and wounded, but another 1,500 fell into Union hands as prisoners.

McClellan had moved with excessive slowness, but he still was on the verge of interposing the Union army between Longstreet and D. H. Hill at Turner's Gap and McLaws in Pleasant Valley and on Maryland Heights. Lee decided that the danger was too great. He had to retreat to safety beyond the Potomac River. At 8:00 P.M., Lee sent a message to McLaws to abandon his position during the night, and to take his force across the Potomac on some ford, but not the ford at Shepherdstown, just south of Sharpsburg, Maryland, for Lee wanted to use it to get Hill and Longstreet back to Virginia.

Shortly thereafter Jackson sent Lee word from Harpers Ferry that caused Lee to change his orders radically. He made a devastatingly bad decision that had the potential of losing the war for the South in a day.

In the Maryland campaign, Robert E. Lee illustrated supreme examples of a fundamental principle of how war can go awry. The renowned Prussian strategist Carl von Clausewitz had explained the axiom three decades earlier in his classic work, *On War:* "The military machine is basically very simple. But none of its components is of one piece: each part is composed of individuals, every one of whom retains his potential of friction. A battalion is made up of individuals, the least important of whom may chance to delay things or somehow make them go wrong." And an important person can make them go very wrong. Clausewitz wrote that in war this tremendous friction is everywhere in contact with chance. "Action in war," Clausewitz wrote, "is like movement in a resistant element. Just as the simplest and most natural of movements, walking, cannot easily be performed in water, so in war it is difficult for normal efforts to achieve even moderate results."[20]

Lee's troubles started with his mistake of rejecting Jackson's proposal to stand east of Frederick and let McClellan attack. His next mistake was to divide his army into four parts to achieve a secondary, and not vital, goal of capturing the Harpers Ferry garrison. This mistake, combined with the enemy's chance discovery of a discarded order, placed the Rebel army in imminent danger of destruction. Although the cost was high, one of the four army parts was able to extricate itself from peril on South Mountain. But then a message from Jackson caused Lee to cancel out the advantage gained, and to make the even greater mistake of fighting McClellan's army of 85,000 men with only a fraction of his own army, about 35,000 men. He intensified the blunder by selecting a cul-de-sac for a battlefield. He did not reconnoiter this field in advance, and discover that he had no space for maneuver. In this frightful situation the Confederate army had no chance of achieving victory. It literally had to fight for its life. Jackson sent his message to Lee at 8:15 P.M. on September 14 telling of the progress he had made at Harpers Ferry and that he looked "for complete success tomorrow. The advance has been directed to resume at dawn tomorrow."[21]

Jackson had encountered some difficulty in communicating by means of flag signals with McLaws and Walker, but by 3:00 P.M. on September 14, Rebel guns were firing from three directions into the town. The Federal guns, located far lower than the Confederate cannons, were unable to reply. Jackson made no attempt to storm Bolivar Heights, where the Union commander Colonel Dixon Miles had lined up his troops. But Rebel forces gained commanding ground near them, and Dorsey Pender's brigade advanced to a good assault location along the west bank of the Shenandoah River. The Union position was hopeless.

When Lee got Jackson's message, he thought he saw a way to retrieve the campaign. If Jackson took the Ferry, his force might then march to Sharpsburg, and so might McLaws and Walker. The strain on these three commands would be horrendous, but they might join with Longstreet's corps and challenge the Union army. But there was no possibility of getting even half as many Rebel troops to Sharpsburg as McClellan already possessed.[22] There was good defensive ground just east of the town along Antietam Creek. But Lee did not know that the Potomac River turned north just west of Shepherdstown, putting Sharpsburg and Antietam Creek into a very tight corner hemmed in on two sides by the Potomac, with no space for any turning movement around the Union army.[23]

There is a cardinal truth about warfare that cannot be avoided. An army requires a leader who can *see* a way to victory. An army can possess extreme valor, dedication, and energy. But if it is led by a general without vision, it will fail. The Confederate army had one such general who could see, Stonewall Jackson. But it was commanded by a general who could not see, Robert E. Lee.

Napoleon Bonaparte recognized the requirement for vision and intelligent leadership in one of his most famous comments: "In war, men are nothing; it is the man who is everything. The general is the head, the whole of an army. It was not the Roman army that conquered Gaul, but Caesar; it was not the Carthaginian army that made Rome tremble in her gates, but Hannibal; it was not the Macedonian army that reached the Indus, but Alexander."[24] As G. F. R. Henderson wrote in his biography of Stonewall Jackson, "no army has ever achieved great things unless it has been well commanded. If the general be second-rate the army also will be second-rate."[25]

Early on September 15, 1862, McClellan's forces advanced cautiously into Turner's Gap and found that the enemy had slipped away. They set off in pursuit, certain that the Rebels were retreating back across the Potomac. At 12:40 P.M., however, a signal observation post reported that they were forming a line of battle at Sharpsburg just beyond Antietam Creek.

Meanwhile, at Harpers Ferry Confederate guns opened on Federal positions. At 8:00 A.M., Confederate troops were just about to storm the Union works at Bolivar Heights when a horseman appeared waving a white flag. The post was surrendering. It was accomplished quickly, but the Union commander, Colonel Miles, was mortally wounded by one of the last cannon rounds.[26]

Jackson wasted no time. Lee wanted him at Sharpsburg as soon as possible. Jackson gave generous terms. All of the 11,500 Union troops were paroled and allowed to go home until exchanged. The officers could keep their side arms and baggage. Jackson left A. P. Hill with his division to superintend the surrender, sent Lee news of the Ferry's capture, and set his remaining two divisions on the march for Sharpsburg.

McClellan came up on Lee's hastily prepared defenses along Antietam Creek during the afternoon of September 15. Lee had perhaps 16,000 men and could easily have been bowled over by a massive Union assault. But McClellan could not act fast. He decided the next day would be soon enough to deal with the problem.

The next morning, September 16, Jackson's two divisions reached Sharpsburg and dropped down in exhaustion after a hard march of sixteen miles. In the afternoon, Walker's division arrived. McLaws's troops were still south of the river. The situation remained critical. McClellan now had 70,000 men forward, the Confederates well under half this number. But on this day, as well, McClellan refused to act. He only moved his troops into position to launch assaults on the morrow, September 17, 1862.[27]

Lee posted Longstreet's corps along Antietam Creek on both sides of the Boonsboro Pike. He had no troops to guard the lower reaches of the stream, and placed only cavalry along this stretch. A short distance north of the pike the Antietam turns sharply northeastward. Thus, when Jackson's two divisions arrived, Lee lined them up a mile west of the stream and along the Hagerstown Pike running on a low ridgeline northward from Sharpsburg. Jackson's troops were on both sides of the Dunker Church, a white-painted brick structure next to a large grove of hardwood trees, known as the West Wood. To the northeast was a huge cornfield filled with ripened corn still on the stalks. Three-quarters of a mile away on the far edge of the cornfield was another block of trees, called the East Wood.

McClellan, approaching from the east, could have executed a classic maneuver to destroy the Confederate army within hours. The maneuver's origins go back to ancient Greece when the Theban commander Epaminondas used it to defeat the Spartans at Leuctra in 371 B.C. It was Napoleon's characteristic mode of winning battles. McClellan could have hidden a large force east of Snavely's Ford on the lower reaches of Antietam Creek. Meanwhile, he could have launched simultaneous attacks all along the Confederate line north of this ford. This would have held all the Confederates in a battle embrace, permitting the hidden force to cross the ford, swing onto the rear of the Rebel army, and block Lee's only retreat route, the road to Shepherdstown and the Potomac. Assailed front and rear, the Confederate army would have been forced to surrender.

Snavely's Ford was guarded only by John G. Walker's small division. By not assaulting the ford at once, McClellan could hope that Lee would move Walker's force to aid the beleaguered Rebels to the north. This is exactly what Lee did during the battle. But even if Lee had left Walker in place, a strong Union assault by two divisions could have overwhelmed him, and allowed the flanking attack to succeed.

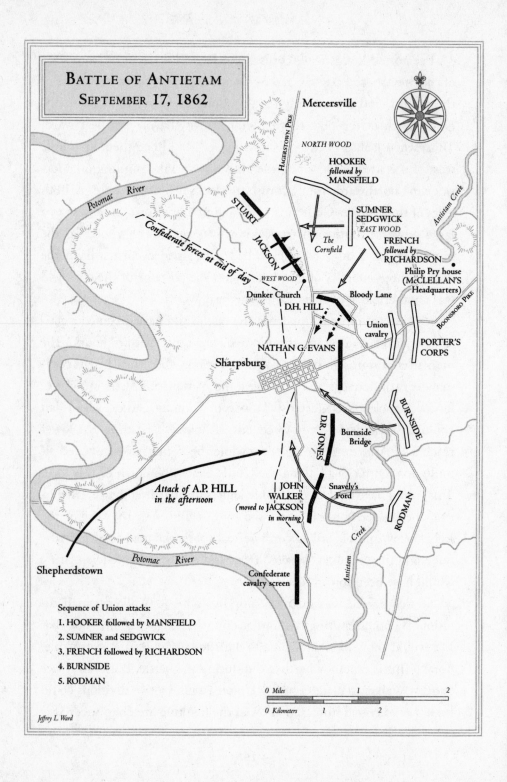

BATTLE OF ANTIETAM
SEPTEMBER 17, 1862

Mercersville

NORTH WOOD

HAGERSTOWN PIKE

HOOKER
followed by
MANSFIELD

SUMNER
SEDGWICK
EAST WOOD

FRENCH
followed by
RICHARDSON

Potomac River

STUART

JACKSON

Confederate forces at end of day

The Cornfield

WEST WOOD

Dunker Church

D.H. HILL

Bloody Lane

Philip Pry house
(McCLELLAN'S
Headquarters)

Antietam Creek

BOONSBORO PIKE

Union
cavalry

NATHAN G. EVANS

PORTER'S
CORPS

Sharpsburg

BURNSIDE

DR. JONES

Burnside
Bridge

*Attack of A.P. HILL
in the afternoon*

JOHN
WALKER
*(moved to JACKSON
in morning)*

Snavely's
Ford

RODMAN

Shepherdstown

Potomac River

Antietam Creek

Confederate
cavalry screen

Sequence of Union attacks:

1. HOOKER followed by MANSFIELD

2. SUMNER and SEDGWICK

3. FRENCH followed by RICHARDSON

4. BURNSIDE

5. RODMAN

0 Miles   1   2

0 Kilometers   1   2

Jeffrey L. Ward

But McClellan did none of this. Classic methods of winning battles meant nothing to him. He kept in reserve along Boonsboro Pike Fitz John Porter's entire corps along with all of his cavalry (4,200 troopers), and did not use them the entire day. He scarcely used William B. Franklin's corps, which came up behind Porter. He launched separate attacks on three separate parts of the line, none at the same time. This allowed Lee to concentrate on each danger as it occurred, and to assemble enough troops to fend it off.

McClellan first launched attacks on the north along the Hagerstown Pike. Here he made five separate assaults. The battle centered on the cornfield. Union forces of Joe Hooker's corps advanced through the cornfield directly on Jackson's forces and D. H. Hill's division lined up along the southern edge of the cornfield to the East Wood. Federal forces knocked D. H. Hill out of the East Wood and forced him to retreat to a sunken road just to the south of the cornfield. Jackson stopped all of the assaults along and near the pike, although the slaughter on both sides was horrible.

Alexander R. Lawton, commanding one of Jackson's two divisions, sent an urgent plea for help to John Bell Hood, whose small division of 2,000 men was in reserve around the Dunker Church. Ignoring the heavy cannon fire, Hood's soldiers pushed into the cornfield, and in a fierce charge drove Union troops all the way back to a rail fence at the northern edge of the field. This attack forced Joe Hooker to commit his last troops, two Pennsylvania brigades of George G. Meade's division. Meade's troops stopped parts of Hood's division in the East Wood. Meanwhile, on the western edge of the cornfield, cannons of Abner Doubleday's Union division destroyed rows of Hood's men with double-shotted canister. Hood pulled his shattered division back to the Dunker Church.

It was now 7:30 A.M. Jackson had stopped all the Federal assaults. In Jackson's two divisions, a third lay dead or wounded, while Hood's division had suffered 60 percent casualties. Hooker had lost about 2,600 men, and most of the survivors had rushed from the field. Afterward, soldiers on both sides remembered this morning as the worst they had ever experienced. Dead and wounded littered the corn-field, the East Wood, and the ground around Hagerstown Pike. Battle lines sometimes had faced each other at fifty or even thirty yards.

Now McClellan launched two more unconnected attacks on the north. The first was Joseph K. F. Mansfield's corps, which advanced from the former position of Hooker. Jackson's troops stopped this assault, but Federal troops reached almost to the Dunker Church. Jackson was frantically trying to re-form his troops in the West Wood when Lee informed him that he was sending John Walker's division from the right flank to support him, and promised to send up Lafa-yette McLaws's force, which had just arrived on the field.

At this time, Edwin V. Sumner launched the third uncoordinated assault on the north, using John Sedgwick's 5,500-man division. But Sumner did not support Mansfield's previous advance, and struck di-rectly *west* from the East Wood. Sedgwick's men crossed the cornfield and collided with a small Rebel force under Jubal Early west of the Hagerstown Pike. But Sedgwick's left flank was unprotected, and Jack-son launched a counterattack directly on it from around the Dunker Church. The assault caused Sedgwick's division to collapse. The survi-vors rushed back to the East Wood.

Soon afterward, Jackson's medical officer, Hunter McGuire, found Jackson in the yard of the Dunker Church. McGuire gave him some peaches, his first food of the day, and reported the staggering prelim-inary casualty figures. McGuire wondered aloud whether the survi-vors could withstand another assault. But Jackson shook his head, and pointed to the Federals huddled behind their guns a mile to the north, and said, "Dr. McGuire, they have done their worst."[28]

The fighting now shifted to the sunken road. This zigzagging track came to be known as the Bloody Lane. After the attacks across the cornfield had collapsed, William French decided to launch his 5,700-man division from the East Wood directly against the sunken road. French sent his brigades one at a time in headlong charges against the 2,500 Rebels in the lane.

As French's first brigade, under Max Weber, reached just under a low ridge in front of the sunken lane, Weber ordered his men to fix bayonets and charge. Colonel F. M. Parker of the waiting 30th North Carolina told his men that he would give the order to fire only when the enemy crossed the ridge, and the men could see the Federals' belts. Aim at these, he told them. The Tar Heels obeyed precisely. The effect was appalling. Nearly the entire first line of Weber's brigade was cut down as if by a scythe, 150 men of the 4th New York falling at virtually the same moment. In a couple minutes the brigade suffered more than 450 killed and wounded. The survivors fell behind the crest and lay down.

French's second brigade, under Dwight Morris, advanced through the shambles. The men had been in service scarcely a month. Some fired into the backs of Weber's men on the ground. Others broke and ran, while still others joined Weber's men lying under the brow of the ridge.

French now sent in his last brigade, under Nathan Kimball. It advanced in double-quick time, bayonets fixed, and met a hail of fire that virtually disintegrated it. Rebels in the rear passed up loaded rifles to men in the front to speed the firing. Federal dead and wounded covered the crest. Although some of French's men remained, the division had been shattered—1,750 men killed or wounded, with most of the survivors streaming in panic for the rear.

Now Israel Richardson's 4,000-man division arrived in the East Wood. He launched it toward the sunken lane as well. D. H. Hill's men were exhilarated by their success, but they were exhausted, and they had suffered many losses, especially among the officers. Command was falling into disarray.

Richardson advanced a bit to the east of where French's men had struck, led by the Irish brigade under Thomas F. Meagher. This brigade had three New York Irish regiments but also the 29th Massachusetts. Waiting was a brigade of North Carolinians under Colonel R. T. Bennett. As the Irish brigade reached the ridge, it, too, met a lightning blast of rifle fire. The assault instantly collapsed. The 63rd and 69th New York lost nearly two-thirds of their men in a minute or two. The survivors could do no more than fall to the ground and return fire.

Throughout the battle, Longstreet had been frantically trying to get reinforcements to help the hard-pressed soldiers in the sunken lane. Just as the Irish brigade's attack disintegrated, soldiers of Roger A. Pryor's and Carnot Posey's brigades reached the lane and squeezed in among the Tar Heels there.

It was now approaching noon, and Richardson's second brigade, under John C. Caldwell, swung to the east of the Irish brigade. Richardson ordered it to outflank the sunken road entirely. But the advance was cautious and slow. Richardson, irritated, searched out Caldwell and found him hiding behind a haystack. Richardson angrily sent the brigade in at double-quick time to relieve Meagher. At this moment, Lieutenant Colonel Joseph H. Barnes of the 29th Massachusetts ordered a surprise attack from Meagher's position. Though the Rebels stopped it quickly, they were unnerved by its suddenness. Meanwhile, Colonel Posey tried to pull out some of his brigade to relieve crowding in the sunken lane. This flurry frightened the stressed-out soldiers nearby and a large group of Rebels fled from the right side of the lane.

Almost at the same moment on the left side of the lane, Lieutenant Colonel J. N. Lightfoot, commanding the 6th Alabama, asked his brigade commander Robert E. Rodes whether he could withdraw from a bend in the road that allowed the enemy to direct enfilade fire on his men. Rodes agreed, but Lightfoot misunderstood the order and told the chief of his adjacent regiment that the withdrawal order applied to the whole brigade. This set off the disintegration of the entire sunken road line, and the flight of the men to the rear.

Richardson's division, with some of French's survivors, rushed gleefully into this void. They directed devastating enfilade fire against the few North Carolinians still grimly holding on to their positions, killing many and forcing the rest to flee.

Richardson's breakthrough was clearly visible from McClellan's headquarters, and officers there agreed that the time had come to launch Fitz John Porter's corps into the center of the Confederate line along the Boonsboro Pike. But McClellan was not capable of seizing the opportunity. He held Porter in place and sent Richardson no reinforcements. Massed Confederate artillery on the hill to the south stopped Richardson's advance. At 1:00 P.M., Richardson, getting no help, ordered his men to safety behind the ridge just north of the sunken road. Richardson was wounded when a Confederate shell exploded nearby. He died six weeks later.

Only after Richardson called off his advance did Ambrose E. Burnside launch his corps across a stone bridge southeast of Sharpsburg. Although this attack failed badly at first, it at last broke over the bridge, and the Federals advanced on the town of Sharpsburg. Later, Isaac P. Rodman's division also crossed now-undefended Snavely's Ford, and joined Burnside's men in driving the Confederates back into the eastern part of the town. But at this moment, A. P. Hill's division, marching hard from Harpers Ferry, swung onto the left flank of Rodman, and drove him and Burnside back to the east edge of Sharpsburg. With that, the battle ended.[29]

Lee had stopped McClellan, but at a frightful price. Antietam was the bloodiest day in American history. The Army of the Potomac suffered 2,108 dead, 9,450 wounded, and 753 missing, most of them dead, a total of 12,401, one-quarter of the men who had gone into action. The Army of Northern Virginia lost about 1,500 dead, 7,800 wounded, and 1,000 missing, most dead, a total of 10,300, or 31 percent of those on the firing lines. The combined American total was 22,700.

McClellan committed only 50,000 men. Well over a third of his army did not fire a shot. Nevertheless, his brave and dedicated soldiers came close to breaking the Confederate line, despite the atrocious manner in which McClellan committed them.

For the Confederacy, Antietam was a catastrophe. Lincoln had been waiting for a victory to issue the Emancipation Proclamation, which transformed the Civil War into a moral crusade. This proclamation guaranteed the persistence of the Northern people in the war, and ended any hope that Britain and France might intervene on the South's side. All the blunders had been made by Robert E. Lee.

CHAPTER 9

---·—

Hollow Victory

On the morning of September 18, 1862, Lee and Jackson reluctantly concluded that the Potomac River was too close to the Union northern or right flank to allow an attack around it. The only course left was to retreat back to Virginia, which the army did over Boteler's Ford, just east of Shephardstown, on the morning of September 19. The Union forces made a modest attempt to inhibit this movement, but were thrown back quickly.

The Army of Northern Virginia withdrew to the vicinity of Winchester and bivouacked for a long-needed rest and refitting. On September 22, 1862, Abraham Lincoln issued the Emancipation Proclamation, effective January 1, 1863. It was a revolutionary presidential edict that struck down constitutional protections for slavery and changed the war into a crusade to free the slaves. The edict did *not* end slavery in the Northern border states that had not seceded, only in the eleven Confederate states that had withdrawn.

Two days later, Lincoln also suspended the writ of habeas corpus, a guarantee in the Constitution (Article I, Section 9) designed to prevent government authorities from illegally detaining people. Lincoln denied habeas corpus to those persons accused of "discouraging volunteer enlistments, resisting militia drafts or guilty of any disloyal practice, affording aid and comfort to Rebels." The Constitution permits suspension of habeas corpus only "in cases of rebellion or invasion" when "the public safety may require it."[1] The suspension led to widespread arrests and imprisonment for many people in the North. Conversely, citizens' rights continued to be respected in the South.

Lincoln wanted McClellan to pursue the Confederates into Virginia at once. But McClellan, reverting to his "slows," demanded that his army be overhauled before he could move. Lincoln was already highly suspicious that McClellan entertained ideas of running for president in 1864 on a ticket of compromise peace with the South, and on October 2 gave him a peremptory order to "cross the Potomac and give battle to the enemy." But McClellan did not move.[2]

McClellan's defiance brought forth an irritated October 13, 1862, letter from Lincoln: "You remember my speaking to you of what I called your over-cautiousness. Are you not over-cautious when you assume that you cannot do what the enemy is constantly doing? . . . You are now nearer to Richmond than the enemy is, by the route that you *can* and *must* take. . . . It is all easy if our troops march as well as the enemy, and it is unmanly to say they cannot do it."[3]

Meanwhile, the Army of Northern Virginia underwent a remarkable transformation. Resting under ideal weather conditions, the Rebels received ample food and got much-needed clothing, shoes, and blankets. The few soldiers still armed with old smoothbore muskets exchanged them for rifles surrendered by the Federals at Harpers Ferry. The army more than doubled in size as stragglers rejoined their units and a small stream of conscripts arrived. On October 10, the army numbered 64,273; by November 20, it reached 76,472. Lee also

reorganized the army formally into two corps, commanded by Longstreet and Jackson, who both were promoted to lieutenant general.[4]

We have a unique, revealing portrait of the Confederate army at
this time. It was written by the English Colonel Garnet Wolseley, later
to become commander of the British army. He had crossed secretly
into Virginia and got a pass to visit the army, along with Francis C.
Lawley, a well-known correspondent for *The Times* of London.

Wolseley was struck by the absence of pomp and circumstance at
Lee's headquarters. It consisted, he said, "of seven or eight pole tents,
pitched with their backs to a stake fence." In front of the tents were
three or four wagons, drawn up without any regularity, while a number
of horses roamed loose about the field.

"Wagons, tents, and some of the horses were marked U.S., showing
that part of that huge debt of the North has gone to furnishing even
the Confederate generals with camp equipment," Wolseley wrote. "No
guard or sentries were to be seen in the vicinity; no crowd of
aides-de-camp loitering about making themselves agreeable to visitors,
and endeavoring to save their generals from receiving those who have
no particular business." A large farmhouse stood nearby, but Confederate rules were firm: private property was to be respected. Lee and the
other generals resided in tents. Only when specifically invited by the
owners did Confederate generals sometimes occupy private homes.
This was opposite the practice of Federal commanders, who routinely
evicted owners from their properties and set up headquarters there.

In talking with Wolseley, Lee "spoke as a man proud of the victories won by his country, and confident of ultimate success under the
blessing of the Almighty, whom he glorified for past successes, and
whose aid he invoked for all future operations." Lee regretted he could
not provide tents for Wolseley and his small party, but provided a two-
horse wagon to drive them six miles north to Bunker Hill and Stonewall Jackson's headquarters.

"With him," Wolseley wrote, "we spent a most pleasant hour, and were agreeably surprised to find him very affable, having been led to expect that he was silent and almost morose. Dressed in his grey uniform, he looks the hero that he is; and his thin compressed lips and calm glance, which meets yours unflinchingly, give evidence of that firmness and decision of character for which he is so famous. He has a broad open forehead, from which the hair is well brushed back; a shapely nose, straight, and rather long; thin colorless cheeks, with only a very small allowance of whisker; a cleanly shaven upper lip and chin; and a pair of fine greyish-blue eyes, rather sunken, with overhanging brows, which intensify the keenness of his gaze, but without imparting any fierceness to it. Such are the general characteristics of his face; and I have only to add, that a smile seems always lurking about his mouth when he speaks; and that though his voice partakes slightly of that harshness which Europeans unjustly attribute to *all* Americans, there is much unmistakable cordiality in his manner; and to us he talked most affectionately of England, and his brief but enjoyable sojourn there. The religious element seems strongly developed in him; and though his conversation is perfectly free from all puritanical cant, it is evident that he is a person who never loses sight of the fact that there is an omnipresent Deity ever presiding over the minutest occurrences of life, as well as over the most important."

The Times correspondent Lawley wrote that Jackson's "chief delight was in the cathedrals of England, notably the York Minster and Westminster Abbey. He was never tired of talking about them, or listening to details about the chapels and cloisters of Oxford."[5]

Wolseley wrote that Jackson's "manner, which was modesty itself, was most attractive. He put you at your ease at once, listening with marked courtesy and attention to whatever you might say. I quite endorse the statement as to his love for beautiful things. He told me that in all his travels he had seen nothing so beautiful as the lancet windows in York Minster."[6]

Wolseley added: "With such a leader men would go anywhere, and face any amount of difficulties; and for myself, I believe that, inspired by the presence of such a man, I should be perfectly insensible to fatigue, and reckon upon success as a moral certainty. Whilst General Lee is regarded in the light of infallible Jove, a man to be reverenced, Jackson is loved and adored with all that childlike and trustful affection which the ancients are said to have lavished upon the particular deity presiding over their affairs."[7]

Wolseley also observed General Longstreet inspecting one of his divisions. "Several regiments were to a man clothed in the national uniform of grey cloth, whilst others presented a harlequin appearance, being dressed in every conceivable variety of coat, both as regards color and cut. Grey wideawake hats, looped up at one side, and having a small black feather, are the most general headdress; but many wear the Yankee black hat or casquette [visored cap] of cloth. . . . Their rifles were invariably in good serviceable order. They marched, too, with an elastic tread, the pace being somewhat slower than that of our troops, and not only seemed vigorous and healthy, but each man had that unmistakable look of conscious strength and manly self-reliance, which those who are accustomed to review troops like to see.

"I have seen many armies file past in all the pomp of bright clothing and well-polished accoutrements, but I never saw one composed of finer men, or that looked more like *work*, than that portion of General Lee's army which I was fortunate enough to see inspected. If I had at any time entertained misgivings as to the ability of Southerners to defend their country and liberties against Northern invasion, they were at once and for ever dispelled when I examined for myself the material of which the Confederate armies are composed. . . . Every man in that service, whether noncommissioned officer or private, will declare to you that it is his fixed determination to fight for his freedom and resist Yankee oppression as long as he has strength to march. A gulf deep and impassable now divides the Southerners from the old Union; and such is the hatred and loathing entertained by them for those who, forgetting the ties of brotherhood which once bound all the states together, have not hesitated to carry fire and sword into the land of their common forefathers."[8]

McClellan didn't move until October 26, when he began a leisurely crossing of the Potomac at Harpers Ferry and at Berlin (present-day Brunswick), five miles east. The movement took eight days. The leading elements advanced forty miles into Virginia east of the Blue Ridge to Warrenton. This allowed McClellan to exchange his difficult supply line through Harpers Ferry for the easier Orange & Alexandria and Manassas Gap railroads.

Lee—not knowing which direction the Union army might move—shifted Longstreet's corps to Culpeper, but left Stonewall Jackson's corps in the Shenandoah Valley. Jackson's corps moved constantly between Winchester and Manassas Gap and Front Royal to keep the Federals off balance and unsure of his intentions.

One day Jackson and his staff were riding at the head of a column near Front Royal when a country woman with a child in each hand stopped them. She inquired anxiously about her son, Johnnie, who was serving, she said, "in Captain Jackson's company." Jackson politely introduced himself as her son's commanding officer, but begged for further information as to his regiment. The woman's interest in the war was limited to her son, however, and she appeared astonished that "Captain Jackson" did not know him. She repeated her inquiries with tears in her eyes. This caused some of Jackson's young staff officers to snicker. Jackson turned fiercely on the officers, silenced their mirth with scorn, and sent them galloping in every direction to find the man in question. Mother and son were soon united for a brief visit.[9]

On November 4, 1862, congressional elections were held in the North. Seven states that had voted Republican in 1860 went Democratic, though the Republicans retained control of both houses of Congress. If a Confederate army had been ranging over the North on Election Day, results would have been much worse for the Republicans.

The modest Republican success gave Lincoln the leverage he needed to oust McClellan. Two days after the election, he replaced him with Ambrose E. Burnside, an officer with little energy, less imagination, and a reputation for ineptitude. Indeed, Burnside himself protested that he was unqualified for high command. But Lincoln said otherwise he'd appoint Joe Hooker. Burnside took the job because he considered Hooker to be a devious conniver who had conspired to get an independent command at Antietam. Lincoln was looking for a general who had no political ambitions, and who could not challenge him in the 1864 presidential election. Military capability was far less important than political irrelevance.

However, Burnside knew that Lincoln required quick action. A directive from Lincoln accompanying his appointment ordered him to report to Lincoln what he expected to accomplish. Two days later, Burnside recommended that the Army of the Potomac move to Fredericksburg, where it could get its supplies by ship through Aquia Creek, twelve miles northeast on the Potomac River. After seizing Fredericksburg, Burnside said, the army would push straight south to Richmond, fifty-five miles away.

In making this recommendation, Burnside ignored Lee's army, which was split in half, with the Blue Ridge intervening. His own army of 119,000 men and 374 guns, on the other hand, was concentrated around Warrenton, and could have fallen on Longstreet's isolated corps at Culpeper before Jackson, two days' march away, could possibly have come to his rescue. But it never occurred to Burnside or to any of the other Federal generals that this opportunity existed.

General Halleck preferred a repetition of John Pope's advance through central Virginia on Gordonsville. But Lincoln agreed to Burnside's decision to transfer to Fredericksburg provided that he moved fast, crossed the Rappahannock River well upstream, and approached the town on the right bank of the river so as to prevent any Confederate occupation of the formidable heights just west of the river at Fredericksburg.[10]

Burnside agreed to these conditions, but he revealed his incompetence at once. Instead of crossing the Rappahannock upstream from Fredericksburg, where the river was narrow and fords numerous, he sent his advance force under General Edwin V. Sumner down the left or upper bank of the river.[11] Sumner arrived at Falmouth just opposite Fredericksburg on November 17. Only a tiny Confederate observation force was on guard and Sumner asked Burnside's authority to cross the river at once and seize the town. But Burnside rejected the idea, telling Sumner to await the arrival of pontoon bridges. They took until November 26 to appear. By that time, Longstreet was occupying the heights in force.

George Washington spent his boyhood near Fredericksburg, and James Monroe practiced law there. The town was a thriving industrial center and port, and in 1862 had about 5,000 people. It was quickly apparent that the town was likely to be the scene of heavy fighting, and Longstreet advised the population to evacuate. Longstreet wrote that the evacuation "was a painful sight. Many were almost destitute and had nowhere to go, but, yielding to the cruel necessities of war, they collected their portable effects and turned their backs on the town. Many were forced to seek shelter in the woods and brave the icy nights to escape the approaching assault from the Federal army."[12]

At last awakening to the difficulties he faced, Burnside reconnoitered crossing sites of the Rappahannock, but he ignored the easy fords upriver, and bizarrely looked only downriver, where the Rappahannock is tidal, broad, and deep. He began preparations for crossing at Skinker's Neck, twelve miles below the town, and also investigated Port Royal, eighteen miles downstream, where the river is a thousand feet wide.

Lee immediately undertook to defend the line of heights west of Fredericksburg. These heights were not continuous, but consisted of several discrete hills, notably Marye's Heights, 130 feet high, directly west of the town, and Prospect Hill, about four miles southwest. There was open ground 1,000 to 1,800 yards deep between the heights and the river. The likelihood of a Federal assault succeeding over such an expanse was practically nil. Burnside, slowly realizing the problem, intensified his efforts to make a flanking movement downriver.

By this time, Jackson's corps was already on the march to the Rappahannock, leaving Winchester on November 22, marching up the Valley Pike to New Market, turning on the road over Massanutten Mountain to Luray, and crossing over the Blue Ridge into the Piedmont at Thornton Gap on November 24.

Early on the march, Jackson wrote his wife, Anna, in North Carolina awaiting the imminent birth of their child. "My heart is with his little darling," he wrote. "Write to me at Gordonsville." He told Anna not to telegraph the news of any birth. Childbirth was a personal gift of God, to be announced in a private letter. Sometime around November 28, a quick note came from Harriet Irwin, Anna's sister. Anna had given birth to a daughter at the Irwin home in Charlotte. Mother and child were both fine. Jackson fell to his knees in thanksgiving.[13] Jackson, in keeping with his very private nature, shared the news of the birth with no one. Some members of his staff didn't know of the birth for a month.

The next day Jackson, with several members of his staff, rode forty miles to Salem Church, Lee's headquarters on the Orange Plank Road (present-day Virginia Route 3), four miles west of Fredericksburg. Refugees from Fredericksburg clogged the road. In his conference with Lee, the commander directed Jackson to protect Skinker's Neck and Port Royal.

Jubal Early moved his division to Skinker's Neck and D. H. Hill took his division to Port Royal. There his gunners emplaced a battery of Parrott rifled cannons on a commanding hill upstream, and an English Whitworth rifle of great power and range three miles below the village. On December 5, 1862, the guns opened on the numerous Federal gunboats in the river. The gunboats couldn't locate the Rebel guns to fire back, and vented their anger by appearing without warning before Port Royal, still occupied by the civilian population, and launching a severe bombardment that destroyed half the houses in the village. By happenstance, no lives were lost, but the wanton destruction deeply angered the Southern people.[14]

On December 4, Jackson wrote Anna: "Oh, how thankful I am to our kind Heavenly Father for having spared my precious wife and given us a little daughter! I cannot tell you how gratified I am, nor how much I wish I could be with you and see my two little darlings. . . . How I would love to see the darling little thing! Give her many kisses for her father." He said their new daughter should be named Julia, after his mother. "My mother was mindful of me when I was a helpless, fatherless child, and I wish to commemorate her now."[15]

Jackson was intensely opposed to the Confederates standing at Fredericksburg, irrespective of the splendid defensive position it presented. There were three overwhelming reasons why the town was a terrible battle site for the Confederates. The first, and most damning, fact was that the Union supply base at Aquia Creek was only twelve miles northeast of Fredericksburg. No matter how successful the Rebels might be, there was no possible way they could prevent the Union army from retreating to Aquia Creek and setting up an unassailable defensive position, its supplies guaranteed, and protected by gunboats in the Potomac River. This is precisely what shielded McClellan at Harrison's Landing on the James River after the Seven Days.

The second deadly disadvantage was that, even if the Confederates stopped Union assaults, they could not swing around the Federal army quickly because this would require Rebels crossing the Rappahannock, a virtually impossible task since the Confederates possessed no pontoon bridge train, and any river assault would be subject to the third disadvantage of the Fredericksburg site—the presence of 180 heavy cannons on Stafford Heights just across the river from the town. These cannons dominated the entire battlefield, and could halt any close move around the Union army. The Rebels would have to march upstream well out of the range of the cannons to make a river crossing. This would take so much time that the Union army could set up an impregnable position at Aquia Creek.

In other words, as Jackson told Lee, "we will whip the enemy, but gain no fruits of victory."[16] No matter how many casualties the South might inflict on the Union army, the North could replace them readily.

Jackson proposed instead that the Confederate army withdraw to the North Anna River, about twenty-five miles south, and there offer battle. The North Anna site presented tremendous strategic advantages that Fredericksburg lacked. It was thirty-seven miles south of Aquia Creek. The North Anna possessed no elevation like Stafford Heights where the superior Union artillery could concentrate and dominate the battlefield. The river itself was easy to ford in a number of places. If Burnside attacked at the North Anna, he would be as certain to lose as at Fredericksburg, but the Rebels could readily swing around the defeated Union flank and force the army into precipitate retreat. There would be no sanctuary short of Aquia Creek. At numerous locations along the way, Jeb Stuart's cavalry could swing around the retreating Union army and force it to stand. Deprived of fresh ammunition and food supplies, the Federals would be compelled to attack. Once more they would be defeated. If the Union army still tried to retreat, Stuart's cavalry once more could swing on its rear and force it to stand. In this fashion, Burnside's entire army could be obliged to surrender. It could spell triumph for the South.[17]

English Colonel G. F. R. Henderson, who wrote the brilliant 1898 biography of Jackson, understood distinctly the advantage Jackson saw on the North Anna. A battle there, he wrote, would have resulted in a great Confederate victory. "A pursuit directed against the flanks, striking the line of retreat, cutting off the supply and ammunition trains, and blocking the roads, a pursuit such as Jackson had organized when he drove Banks from the [Shenandoah] Valley, if conducted with vigor, seldom fails in its effect. And who would have conducted such an operation with greater skill than Stuart, at the head of 9,000 horsemen? Who would have supported Stuart more expeditiously than the 'foot-cavalry' of the Second Army Corps?"[18]

But Lee had already demonstrated that he did not understand strategic advantages, no matter how clearly Jackson pointed them out to him. He had failed to see that a swing around John Pope's unguarded eastern flank on the Rapidan could drive his army against the river or the mountains to the west and force his surrender. He had failed to take advantage of his position on Pope's flank at Second Manassas until the very end of the second day of the battle. He had refused to stand east of Frederick, Maryland, and threaten Washington, Baltimore, and Philadelphia, all at the same time. Lee could think only of short-term gains, like the capture of Harpers Ferry. He could see a short-term gain of a victory at Fredericksburg. He could not see the war-winning potential of pulling back to the North Anna River.

So for the fourth time, Lee rejected Jackson's proposals to gain military victory for the South. The Confederacy was crippled by a fatally flawed leadership.

When Burnside realized that Jackson was barring his passage at Skinker's Neck and Port Royal, he conceived a new plan to strike quickly *between* Longstreet's corps at Fredericksburg and Jackson's corps downriver. He believed he could destroy Longstreet's force before Jackson could reinforce him. Then he could turn with his whole army on Jackson. The idea was to cross the Rappahannock on pontoon bridges at and below Fredericksburg, and then drive around Longstreet's right or south at Hamilton's Crossing. Here both the railroad and the Richmond Stage Road turned around the edge of Prospect Hill.

The plan actually was imaginative, and, if carried out before Jackson could arrive, offered possibilities for victory. It would require the utmost speed and resolve on the part of Burnside as commander and the Army of the Potomac as executioner. But there were several places where Clausewitz's friction could slow the operation and affect the outcome. Most especially, the Union army had to cross the river very quickly. It then had to march down the narrow plain between the river and the heights, directly under Longstreet's guns. At Hamilton's Crossing it had to swing swiftly around Longstreet's flank and onto his rear. It was a dazzling concept and excited Burnside tremendously. In late November he pointed out Prospect Hill and the gap around it to William Farrar Smith, commander of the 6th Corps. "I expect to cross and occupy the hills before Lee can bring anything serious to meet me," he told Smith.[19]

But Burnside was an incompetent general, and he committed one error after another to prevent his grand scheme from being accomplished. His first mistake was to take so long in getting his army over the river that Lee had enough time to move Jackson's corps firmly into position on Prospect Hill.

The original plan was to throw pontoon bridges across the river at

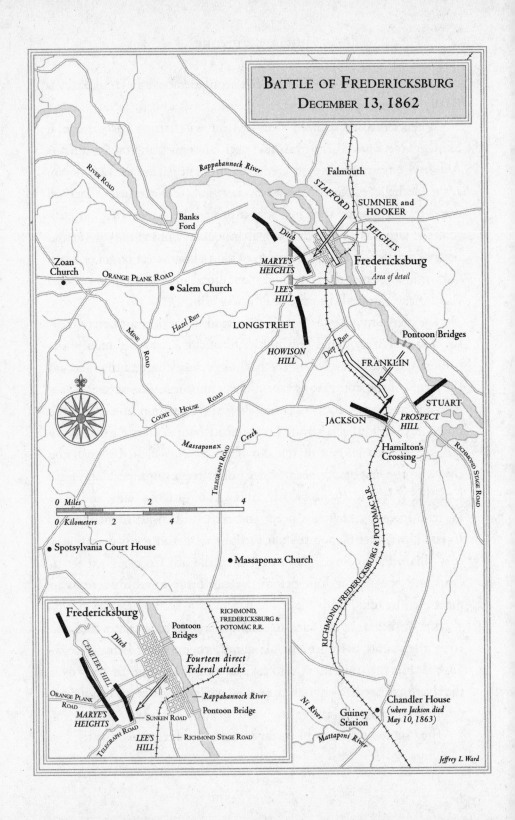

BATTLE OF FREDERICKSBURG
DECEMBER 13, 1862

River Road

Rappahannock River

Falmouth

STAFFORD

Banks Ford

HEIGHTS

SUMNER and HOOKER

Ditch

Zoan Church

ORANGE PLANK ROAD

MARYE'S HEIGHTS

Fredericksburg

Area of detail

• Salem Church

LEE'S HILL

Hazel Run

LONGSTREET

Pontoon Bridges

MINE ROAD

Deep Run

HOWISON HILL

FRANKLIN

COURT HOUSE ROAD

STUART

Massaponax Creek

JACKSON

PROSPECT HILL

TELEGRAPH ROAD

Hamilton's Crossing

RICHMOND STAGE ROAD

0 Miles 2 4

0 Kilometers 2 4

RICHMOND, FREDERICKSBURG & POTOMAC R.R.

• Spotsylvania Court House

• Massaponax Church

Fredericksburg

RICHMOND, FREDERICKSBURG & POTOMAC R.R.

Pontoon Bridges

Ditch

Fourteen direct Federal attacks

CEMETERY HILL

ORANGE PLANK ROAD

Rappahannock River

MARYE'S HEIGHTS

Pontoon Bridge

SUNKEN ROAD

RICHMOND STAGE ROAD

TELEGRAPH ROAD

LEE'S HILL

Ni River

Guiney Station

Chandler House *(where Jackson died May 10, 1863)*

Mattaponi River

Jeffrey L. Ward

the town and a couple miles downstream by daybreak on December 11, 1862. Union troops were immediately to cross and form up to carry out Burnside's plan. But Lafayette McLaws's division had arrived at Fredericksburg on November 25, and he sent William Barksdale's Mississippi brigade to dig rifle pits close to the edge of the river. Union commanders were completely unaware of these rifle pits, and Rebel snipers stopped all attempts to throw bridges across the river. Finally, at 10:00 A.M., Burnside called off the effort and ordered a massive bombardment of the town by the heavy Union cannon massed on Stafford Heights. The barrages shattered many buildings, and forced Barksdale's brigade to withdraw. At 4:30 P.M., Union infantry crossed the river in boats, secured the town, and allowed the engineers to finish building the bridges.

Meanwhile, at the bridge-building sites downriver, progress was so slow that it was 4:00 P.M. before Union troops were able to cross. They had scarcely reached the west bank when Burnside recalled them to the east bank, because Union forces still had not occupied the town in force.

As a result, Burnside lost an entire day, and revealed that his effort was going to be at Fredericksburg, not the fords downstream. This allowed Lee to order Jackson's whole corps to join Longstreet's men on the heights west of Fredericksburg. The Union army did not occupy the plain on the west bank until the morning of December 12. Burnside had complicated matters even further by dividing his army into three awkward "grand divisions," each of two corps with three divisions, the left under William B. Franklin facing Jackson on Prospect Hill, the right under Edwin Sumner facing Longstreet on Marye's Heights and adjacent hills to the north, and the center under Joseph Hooker, kept across the river in reserve. Both Franklin and Sumner's wings were too far apart to assist each other. Each was destined to fight entirely separately and alone.

Now, when speed was all the more imperative, Burnside lost another day in trying to decide what to do. Franklin's wing still could have continued Burnside's original plan, and could have mounted a massive assault directly onto Hamilton's Crossing. General Smith urged this movement, and pointed out that Franklin had 60,000 men in place to do the job.[20] Burnside at first agreed, but then began to have doubts. The massed Confederate army on the heights hypnotized him. Like so many uninspired generals over the aeons, he forgot the creative indirect approach he had originally envisioned and could think only of the enemy army directly in front of him. The real possibility of going around that force disappeared from his mind.

While Burnside was pondering his actions, Jackson brought up A. P. Hill's division and emplaced it for a little over a mile along Prospect Hill, and he located W. B. Taliaferro's division directly behind. Meanwhile, D. H. Hill's division from Port Royal and Jubal Early's division from Skinker's Neck were on a hard march for the heights. They arrived on the morning of December 13, forming a reserve on Prospect Hill, and thus uniting the entire Confederate army of 78,000 men.

Jackson's line was so short that he had space only for A. P. Hill's division along the firing line, leaving his remaining forces to hide in the woods behind. Protecting Jackson's line were fourteen cannons emplaced just above Hamilton's Crossing on the crest of Prospect Hill, twelve guns advanced beyond the railroad line that ran at the base of the ridgeline, and twenty-one more guns emplaced on the hill about 200 yards behind.

Because the weather was cold, the ground frozen, and the time short, Jackson's troops did not build field fortifications. The results of the battle, however, convinced everyone that field emplacements to deflect rifle and cannon fire were mandatory.[21]

In the plain just east of Hamilton's Crossing and directly on the left or southern flank of Franklin's whole force, Jeb Stuart had located his cavalry to guard against a Union sweep around Jackson's flank. There Stuart's artillery chief, Major John Pelham, had posted two cannons, a canister-firing Napoleon twelve-pounder, and a high-velocity English Blakely rifle.

A. P. Hill had placed his six brigades well on Prospect Hill, except for one glaring error. Between the brigades of James J. Archer and James H. Lane, he had left a gap of about 500 yards because the area consisted of marshy woodland overgrown with underbrush.[22] These marshy woods extended beyond the railroad line, and thus offered a covered route by which the enemy could advance onto the ridgeline. Here was a case of Clausewitzian friction—the mistake of a single person can have doleful consequences for an entire army. Hill didn't think the enemy would move over the boggy ground. But he also didn't inform Jackson on December 12, when there would have been time to rectify the error. Only on the morning of December 13 did Jackson have a chance to ride the line. He stopped to study the boggy ground. "The enemy will attack here," he said grimly. With battle imminent, it was too hazardous to make major realignments.[23] Behind the wood, Maxcy Gregg's brigade was posted as a second line along the ridge. And behind Gregg were Early and D. H. Hill's divisions. Any Union assault into the void would not go far, but it could inflict many unnecessary casualties.

The orders that Burnside finally issued on the morning of December 13 commanded headlong assaults against both Jackson and Longstreet on the heights. He ordered Franklin to send "a division, at least" to seize Prospect Hill, but confused the matter by telling Franklin to keep his "whole command" ready for a rapid movement around Hamilton's Crossing. He directed Sumner to march "a division or more" up the Orange Plank Road and along the Telegraph Road "with the view to seizing the heights to the rear of the town."[24] The Plank Road was two blocks (an eighth of a mile) north of the Telegraph

Road, which ran parallel with the Plank Road for a quarter mile, then veered off to the southwest, skirted the base of Marye's Heights, and proceeded through the valley of Hazel Run.

Burnside's order to Franklin called for a headlong assault on Jackson, but gave the impression that he still contemplated a sweep around Jackson's flank. These contradictory messages caused Franklin to attack Prospect Hill with only two of his six divisions. Yet Burnside later told the Congressional Committee on the Conduct of the War that he never intended such a move, and hoped to crack Jackson's position by a direct assault.

In the plain between Jackson's position and the river, Franklin lined up George G. Meade's division on his left or south, with John Gibbon's division supporting it on the right rear or north. He deployed Abner Doubleday's division on the extreme left or south to defend against Stuart's cavalry. Just as Meade's three brigades started forward, John Pelham, Stuart's artillery chief, advanced his two cannons directly on the flank of Meade's brigades and opened fire. More than a dozen Federal guns tried to silence Pelham, but he moved his Napoleon so swiftly that they failed, although they did disable the heavier, less nimble Blakely rifle. Pelham's dramatic action held up Meade's action for an hour before Stuart called on him to withdraw.

The Confederates standing on Prospect Hill were awestruck by the spectacle of 60,000 Union soldiers maneuvering in the plain in front of them. Heros von Borcke, a Prussian officer on Stuart's staff, turned to Stonewall Jackson and expressed doubt whether the Rebels could stop such a tremendous Yankee assault. Jackson answered: "Major, my men have sometimes failed to take a position, but to defend one, never!"[25]

Pelham's unexpected effectiveness with just two guns convinced Franklin that it was necessary to silence all the Confederate artillery before Meade advanced again. He ordered a massive bombardment that rained down on Jackson's entire position for an hour. The aim was to draw Rebel counterbattery fire so as to locate the guns and con-centrate on silencing them. But Jackson ordered his gunners to remain completely silent during the entire barrage.

About 11:30 A.M., Franklin, believing his bombardment had destroyed the Confederate cannons, ordered forward Meade's di-vision, with Gibbon supporting. Meade formed up two brigades on his front with his third brigade behind in close support. Gibbon drew up a column of brigades—that is, one brigade deployed in long lines, followed by his other two brigades directly behind—and advanced in parallel with Meade.

The broad lines of blue infantry advanced in silence. Not a gun fired at them. But the Rebel gunners on Prospect Hill were still in place, along with eight pieces from the reserve artillery that had joined Pelham's one gun on the southern flank. All the guns were loaded, ranges set. When Meade's lines reached within 800 yards of the Con-federate position, all the cannons erupted in a great burst of flame.

The shells tore great gaps in Meade's brigades. The soldiers wavered, halted, and re-formed. The Federal gunners had discovered the loca-tion of the Confederate cannons, however, and they recommenced a heavy cannonade on these positions. This largely silenced the Rebel artillery. Jackson pulled the exposed guns beyond the railroad line back up on the heights.

The real danger to the Union infantry now was rifle fire pouring down from the crest of Prospect Hill in sheets on the advancing Fed-eral lines. The fire staggered Meade's brigades, while Gibbon got no farther than the railroad line, losing more than 1,200 men in a few minutes.

Meade's men had been aiming all along at the boggy woods be-cause no fire was coming from that sector. All three brigades now pressed into the woods, where they were mercifully free of Confederate bullets and shells. They found the ground firm enough to continue their advance up to and over the railroad line, and straight up the slope of Prospect Hill. The left-hand brigade fell on Archer's left flank, while the right-hand brigade collided with Lane's right flank. The Confederates were surprised by the sudden appearance of the Union soldiers, and recoiled in confusion. Two of Archer's regiments collapsed, and Lane's brigade fell back into the woods.

Meanwhile, the third brigade coming up between the other two encountered no Rebel resistance, and advanced right through the Confederate position to a rear military road along the ridge crest where Maxcy Gregg's South Carolina brigade was resting in reserve. When they discovered the Union brigade descending on them in a long line, the Rebel soldiers sprang for their rifles. But Gregg was convinced the advancing force was Confederate, and rushed forward to stop the firing. He was almost instantly mortally wounded. One of his regiments collapsed, but the remainder held firm.

Meade's other two brigades were being hotly challenged by Rebel forces on either side, and the third brigade was now deep into the Confederate position with no hope of help. Just as the fight with Gregg's brigade was ending, the Union soldiers looked up and saw that two of Jubal Early's brigades were deployed in line of battle and were advancing directly on them. Before the Union troops could even respond, Early's men crashed into them, and sent them flying back down the hill in panic. Their flight drew in both of Meade's other brigades, and the entire division fled back across the railroad tracks, through the woods, and out into the plain. The panic pulled in Gibbon's division, and it fled back in chaos as well.

Early's counterstroke was wild and carried out with passion, but it was not organized as a real advance, and the men quickly withdrew to the safety of Prospect Hill.

Franklin realized that Meade and Gibbon's divisions were wholly broken, and he moved some of William Farrar Smith's 6th Corps troops over from the right to shore up the position. Burnside wanted him to renew the attack, but Franklin thought another assault would be as hopeless as the first, and he did nothing. This was going to cost him his job. The losses on both sides were about equal, 3,000 Confederates and 3,100 Federals. If A. P. Hill had not committed the blunder of leaving a great gap in his line, the Rebel casualties would have been far fewer.

While the fight against Jackson on Franklin's front was going on, Sumner was preparing to assault Longstreet at Marye's Heights. The assaults that Burnside had ordered were absolutely insane, and the senseless manner in which they were carried out constitutes one of the most appalling tragedies in military history. The Union commanders had the entire day of December 12 and the morning of December 13 to ascertain Confederate positions and to adjust their assaults accordingly. But they did not do so. Rather, they aimed *all* of their attacks against the one Confederate position that was impregnable—the Sunken Road in front of Marye's Heights, and ignored all other avenues of approach, though there were several.

After the Federals drove Barksdale's Mississippi brigade out of the town on December 11, Lafayette McLaws pulled his division back to Marye's Heights. The Telegraph Road ran along the base of these heights. For about a quarter of a mile, this road was sunken below the grade, and was flanked on the east or toward the town by a stone wall about four feet high. McLaws saw that if earth were thrown up from the road onto the wall, it would be impervious to enemy rifle fire and most artillery shells, and troops could stand in the road and easily fire over the wall at oncoming Union forces. He immediately ordered these preparations to be carried out, and sent Thomas R. R. Cobb with three of his Georgia regiments into the Sunken Road. McLaws extended this line by ordering the 24th North Carolina Regiment to dig a trench from the Sunken Road northward to the Orange Plank

Road. About 2,000 Rebel soldiers thus were holding the Sunken Road and the infantry trench.

In support on Marye's Heights above were about 7,000 more Confederate infantry of the divisions of McLaws and Robert Ransom Jr., plus nine cannons of the Washington Artillery of New Orleans in easy canister range of any enemy approaching the Sunken Road. On Cemetery Hill to the left or north of Marye's Heights were eight more Confederate cannons under Porter Alexander, while eight additional guns, including two Parrott rifles, were on Lee's Hill, a 210-foot elevation a mile south, where Lee had set up his observation post. These guns could strike the flanks of any advance against Marye's Heights.

When Longstreet suggested to Alexander that he needed more guns, Alexander replied: "General, we cover that ground now so well that we will comb it as with a fine-tooth comb. A chicken could not live on that field when we open on it."[26]

In front of Marye's Heights an open plain stretched for 900 yards to a south-flowing drainage ditch right at the edge of the town. Union troops were able to cross the ditch at several bridges, and just beyond was a low-lying area where the troops could form up. But as they moved to the crest of the plain, where they could be seen by Rebels on the Sunken Road and the heights, there were still about 400 yards of a long, sloping glacis with only a few houses, gardens, and fences that might provide a small bit of shelter. Otherwise, the Union troops were exposed for the entire distance to the Sunken Road.

Sumner's attack started about noon. But he demonstrated no judgment whatsoever. Burnside had ordered him to launch "a division or more" both over the Telegraph Road and the parallel Orange Plank Road, which ran up and over the northern edge of Marye's Heights. The Plank Road was not nearly as well defended as the Sunken Road, and a simultaneous assault both at the Sunken Road and along the Plank Road could well have yielded results.

But Sumner ignored the Plank Road and directed all of his efforts at the Sunken Road. In other words, he assaulted the single-most powerful position on the Confederate line. He continued to assault this one position for the entire day. Burnside supported him. He never told Sumner to change his effort, or part of it, to the Plank Road or any other point. All he and the other Union generals could think to do was to crash headlong against the Sunken Road. It was total madness, a supreme example of collective hysteria.

The attack commenced with two divisions—William H. French's and Winfield S. Hancock's—but with the entire force stacked up in a row, one brigade behind the other, each separated by about 200 yards. So the entire assault was limited to one brigade at a time approaching the Sunken Road. Each brigade ranged from about 1,000 to 1,500 men, giving the Confederate riflemen and gunners a concentrated target on which they could direct all their fire.

Nathan Kimball's brigade of French's division was the first to go. The brigade formed a long line two men deep, fixed bayonets, climbed over the crest beyond the ditch, emerged on the sloping glacis, and moved resolutely toward the Sunken Road, 400 yards away. Confederate fire commenced the moment the brigade appeared in view. The men bent their heads against the hail of bullets and shells screaming at them. Men fell all the way across the plain, but incredibly the brigade reached within a hundred yards of the Sunken Road, before the assault collapsed and the survivors fled or dropped to the earth in despair. The brigade lost 520 men in just minutes.

Next in line came the brigade of John W. Andrews, which traversed the same path and encountered the identical sheets of fire. This brigade broke sooner than the first brigade, and retreated back, seeking whatever small cover the men could find in small depressions or in the few buildings on the plain. Andrews's brigade lost 342 men.

Third in the row was the brigade of Oliver H. Palmer. The men in this brigade saw what was happening to their fellows, and retreated sooner, losing 291 men.

Major General Darius N. Couch, commanding the Union 2nd Corps, was observing the assault from the steeple of the courthouse in Fredericksburg. Couch exclaimed to Brigadier General Oliver O. Howard, who was with him: "Oh, great God! See how our men, our poor fellows, are falling!" Couch reported that "the whole plain was covered with men, prostrate and dropping, the live men running here and there, and the wounded coming back. The commands seemed to be mixed up. I had never seen fighting like that, nothing approaching it in the terrible uproar and destruction. . . . As they charged, the artillery fire would break their formation and they would get mixed; then they would close up, go forward, receive the withering infantry fire, and those who were able would run to the houses and fight as best they could; and then the next brigade coming up in succession would do its duty and melt like snow coming down on warm ground."[27]

Hancock's three brigades followed in close succession to French's division, and they suffered the same fate. The leading brigade of Samuel K. Zook got the closest of all to the Sunken Road, about thirty or forty yards away, but lost 527 men before it vanished in chaos. Next came the Irish brigade of Thomas F. Meagher, which lost 545 men before dissolving. Hancock's last brigade, John C. Caldwell's, caught the full brunt of the Rebel fire, and lost 952 men, virtually destroying it.

All these disasters had occurred in the space of only an hour or so. But Confederate fire was actually rising, not falling. General Ransom, seeing that the Federals were concentrating their entire effort against Marye's Heights, reinforced the position with the North Carolina brigade of John R. Cooke, with one regiment going into the Sunken Road and three occupying the crest of the hill.

Two complete Union divisions had been shattered, and the pattern of absolute destruction was plain to all. But Burnside refused to stop the attacks. He ordered Oliver O. Howard's division to follow the same path. By now the Union soldiers realized they were being sent to their deaths or maiming, and when Howard's first brigade, Joshua T. Owen's, advanced, the men did not push far, and instead lay down where they could find a bit of cover. There the men remained until nightfall, losing 258 men. The brigade of Norman J. Hall went in a little to the right or north of the path followed by the previous brigades, but got no farther. The brigade broke under the hail of fire, rallied, charged again, broke again, fell back, and sought whatever cover it could find. It remained pinned down until nightfall, losing 515 men. Howard kept his last brigade, Alfred Sully's, in reserve, but two of its regiments went to reinforce other brigades, and lost 122 men.

One entire Union corps had been wrecked, more than 4,000 men lost. Eight separate charges had been attempted, all at the same spot, and all had failed miserably. The Confederate defenders amounted to far less than half the numbers of a Union corps, and they had scarcely been tested.

It was madness to continue the attacks, and a monstrous misuse of men. But Burnside refused to stop them, and Sumner ordered up the two-brigade division of Samuel D. Sturgis, positioned on French's left. Sturgis brought forward the brigade of Edward Ferrero, along with a battery, which he intended to use to crack the stone wall on the Sunken Road. But gunners and horsemen were easy targets. Cannon fire from Lee's Hill quickly disabled the battery, and it withdrew. Ferrero's brigade advanced a little to the left or south of the path French and Hancock had followed, but it met equally severe fire. The men hid in small depressions and waited out the day. The brigade lost 491 men.

Now Sturgis's other brigade, James Nagle's, marched to the support of Ferrero. But, finding a bit of cover in Ferrero's rear, the men dropped down and spent the day firing at the Rebel lines. They did little damage, but, even so, the brigade lost 500 men.

Ferrero was in an extremely exposed position, and at 3:00 P.M. he asked for reinforcements. By this time, Charles Griffin's division of Joe Hooker's center "grand division" had crossed the river, and Sumner called it forward. Griffin sent the brigade of James Barnes to Ferrero's aid, but despite a gallant advance, it, too, collapsed in chaos, and took whatever cover it could find, losing 500 men.

Meanwhile Amiel W. Whipple, commanding a division under Hooker, had occupied the town, and he sent one of his brigades, Samuel S. Carroll's, to the aid of Griffin. Griffin placed one of his brigades, under Jacob B. Sweitzer, alongside Carroll's brigade, and two brigades now for the first time advanced side by side, supported by Griffin's last brigade, under T. B. W. Stockton.

This was now the eleventh charge of the day. The Confederates had lost some men from random fire, including General Cobb, who had been killed, and General Cooke, severely wounded. General Ransom sent down into the Sunken Road the last three regiments of Cooke's North Carolina brigade, and General Joseph B. Kershaw brought down into the road his South Carolina brigade. There were now six ranks of riflemen in the road. Each rank fired, then moved to the rear to reload, while the next rank fired, and followed the same process. In this fashion a virtually continuous sheet of fire raged out from the Sunken Road, killing or wounding anyone who lifted his head.

Against this curtain of fire, Griffin's charge reached only the point where the men, seeing they had no chance of carrying the road, dropped down to seek whatever cover they could find. The three brigades lost 541 men, less than some of the other charges. But a grim panorama of dead, dying, and wounded men covered the entire glacis from the crest above the drainage ditch to thirty or forty paces in front of the Sunken Road.

It was now about 4:00 P.M. The attacks had been going on for four hours. The total failure of the entire process was manifest to everybody who witnessed it. Even the Confederates were appalled at the carnage. General McLaws wrote in his official report: "The body of one man, believed to be an officer, was found within about thirty yards of the stone wall, and other single bodies were scattered at increased distances until the main mass of the dead lay thickly strewn over the ground at something over one hundred yards off, and extending to the ravine [drainage ditch]."[28]

The Confederates were in disbelief that Burnside was persisting in the impossible task he had given his men. But Burnside was a person of poor judgment to begin with. In the intense crisis he had brought about, what little judgment he did have simply vanished. He demanded of Hooker that he attack with his whole force.

Hooker had two intact divisions left, those of George Sykes and Andrew A. Humphreys. But Hooker was certain no Union force could carry the Sunken Road by frontal attack, and he rode back across the river to try to persuade Burnside in person to call off the attacks. But Burnside would not budge.

Hooker was intensely unhappy with Burnside's blindness, but he advanced as many batteries as he could find and emplaced them at the edge of the town, and even advanced two batteries across the ditch within 300 yards of the Sunken Road. Rebel sharpshooters promptly shot down gunners and horses, and put the guns out of action before they could do any damage.

While all this was going on, Union soldiers hiding in dips and hollows noticed activity on the Confederate line, and called back that the Rebels were abandoning the Sunken Road. What actually was happening was that Porter Alexander was shifting a portion of his artillery to replace the Washington Artillery on the top of Marye's Heights because it had run out of ammunition.

But Humphreys at once ordered one of his two brigades, Peter H. Allabach's, to attack, without waiting for his other brigade, under

Erastus B. Tyler, to move forward. Humphreys and Allabach led the charge in person. About 200 yards past the crest above the ditch they reached men from previous charges lying prone. Despite all their commanders could do, the soldiers of Allabach's brigade also lay down, and began firing from prone positions, a virtually useless process. Humphreys finally pressed the men to get back on their feet and resume the charge. But they went forward only about another fifty yards before the entire brigade broke under a hail of Confederate fire. Some of the men dropped to the ground, but many others ran back to the low ground around the ditch.

After a delay, Humphreys was able to get Tyler's brigade formed up and ordered it to charge with fixed bayonets. Tyler told the men not to fire, but to carry the Sunken Road entirely with cold steel. His idea was that the Union soldiers had failed because they stopped and fired volleys. These halts had brought colossal Rebel fusillades and led to the Union brigades' disintegration.

Tyler's men advanced with loud hurrahs, passing over the men lying on the ground. The prone soldiers resented the new assault, because it seemed to reflect on their courage. They did everything in their power to stop the charge, even trying to tackle some of Tyler's men personally. The brigade passed on, but fears arose that the prone men would fire into the backs of Tyler's soldiers.

The loud huzzahs of the Union soldiers had alerted Alexander's gunners. They set to work firing full loads of canister into the line of Tyler's brigade. At the same time the riflemen in the Sunken Road unleashed a violent fury of fire directly into the brigade.

Tyler gave the dreadful report of what happened: "When we were within a very short distance of the enemy's line a fire was opened on our rear, wounding a few of my most valuable officers and, I regret to say, killing some of our men. Instantaneously the cry ran along our lines that we were being fired into from the rear. The column halted, receiving at the same time a terrible fire from the enemy. Orders for the moment were forgotten and a fire from our whole line was immediately returned. Another cry passed along our line that we were being fired on from our rear, when our brave men, after giving the enemy several volleys, fell back."[29]

Humphreys's 4,500-man division lost 1,000 men in its two short advances.

These were the twelfth and thirteenth separate charges against the Sunken Road. One more was to still to come. As sundown neared, Burnside called on George W. Getty's two-brigade division on the left to move over and attack the Sunken Road. It arrived after Tyler's abortive charge had failed, and the survivors retreated to the ditch.

The brigade of Rush C. Hawkins of Getty's division led this last charge as night was falling. Edward Harland's brigade was to follow. Hawkins aimed his charge a bit to the north of the other charges, and the darkness permitted his men to get fairly close to the Confederates. Then, some yards away from the Sunken Road, Hawkins's men stopped and unleashed a volley. Their rifle flashes defined the line for all the gunners, and they immediately laid a curtain of shells and canister directly on the hapless brigade. Even so, the brigade continued to advance to within a few yards of the Sunken Road when the Rebel infantry unleashed a withering fire while, at the same time, some of the Union soldiers lying prone in their rear, also fired into them. Hawkins's men endured the fire front and rear for only a few moments before they broke and ran back to the ditch. Getty, seeing what had happened to Hawkins's men, stopped Harland's brigade and did not send it forward.

The horrible day of battle finally ended. Only four of nine Confederate divisions had been engaged, less than half the army. The Federals lost 12,647 men, most killed or wounded, the Confederates 5,309. The Rebel losses would have been much lower except for the inexcusable blunder of A. P. Hill in leaving a large part of his front unguarded.

The Confederates expected the Federals to renew the battle the next day, and Jackson made intense preparations for the expected attack, moving forward D. H. Hill's division and distributing fresh ammunition to the troops. Riding back from a visit to the dying Maxcy Gregg, Jackson looked up at the sky and exclaimed: "How horrible is war!" Hunter McGuire, his medical officer, said: "Horrible, yes, but we have been invaded. What can we do?" "Kill them, sir!" Jackson answered fiercely. "Kill every man!"[30]

Burnside indeed planned to renew the battle. His only idea was to form the entire three-division 9th Corps into a column of regiments and lead it in person upon Marye's Heights. It was an utterly stupid idea, but it took Sumner, Hooker, and Franklin a long time to talk him out of it. Hooker sealed the argument with this comment: "There has been enough blood shed to satisfy any reasonable man, and it is time to quit."[31]

The Union dead and wounded lay untended all day on December 14. On December 15, Hooker and Franklin applied to Burnside for a truce to allow removal of the Federal wounded. But Burnside refused. The wounded men around Marye's Heights remained to suffer, and many to die, in the very cold weather. Jackson, however, honored an informal truce on his front, and Union medical people tended the survivors and buried the dead. The dark and rainy night of December 15 gave Burnside cover to withdraw his entire army back across the river to the eastern bank.

Abraham Lincoln disclosed his cold indifference to the human tragedy that was unfolding for North and South. He told his secretary, William Stoddard, "that if the same battle were to be fought over again, every day, through a week of days, with the same relative results, the army under Lee would be wiped out to its last man, the Army of the Potomac would still be a mighty host, the war would be over, the Confederacy gone."[32]

Confederate losses in killed and wounded since Lee had become commander were actually far more than Lincoln imagined. They were *greater* than Union losses—44,094 to 41,345. The Confederates had captured almost 30,000 Union men, while the North had captured 4,000 Rebels, but these men were routinely exchanged.[33] With less than a third the white population of the North, the South could not endure Lee's method of waging war.

The day after Christmas 1862, Jeb Stuart led 1,800 of his troopers on a raid into the Federal rear. They did much damage to Federal facilities around Occoquan and Dumfries, twenty miles north of Falmouth, then they penetrated to Burke Station, only fourteen miles from Alexandria. There Stuart sent a telegram to Montgomery C. Meigs, the Union quartermaster general, saying that the mules furnished to the Army of the Potomac were of such poor quality that he was embarrassed to take them with the wagons he had seized into the Confederate lines. He asked that better-quality animals be provided in the future for the Rebels to capture.[34]

Fredericksburg had proved how utterly incompetent Burnside was as a general. Lincoln removed him on January 26, 1863, and replaced him with Joe Hooker. Hooker didn't fit within Lincoln's job requirements, because he had announced publicly that the country needed a dictator to take charge of both the army and the government. But Lincoln figured that Hooker's political savvy was so low that he posed little danger. Lincoln wrote Hooker: "Only those soldiers who have gained successes can set up dictators. What I now ask of you is military success, and I will risk the dictatorship."[35] Hooker pledged not to become a presidential candidate if he won a great victory.

Jackson had been right. The Confederates achieved a success, but it was pointless. The 12,000 Federal losses could easily be made up by forming new regiments. No permanent damage had been done to the Northern cause.

Colonel Henderson summarized the effects of Fredericksburg vividly: "It was not by partial triumphs, not by the slaughter of a few brigades, by defense without counterstroke, by victories without pursuit, that a power [the Union] of such strength and vitality could be compelled to confess her impotence." A crowning victory like Waterloo, which forced the downfall of Napoleon Bonaparte in 1815, was the only hope for the South. "Had the Army of the Potomac, ill-commanded as it was, been drawn forward to the North Anna, it might have been utterly destroyed." Halfhearted efforts that aim only at repulsing the enemy's attack are not the path to decisive victory.[36]

The South could not win the war by brute force. It had to win by guile. Stonewall Jackson knew this, but Robert E. Lee did not. Jackson continued to try to show him the way and continued to hope that Lee would finally comprehend.

CHAPTER 10

The Fatal Blow

Both armies now went into winter quarters. While Longstreet remained at Fredericksburg, Jackson's corps moved eastward to guard the lower passages over the Rappahannock. Jackson set up his headquarters at Moss Neck Manor, a 1,600-acre estate eleven miles downriver from the town and two miles from the river. But Jackson did not occupy the main house, built like an English country residence and stretching 250 feet from one wing to the other. Instead, he occupied a small wooden "office" fifty yards in front of the manor house.

Jackson wrote his wife, Anna, that he hoped she and the baby would come to visit him before spring. Anna, however, was trying to get Jackson to take leave and travel to her at her father's house north of Charlotte, North Carolina. But Jackson responded that duty required him to remain with his command.

Jackson routinely refused requests of other officers for leave, including his capable young engineer, Captain J. Keith Boswell, who wanted to visit his sweetheart. Boswell turned to his friend General Jeb

Stuart, who was more understanding. Stuart requested Boswell's service for a week or two. Jackson agreed, and Stuart dispatched Boswell "on duty" to the locale where his sweetheart lived.[1]

In mid-March 1863, Jackson moved his headquarters closer to Lee, occupying a frame house about half a mile from Hamilton's Crossing. In mid-April, Anna at last left Charlotte with her baby to visit Jackson. Late on the evening of April 18, Jackson received a message from his friend Governor John Letcher that Anna and the baby had arrived in Richmond and had spent the night in the governor's mansion. Early on April 20, Jackson wired Letcher and asked him to send Anna and the baby by train to Guiney Station, about eight miles south of Hamilton's Crossing.

When the train stopped, Jackson in a wet raincoat pushed through the people getting off the train, searching for his wife and his child. Anna described the moment he saw them: "His face was all sunshine and gladness, and, after greeting his wife, it was a picture, indeed, to see his look of perfect delight and admiration as his eyes fell upon that baby! He was afraid to take her into his arms with that wet overcoat, but as we drove in a carriage to Mr. [Thomas] Yerby's, his face reflected all the happiness and delight that were in his heart."[2] Jackson had secured quarters at Belvoir, Yerby's Georgian-style brick home, only a mile from his headquarters.

Told often over the days ahead that the baby looked like him, Jackson always responded, "No, she is too pretty to look like me." Anna disagreed, and later wrote: "I never saw him look so well. He seemed to be in excellent health and looked handsomer than I had ever seen him."[3] Anna noted that Jackson seldom let Julia out of his arms, and when she slept during the day, he would often lean over her cradle and gaze on her.

The baby was christened Julia Laura on April 23, 1863, in honor of

Jackson's mother and sister, by Jackson's chaplain, the Reverend Beverly Tucker Lacy.

Federal forces at last were stirring. On April 28, Rebel outposts reported that Union forces of uncertain size were moving westward along the north bank of the Rappahannock. Lee believed they were heading for the Shenandoah Valley. Early the next morning, April 29, a wholly new threat materialized. A rider galloped into the yard of the Yerby home. It was a messenger from Jubal Early that Federal troops were fording the Rappahannock at Deep Run, a couple miles below Fredericksburg. Yerby's was no place for a mother and child. Jackson told Anna that they must depart at once. They bade a quick farewell, before Jackson sent Reverend Lacy to escort Anna and Julia to Richmond.

Early informed Lee of the landings, and Jackson rode to Hamilton's Crossing to find that Early had deployed his forces to defend against Union General John Sedgwick's 6th Corps, now spreading out on the west bank of the Rappahannock, but showing no inclination to advance.

The year 1863 had already presented a crisis in leadership for both the North and the South. The Northern crisis was open and public, the Southern crisis chronic and unpublicized. Lincoln had gone through a panoply of generals: Irvin McDowell, George B. McClellan, John Pope, McClellan again, Ambrose E. Burnside, and now Joseph Hooker. All before Hooker were inadequate and incapable of gaining success, and Hooker had a reputation for pugnacity, not brilliance.[4] But the Confederacy had replaced an incompetent Joseph E. Johnston with Robert E. Lee, whose direct challenges of Union forces were causing irreplaceable losses, and were leading the South to ruin. The Confederacy had refused to name a proven military genius, Stonewall Jackson, to command its forces. While the Northern generals proposed only vague and uncertain campaigns that required enormous resources and vast expenditures of manpower, Stonewall Jackson had shown step-by-step how to produce victory with virtually no new troops and very few losses in human lives.

Colonel G. F. R. Henderson saw the Northern situation quite accurately: "The government which commits the charge of its armed forces to any other than the ablest and most experienced soldier the country can produce is but laying the foundation of national disaster. . . . The Federal administration, confident in the courage and intelligence of their great armies, considered that any ordinary general, trained to command, and supported by an efficient staff, should be able to win victories."[5]

Henderson did not see, however, that the Confederacy's practice of appointing senior generals distinguished by their social status was more disastrous than the Lincoln administration's belief that leadership was not important. For the North possessed so many resources that, even with atrocious commanders, its armies could ultimately beat down Southern resistance. But the South, with few resources, *had* to have outstanding leaders if it was going to succeed. The ruling Southern aristocracy, however, still believed there was a strong connection between social prominence and leadership of all kinds. Such a belief is most destructive and completely false. A nation that restricts its leadership to a narrow aristocracy deprives itself of most of its brainpower. Unless this belief changed, the Confederacy was facing a death sentence.

Stonewall Jackson was not the only outstanding leader who was being kept in a subordinate role. In the Western Theater, Nathan Bedford Forrest had emerged as a brilliant commander who mystified Union commanders and achieved dazzling successes with small forces and few losses. But Forrest had virtually no education and, before the war, had been a slave trader. Although the Southern aristocracy depended on slave labor for its wealth, it despised men who traded in slaves as being socially contemptible. Therefore, Forrest, whatever his brilliance, had no possibility of ascending to high command in the Confederacy.

By 1863 the military and political situation had tilted decidedly against the South. The Emancipation Proclamation had eliminated any possibility that Britain or France would intervene on the side of the South. In the West, where Confederate leadership under Braxton Bragg was abysmal, the North had wrestled control of Kentucky and Tennessee and had seized all but a narrow stretch of the Mississippi River. In the East, Lee's system of warfare had cost more casualties than the Northern armies had suffered.[6] The South could not replace its losses, whereas the North had virtually unlimited human resources.

Also, President Jefferson Davis and his cabinet members, who had little strategic understanding, were being distracted by peripheral problems, and were diverting more and more resources to them rather than to the main arena—which was along the Rappahannock River facing the Army of the Potomac.

In December 1862 a Union garrison on the North Carolina coast at New Bern raided westward and temporarily broke the Wilmington and Weldon Railroad at Goldsboro. This aroused fears that the Federals were going to close this crucial supply line. Wilmington was the port of most of the Confederacy's blockade runners. These fast vessels carried on regular trade with the British colonies of Bermuda and the Bahamas, and were vital for bringing in the most desperately needed weapons and supplies. On January 3, 1863, the War Department removed Robert Ransom Jr.'s small division from Lee's command and sent it down to block further attacks on the railroad, and on January 14 it sent D. H. Hill to direct military operations there.

In February 1863 the Federal 9th Corps moved through the Chesapeake Bay to Fort Monroe, arousing fears that the Federals intended to advance once more up the James River valley toward Richmond, or that the corps might be sent on to New Bern to commence a campaign in eastern North Carolina. The War Department transferred George Pickett's and John Bell Hood's divisions, both from James Longstreet's corps, south to meet 9th Corps, and on February 17, it detached Longstreet himself to direct operations. This left Lee with just 60,000 men and 170 guns to meet Hooker's army of 138,000 men and 428 guns.

The 9th Corps soon departed for the Western Theater, so that danger in the east vanished. But Longstreet became excited about a proposal of James A. Seddon, the secretary of war, to attack 20,000 Union forces that had occupied Suffolk, a few miles west of Norfolk. Though the Federals interfered somewhat with Confederate commissary officers securing hams and bacon from the rich hog-raising country west of Suffolk, the Union garrison presented no strategic danger.

Lee understood the folly of a campaign to secure Suffolk, and he wrote Gustavus W. Smith, commanding the Richmond defenses: "Partial encroachments of the enemy we must expect, but they can always be recovered, and any defeat of their large army will reinstate everything."[7] But Davis, Seddon, and Longstreet ignored Lee's protests, and opened a campaign against Suffolk. Longstreet failed badly as an independent commander, and the campaign went nowhere. But it held 20,000 Confederate troops out of the colossal confrontation about to take place along the Rappahannock, and Lee was forced to fight with an army less than half the size of Hooker's.[8]

The first collision of the 1863 campaign was a cavalry engagement on March 17 at Kelly's Ford, twenty-three miles upstream from Fredericksburg. Federal cavalry had improved markedly over the winter. They now numbered 11,500 troopers, and at Kelly's Ford did well against Jeb Stuart's 4,400 veterans. The famous horse-artilleryman John Pelham died from a shell burst. But the Union troopers withdrew after the clash. Even so, the skirmish informed Lee that Hooker was looking westward for at least a part of his effort.

Lee decided that Hooker would make a turning movement at United States Ford, twelve miles upstream from Fredericksburg. He picked this ford because it gave access to Chancellorsville, a crossroads three miles south, where five roads came together, including the main artery in this region, the Orange Plank Road and Orange Turnpike (present-day Virginia Route 3).[9] Lee saw that if Hooker reached Chancellorsville with a large part of his army, he could press eastward on the flank of the Rebel army, and drive it off the Rappahannock.

Chancellorsville was only a clearing a couple of miles from the eastern edge of a vast cutover forest called the Wilderness, which stretched fourteen miles along the Rappahannock and eight to ten miles to the south. The virgin forest had been cut down over the previous half century to supply charcoal for iron furnaces in the area. A dense second growth of low-branched hardwood, pines, and cedars, along with briars and underbrush, had created a tangled, difficult landscape with few roads, poor visibility, and only a few small open places. Jackson had observed the dense nature of the Wilderness when he rode through it the previous November, but it was doubtful whether Joe Hooker was aware of its major limitation—his greatest asset, his overwhelming artillery, would be crippled there.

Actually, Hooker's original plan did not involve the Wilderness. He intended merely to feint with minor forces at United States Ford, and to make his major move downstream from Fredericksburg, with the aim of cutting the Richmond, Fredericksburg & Potomac Railroad (RF&P), Lee's major supply line. He also wanted to strike downstream to keep Lee away from Aquia Creek, which he thought, incorrectly, that Lee was planning to attack.

Hooker intended to combine this move on the RF&P with a

long-distance strike using most of his cavalry to break the Virginia Central Railroad at Gordonsville and other points. This move was to culminate with the horsemen cutting the RF&P at Hanover Junction, a few miles north of Richmond. He planned for his cavalry to hold this intersection, and thereby break Lee's supply line from Richmond. Caught between the Army of the Potomac pressing on him from the north, and the Union cavalry firmly holding the rail junction above Richmond, Lee would be forced to fall back in chaos.[10]

Hooker's idea that Federal cavalry could seize and hold a major rail interchange deep in enemy territory was strategic nonsense. Cavalry's main advantage was mobility. When horsemen were called on to defend a position, they lost their mobility. Confederates could send cavalry flying by marching on them. Federal cavalry were largely armed with the Sharps single-shot, breech-loaded carbine. The Sharps bullet had an effective range of only 175 yards, and—because the bullet was big and the muzzle velocity low—followed an extreme parabolic trajectory that was very difficult to control at long range. The Minié-ball infantry rifle had an effective range of 400 yards. Thus cavalry at best could deflect an infantry attack temporarily, not hold a position, especially since cavalry brought along few cannons, and these light pieces. Cavalrymen would also soon run out of supplies, notably ammunition. Their position could only be maintained if Federal infantry moved quickly to their support.

So, Hooker's grand idea of knocking Lee off the Rappahannock with the use of cavalry was hopelessly flawed. The plan failed anyway because heavy rains set in on April 15, making the Rappahannock unfordable. In response, Hooker abandoned his projected strike around Lee's eastern flank, and substituted a major move around his western flank. Confederate Porter Alexander called this substitution "decidedly the best strategy conceived in any of the campaigns set on foot against us."[11]

Hooker directed that two Union corps (the 1st and 6th), 40,000 men under Major General John Sedgwick, were to cross the Rappahannock near where William B. Franklin's divisions had crossed in December, and hold in place the main Confederate army on the heights west of Fredericksburg. Meanwhile, three additional corps (the 5th, 11th, and 12th), 42,000 men under Major General Henry W. Slocum, were to march upstream all the way to Kelly's Ford, twelve miles above the confluence of the Rappahannock and the Rapidan rivers. From Kelly's Ford, the three Union corps were to turn back and march down the right or southern bank of the Rappahannock directly on Lee's western flank. Lee would not expect so long and so roundabout an approach, especially since it involved fording two rivers. Slocum's goal was to seize both United States Ford and Banks Ford, four miles west of Fredericksburg. Capturing these two fords would put the two wings of the Union army once more in contact, while, at the same time, dislodging Lee from Fredericksburg and forcing his precipitate retreat.

Hooker intended to confront Lee well east of the Wilderness in the broad, open, cultivated fields opposite Banks Ford, where the Union army could be fully deployed and the Federal artillery could be completely exploited. In such circumstances, Hooker felt, the Federal army would be invincible.

Hooker's new plan was actually an example of the oldest method of winning battles. Its origins go back to the beginnings of warfare, but the first recorded mention we have of it is in the Bible (2 Samuel 5:23–25). In this account, the Lord told David to hold the Philistines in place with his main force, while using a flanking force "to fetch a compass behind them, and come upon them over against the mulberry trees." When David heard the sound of this collision, he was to attack the Philistines frontally, thus accosting the enemy front and rear. "And David did so, as the Lord had commanded him; and smote the Philistines from Gaba until thou come to Gazer."

Napoleon Bonaparte applied the same principle on a vast geographic scale in the Marengo campaign in Italy in 1800. The Austrians were absorbed in their siege of a French army under André Masséna at Genoa. Bonaparte launched a new army through the St. Bernard Passes between Switzerland and Italy. He seized the main Austrian base of Milan, thus cutting off Austrian supplies, and drove on the Austrian rear. At Marengo near Alessandria, thirty-five miles north of Genoa, he defeated the Austrian army. This defeat resulted in the Peace of Lunéville in February 1801, which gave most of Italy and Germany west of the Rhine River to France.[12]

There are countless other examples of this principle of holding at one place and striking at another. It remains the most effective means of winning battles and campaigns to this day. But, as simple as the concept is, few generals over the centuries have implemented it. Robert E. Lee, for example, ordered an imperfect version of it as the opening act of the Seven Days. He called on Stonewall Jackson to descend on Fitz John Porter's right flank at Hundley's Corner on June 26, 1862, but he did not order a threat or a simulated attack at the same time to hold Porter's corps along Beaver Dam Creek. When impatient A. P. Hill launched an actual attack on the creek before Jackson arrived on Porter's flank, Lee forgot his original purpose and ordered D. H. Hill to assist A. P. Hill in a headlong assault, which failed and cost nearly 2,000 men.

Hooker, therefore, applied an ancient, but—given the reputation of Union commanders for incompetence—quite unexpected, method of exploiting his vastly superior force to defeat Lee. The question now was whether he would be able to carry it out.

The campaign commenced on April 27 when Slocum with his three corps marched toward Kelly's Ford. The next day Darius N. Couch's 2nd Corps, 17,000 men, marched to the north sides of United States and Banks fords. Couch's job was to divert Lee's attention from

Slocum's march, and convince him that Hooker was preparing to force crossings on these two fords. The Union army's entire reserve artillery force moved up with Couch to Banks Ford, intending to cross the river there as soon as Slocum's men secured the south bank.

On April 29, Sedgwick crossed the river below Fredericksburg, but did not directly challenge Jackson on the heights. Instead his men dug in along the riverbank. Hooker's last corps, the 3rd, 18,700 men under Major General Daniel E. Sickles, remained on Stafford Heights, ready to reinforce either Slocum or Sedgwick as required.

Meanwhile Hooker launched 10,000 of his cavalry southward under George Stoneman to carry out strikes on the railroads. But the horsemen were no longer charged with seizing and holding the rail crossing at Hanover Junction. Hooker left only 1,300 cavalry under Alfred Pleasonton to scout ahead of Slocum's infantry.

Jeb Stuart could not figure out the Union plan at first, thought Slocum's force was only a third its actual size, and believed it was headed toward Gordonsville. He posted his patrols accordingly, and therefore Slocum was able to cross at Kelly's Ford on the morning of April 29 and turn back eastward without hindrance. Slocum's soldiers waded across two fords on the Rapidan, Germanna (on present-day Virginia Route 3) and Ely's (on present-day Virginia Route 610), ten miles east of Kelly's.

Couriers alerted Lee on the afternoon of April 29 that Stuart was wrong, and that a major Union force was descending on his flank. He dispatched Richard H. Anderson's division to the Chancellorsville crossroads at once.

Stuart sent only W. H. F. "Rooney" Lee's brigade of 1,000 troopers to deal with Stoneman, and concentrated the bulk of his horsemen where they were most needed, at the front of both armies. This gave Lee fast and accurate information, while Pleasonton was unable to penetrate Stuart's screens and knew nothing of the actions of the Confederates.

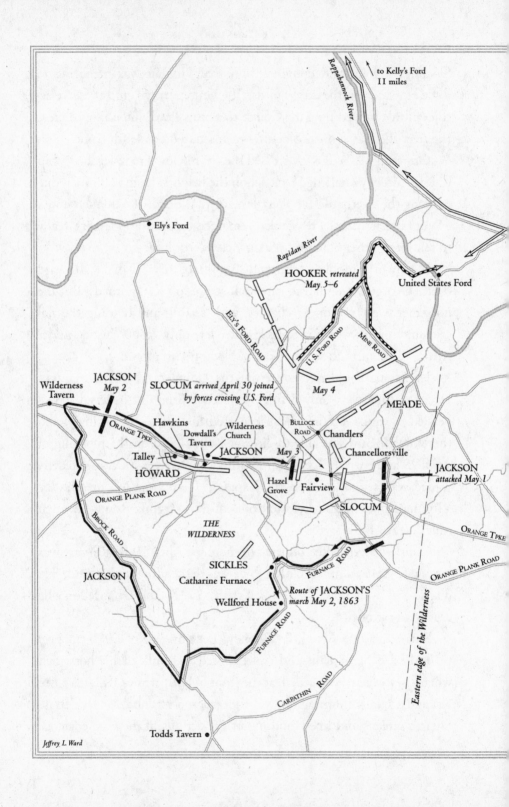

to Kelly's Ford
11 miles

Rappahannock River

Ely's Ford

Rapidan River

HOOKER *retreated*
May 5–6

United States Ford

ELY'S FORD ROAD

U.S. FORD ROAD

MINE ROAD

May 4

Wilderness
Tavern

JACKSON
May 2

SLOCUM *arrived April 30 joined*
by forces crossing U.S. Ford

MEADE

ORANGE TPKE

Hawkins

Dowdall's
Tavern

Wilderness
Church

BULLOCK
ROAD

Chandlers

Talley

JACKSON   *May 3*

Chancellorsville

HOWARD

ORANGE PLANK ROAD

Hazel
Grove

Fairview

JACKSON
attacked May 1

BROCK ROAD

THE
WILDERNESS

SLOCUM

ORANGE TPKE

JACKSON

SICKLES

Catharine Furnace

FURNACE ROAD

ORANGE PLANK ROAD

Wellford House

Route of JACKSON'S
march May 2, 1863

FURNACE ROAD

CARPATHIN ROAD

Eastern edge of the Wilderness

Todds Tavern

Jeffrey L. Ward

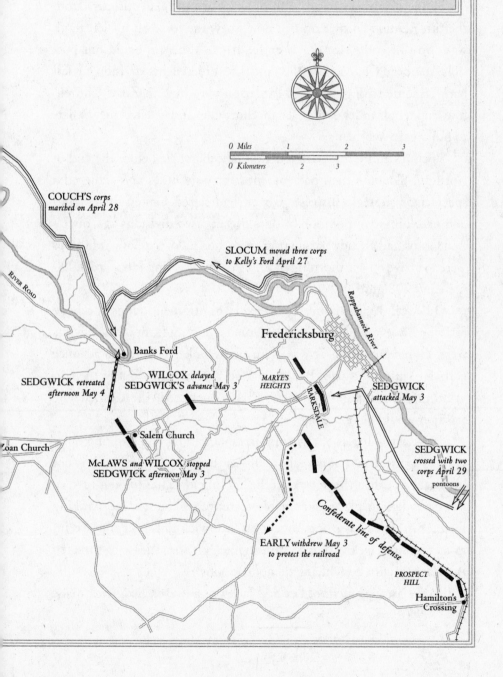

THE CHANCELLORSVILLE CAMPAIGN
APRIL 27–MAY 6, 1863

0 Miles 1 2 3

0 Kilometers 2 3

COUCH'S *corps marched on April 28*

SLOCUM *moved three corps to Kelly's Ford April 27*

RIVER ROAD

Rappahannock River

Fredericksburg

Banks Ford

WILCOX *delayed* SEDGWICK'S *advance May 3*

MARYE'S HEIGHTS

BARKSDALE

SEDGWICK *attacked May 3*

SEDGWICK *retreated afternoon May 4*

Zoan Church

• Salem Church

McLAWS *and* WILCOX *stopped* SEDGWICK *afternoon May 3*

SEDGWICK *crossed with two corps April 29* pontoons

EARLY *withdrew May 3 to protect the railroad*

Confederate line of defense

PROSPECT HILL

Hamilton's Crossing

Lee ignored the breaks of the railway lines that Stoneman's troopers made, and his sweep south degenerated into a giant, but pointless, raid.

By the morning of April 30, Stuart had captured prisoners from the three Union corps, and Lee now knew the force on his left flank was two-thirds the size of his entire army. Anderson could not possibly stand at Chancellorsville, and Lee ordered his division to fall back to some strong position. Anderson withdrew to Zoan Church, four and a half miles east of Chancellorsville, and ordered his soldiers to build entrenchments.[13]

Slocum's entire force arrived at Chancellorsville before the end of April 30. Slocum's men had marched forty-six miles and achieved a spectacular strategic surprise. Couch had seized United States Ford and had flung two pontoon bridges over it. Two divisions of Couch's 2nd Corps had already passed over them, and all of Sickles's 3rd Corps were to arrive on the morning of Friday, May 1, giving Hooker 70,000 men and 208 guns.

On April 30, therefore, Lee faced two imminent dangers, a huge force on his left flank and 40,000 Union troops in front of the heights west of Fredericksburg. It was plain that Hooker planned to advance eastward quickly to seize Banks Ford and get his army out of the labyrinthine, confusing Wilderness. If this happened, the Confederate position would be hopeless.

The key to success of any combination holding and flanking operation is a threatened or actual assault on the defending force. It is not necessary to defeat this force. All the holding force has to do is to keep the defenders in place and unable to move to counter the flanking force. Therefore, it was incumbent on Sedgwick to launch a powerful assault against Jackson's forces on the heights, or at least to threaten those forces with convincing demonstrations.

To the astonishment of Lee and Jackson, however, Sedgwick made no aggressive gestures. Hooker had committed a potentially lethal blunder. He had given Sedgwick the option of deciding whether or not he would advance. He did not insist on an attack, or even a threat. And Sedgwick decided not to do anything! He only hunkered down on the banks of the river and waited. Here was an extreme case of Clausewitzian friction—how the action, or in this case the inaction, of a single individual can affect the outcome of battles and of wars.

Seeing that Sedgwick was not moving, Lee sent Lafayette McLaws's division to reinforce Anderson at Zoan Church, leaving only William Barksdale's Mississippi brigade to defend Marye's Heights. He also ordered Jackson to march three divisions of his corps at daylight the next day, May 1, to Zoan Church, take charge of the western flank, and "repulse the enemy." Jackson left his fourth division, under Jubal Early, along with the army's reserve artillery, under William N. Pendleton, to watch Sedgwick.

Accordingly, at nightfall on April 30, Lee turned his back on Sedgwick's huge force of 40,000 men, and concentrated 45,000 men and 114 guns on the west to confront Hooker. He left only 10,000 men under Early on the Fredericksburg heights.

Hooker was certain of victory. His order of the day on April 30 read: "Our enemy must either ingloriously fly or come out from behind his defenses and give us battle on our own ground, where certain destruction awaits him."[14] Hooker did not think Lee would actually turn on him, however. He thought he would flee the moment he realized how powerful the force on the western flank was. But he had not reckoned on his failure to require Sedgwick to attack. In doing so, Hooker had eliminated 40,000 of his own troops from the upcoming battle, and he had freed the mass of the Confederate army to challenge him at Chancellorsville.

Hooker planned a modest but crucial advance on May 1—to get

out of the Wilderness and to seize Banks Ford. He sent columns east-ward on the Orange Plank Road to the south, the Orange Turnpike in the center, and the River Road to Banks Ford to the north.

When Jackson arrived at Zoan Church on the morning of May 1 with his three divisions, he had already made up his mind what to do. It was a stunning reversal of orthodox practice. But, in an instant, it transformed a desperate situation for the Confederacy into an oppor-tunity for great victory. Jackson knew that if the Federal army could deploy in the wide, open country around Banks Ford, it would be un-beatable. But if Hooker could be kept within the Wilderness, his army could not deploy effectively, his maneuverability would be hindered, and his greatest weapon, his artillery, would have great difficulty find-ing targets and would be exceedingly diminished.

Accordingly, Jackson told Anderson and McLaws to stop building fortifications, and begin forming up to *advance* directly on the Feder-als! Since Hooker expected the Confederates to retreat without a bat-tle, Jackson's attack completely stunned him. In response, he ordered his whole force to withdraw at once back to Chancellorsville, and to build a defensive line in a semicircle of earthworks and logs just east and south of the crossroads. Porter Alexander, who was present on the field when Hooker began pulling his troops back, remarked on "the perfect collapse of the moral courage of Hooker, as commander in chief, as soon as he found himself in the actual presence of Lee and Jackson."[15]

Hooker's distraction can be seen in a strange wire he sent at 2:00 P.M. May 1 to his chief of staff, Major General Daniel Butterfield, at Fal-mouth: "From character of information have suspended attack. The enemy may attack me—I will try it. Tell Sedgwick to keep a sharp lookout and attack if he can succeed."[16]

Hooker's generals were deeply angered by the retreat. When Gen-eral Couch reported to Hooker on the night of May 1, Hooker told him: "I have Lee just where I want him. He must fight me on my own ground." Couch wrote later: "To hear from his own lips that the advantages gained by the successful marches of his lieutenants were to culminate in fighting a defensive battle in that nest of thickets was too much, and I retired from his presence with the belief that my commanding general was a whipped man."[17]

A further indication of Hooker's distraction was an order he sent on the night of May 1 to detach the 16,000-man 1st Corps under John F. Reynolds from Sedgwick's command and to march it to Chancellorsville. This left Sedgwick with 24,000 men in his 6th Corps. Hooker thus abandoned the holding operation against the heights at Fredericksburg that he had originally planned. Now he was standing on the defensive at Chancellorsville. All thought of advance had vanished from his mind, though he commanded an army twice the size of the challenging force.

General Lee arrived on the afternoon of May 1. He rode out to the north to see if there was a chance of turning the Federal line in this direction, but Union troops were flowing over United States Ford, ruling out any move there.

Lee and Jackson met around 7:30 P.M. It was plain to both officers that they had only three choices—to assault frontally the Federal field fortifications around the crossroads, to go around them on the south, or to withdraw the whole army and retreat. Jackson sent off two engineers to examine the Union entrenchments. They reported back that they were entirely too strong to be carried by assault.

Just about this time, Jeb Stuart rode up and informed Lee and Jackson that his patrols had discovered that the Federal right was spread out along the Orange Turnpike west of Chancellorsville, and that it was facing south. Hooker expected no danger from the west. Accordingly his far-right corps, the 11th under Oliver O. Howard, made up mostly of German immigrants, had placed no troops and had built no field fortifications facing west. In the terminology of the time, Hooker's right flank was "floating in the air."

A windfall had materialized for the Confederacy. Jackson saw that if Rebel troops could swing all the way around Hooker's southern flank and emerge on the turnpike on the extreme west, they could drive straight east down the turnpike directly into the rear of the Union position at Chancellorsville. More important, they could then cut off all access to United States Ford three miles north, and place the Union army in an impossible position, with Rebel forces pressing on their rear while other Rebel forces held them in place in front of the crossroads. The Union host would be compelled to surrender.

Here was a potential tactical move that mirrored Jackson's strategic sweep around Pope's army to Manassas Junction, but with even greater implications. It was extremely unlikely that Hooker would expect a Confederate assault on his absolute rear, and a surprise assault there could dissolve his army.

It is clear from what happened subsequently that Jackson saw immediately the possibility of a massive strike on Hooker's rear. Whether Lee saw this same opportunity is unknown, because he never commented on it. But his failure to see a similar opportunity that Jackson had proposed against Pope's exposed eastern flank along the Rapidan River in August 1862 gives rise to wonder whether he saw the chance here. He most certainly did not propose it. All the decisions to follow were originated by Jackson.

We do not know precisely what transpired between Lee and Jackson, but Lee approved a swing around Hooker's southern flank, and appointed Jackson to carry it out. But where Jackson would strike and the forces he would employ were not decided on. Jackson rose, smiling, touched his cap, and said, "My troops will move at 4 o'clock."[18]

Early on the morning of Saturday, May 2, 1863, Jackson awoke from a short sleep and questioned his chaplain, Tucker Lacy, whose family owned land in the region, about a route to reach the far end of the Union line on the turnpike. Lacy remembered that Charles C. Wellford, owner of Catharine Furnace, lived a couple of miles southwest. Jackson called for his map maker, Jedediah Hotchkiss, to seek out Wellford. Hotchkiss and Lacy rode at once to Wellford's house and rousted him from bed. Wellford traced out on a map the course of a road he himself had recently opened through the Wilderness to haul cordwood and iron ore to his furnace. His adolescent son, Charles, knew the route well, Wellford said, and would serve as guide.[19]

When Hotchkiss returned, Jackson and Lee were conferring, each sitting on a cracker box from a pile discarded by the Federals. Hotchkiss pulled another cracker box between them, and spread out the map with Wellford's road marked on it. The two generals studied the map closely. At last, Lee said: "General Jackson, what do you propose to do?" Jackson replied: "Go around here," moving his finger over the road that Hotchkiss had marked. General Lee said: "What do you propose to make this movement with?" Jackson answered: "With my whole corps." Lee was startled by the answer, and responded, "What will you leave me?" Jackson replied: "The divisions of Anderson and McLaws." General Lee was silent for a few moments, then he said, "Well, go on." Jackson, with an eager smile on his face, rose, saluted, and said, "My men will move at once, sir."

This was the transcendent moment in the Civil War. The implications were prodigious: Jackson intended to advance directly into the Union rear and to sever the enemy's connections with United States Ford. The aim was the complete destruction of the major portion of the Army of the Potomac. The fate of the Confederacy hung by a hair. If the Army of Northern Virginia could not strike a pivotal blow against the enemy, it would be compelled to withdraw, with the great likelihood that it would be torn to pieces in a retreat. But Jackson had offered a spectacular alternative. Lee, for the first time, accepted a decisive movement proposed by Jackson that could win the war.

Jackson's end objective was United States Ford, in order to block this, the only retreat path for the Union army. Ideally his advance from the western end of the Union line should be straight northeast to the ford. But this way was barred because of the dense growth of the Wilderness and the absence of any direct roads there. Jackson's only access to the ford was right down the turnpike to Chancellorsville, then northward to United States Ford. Just west of the Chancellorsville crossroads the Bullock Road led northeast less than a mile to Chandlers or White House on the road leading to United States Ford. If the Confederates could get to Chandlers, they would block Hooker's main retreat route. From Chandlers they could push northeast for two more miles and block Mine Road, the only other route leading to the ford.

We know that this was Jackson's intention, because he expressed it precisely to his medical officer, Hunter McGuire, after the battle. McGuire wrote that "he told me that he intended, after breaking into Hooker's rear, to take and fortify a suitable position, cutting him off from the river and so hold him until, between himself and General Lee, the great Federal host should be broken to pieces. He had no fear. It was then that I heard him say, 'We sometimes fail to drive them from position, they always fail to drive us.' "[20]

The head of Jackson's column swung southward toward Catharine Furnace around 7:00 A.M. May 2, 1863. Jackson rode a short distance behind with his staff. Lee stood by the road to say good-bye. Jackson drew rein and they talked briefly. Jackson pointed ahead, Lee nodded, and Jackson rode on. One of the greatest marches in the history of warfare had begun.

The actual move around Hooker's army was largely uneventful for the soldiers of Jackson's corps. It was a hard trek of twelve miles along narrow dirt roads cut through the forest. There was little dust because of recent rains. Stuart's horsemen shielded the corps from any disturbances from Union troops.

The forces left with Lee, about 18,000 men, commenced demonstrations to deceive the Federals into believing an attack was coming on their entrenchments around Chancellorsville. Even so, the Federals discovered Jackson's march soon after it started. David B. Birney, commanding a division in Daniel Sickles's 3rd Corps, had placed forces on a cleared elevation known as Hazel Grove, a little over a mile southwest of Chancellorsville. Around 8:00 A.M. observers there reported passage of a long column heading southwest on the Furnace Road, about a mile and a quarter south of Hazel Grove.

Birney related the movement to Hooker, who decided the Confederates were retreating toward Gordonsville. He sent a warning to Henry W. Slocum, commanding 12th Corps, and Oliver O. Howard, commanding the 13,000-man 11th Corps, about a possible attack from their south. Hooker didn't regard the danger as great, and neither Slocum nor Howard gave it much attention. Birney ordered a Union battery on Hazel Grove to fire on the spot on the road where the Rebel column was visible, but the distance was so great that the shells did no damage, although the firing caused Jackson's wagons to be diverted to the unexposed Catharpin Road a bit south. Around noon Hooker authorized Sickles to advance on Catharine Furnace to attack Lee's "trains." Birney and Amiel W. Whipple's divisions moved forward, but were checked by Carnot Posey's Mississippi brigade of Richard Anderson's division, posted just east of the furnace. The 21st Georgia Regiment defended the actual furnace.

After marching to the end of the Furnace Road, three and a half miles southwest of the Orange Plank Road, Jackson's column turned northwest on the Brock Road (present-day Virginia Route 613). About

1:00 P.M. troopers of the 2nd Virginia Cavalry rode east on the Orange Plank Road and discovered the right of the 11th Corps' line. Troopers reported this to Fitz Lee, and he, with Jackson, rode on the Plank Road to an elevated point southwest of Dowdall's Tavern, near the junction of the Plank Road with the Orange Turnpike. There they saw that the Union entrenchments lay a few hundred yards away, facing south.

Jackson had planned to turn up the Plank Road, thinking the western end of Howard's corps was farther east. But since it continued on west, Jackson kept his corps marching on the Brock Road for another mile and a half to the turnpike. There he turned the column back east, certain he would be beyond the farthest western Federal element.

While Jackson was finishing his march around Hooker, General Sickles decided he could break the Confederate column, which he and Hooker believed was retreating toward Gordonsville. He surrounded the 21st Georgia at the furnace, and captured most of the members. But, fearing Rebel rear guards would be on the alert, he called for reinforcements. Accordingly, Hooker told Howard to send Francis C. Barlow's 1,500-man brigade to the furnace.

Thus Howard's corps was reduced to 11,500 men. It was spread out for nearly two miles along the Orange Turnpike. Most troops faced south, though a small part of the most westerly force, two regiments of Leopold von Gilsa's brigade from Charles Devens's division, were facing west. They were behind a weak abatis of small felled trees and bushes. This emplacement was just north of the turnpike and a little more than a mile west of Dowdall's Tavern. With these two regiments were two cannons deployed to fire on the road, not to the west. Another regiment, the 75th Ohio, was some distance east of von Gilsa, in reserve. The remainder of Devens's divison was on either side of

Talley's house and farm, three-quarters of a mile west of Dowdall's Tavern, and this force was facing south along the pike.

About a quarter of a mile east of the Talley farmstead was the Hawkins farm, on cleared high ground. Here was Carl Schurz's two brigade division. Most of this division also faced south, but two regiments of Alexander Schimmelfennig's brigade faced west, also shielded by a weak abatis.

The final brigade, commanded by Adolphus Buschbeck, of Adolph von Steinwehr's division, was facing south at Dowdall's Tavern, where a considerable area was clear of trees. Here a shallow shelter trench or ditch ran several hundred yards, just north of the road, with several cannons behind it. The trench, however, was unoccupied.

Between Howard's 11th Corps and Slocum's 12th Corps around Chancellorsville was a mile of unoccupied ground, previously held by Barlow's brigade, now marching to the aid of Sickles. Below Catharine Furnace were two divisions of Sickles's corps, Barlow's brigade, and one regiment of Alfred Pleasonton's cavalry, perhaps 16,000 men, who believed they were pursuing Lee's fleeing army.

In summary, two weak lines of Howard's corps faced west, but most of his men and guns were facing south. Sickles's corps was so far south as to be beyond the fight. The remainder of Hooker's army faced largely east or south around Chancellorsville, defending against Lee's two divisions, and was in no position to block Chancellorsville from the rear. Only one division, Hiram G. Berry's of Sickles's corps, was in the vicinity of the crossroads and might be called on in an emergency.

Jackson's aim was to move eastward along the turnpike, roll up Howard's 11th Corps, and drive it into the rear of the corps of Couch, Sickles, and Slocum. His primary aim was to get to the crossroads of Chandlers, just north of Chancellorsville. Jackson deployed his men. In the first line went Robert E. Rodes's division. In the second line,

200 yards back, was Raleigh E. Colston's division. Behind, partly in column, came A. P. Hill's division.

The main Rebel thrust was going to be made by three brigades of Rodes's division near the turnpike—George Doles's Georgia brigade, lined up just south of the road; Edward A. O'Neal's Alabama brigade, just north, and Alfred Iverson's North Carolina brigade to O'Neal's left or north. On the right or south, in the first line was Alfred H. Colquitt's Georgia brigade. Behind and a bit to the south was S. Dodson Ramseur's North Carolina brigade. A short distance farther south was E. P. Paxton's Stonewall Brigade of Colston's division, positioned to march straight up the Plank Road to Dowdall's Tavern as the assault lines moved out. Paxton's job was to clear out any Union detachments that might be south of the main line along the turnpike.

Neither Colquitt's, Ramseur's, nor Paxton's brigade was likely to face many Union forces. But their advance would lead over Hazel Grove and Fairview, an elevated, open area about two-thirds of a mile southwest of Chancellorsville. These heights were the only places where significant numbers of cannons could be mounted, and their capture would imperil Hooker's entire position. Also, seizure of Hazel Grove would split Sickles's large force from Hooker's main body, and probably lead to its surrender.

Jackson, of course, did not realize the significance of Fairview and Hazel Grove at the moment, but he was cautious enough to insist on his troops pushing resolutely ahead and not allowing anything to hold them up, even disorder in their ranks. Under no circumstance was there to be a pause.

About 5:15 P.M., Jackson released his eager soldiers. They descended like a storm on the Union army, which only became aware of danger when stirred up deer, wild turkeys, foxes, and rabbits ran in fright through the Union positions.

Doles's Georgians encountered von Gilsa's soldiers just as they were preparing their evening meal. The surprised Federals hastily formed a line of battle, but Doles's troops unleashed three quick volleys, and smashed right into the position, sending the Union soldiers flying in panic. The other regiments of von Gilsa's brigade, facing south, disintegrated without firing a shot. A few Union soldiers rallied around the 75th Ohio, but its members, seeing the wide sweep of the Confederate column advancing on them, turned and fled. The vast bulk of Devens's division abandoned their positions and ran headlong down the turnpike toward Chancellorsville. General Howard watched the disaster unfold from the elevation around Dowdall's Tavern. "More quickly than it could be told," he wrote, "with all the fury of the wildest hailstorm, everything, every sort of organization that lay in the path of the mad current of panic-stricken men had to give way and be broken into fragments." Howard's aide was struck dead by a shot, and Howard's horse sprang up on its hind legs and fell over, throwing Howard to the ground.[21]

As Rodes's three brigades pressed eagerly toward Dowdall's Tavern, Colquitt, on the south side of the pike, advanced only a few hundred yards, then halted in direct disobedience of orders. Another case of Clausewitzian friction occurred: Colquitt had gotten a report of Federals on his southern flank. He had been informed that Paxton's brigade was positioned to deal with any Federals in that direction, but he stopped anyway. Ramseur assured Colquitt that he would take care of any Federals who appeared, and at last Colquitt moved on. But three brigades, 5,000 men, had been delayed by the foolish fear of one man. This delay prevented the Confederates from seizing Hazel Grove and Fairview and severing Sickles's large force from the main army. After the battle, Lee shipped the disgraced Colquitt south, swapping his brigade for a North Carolina outfit.

The final Union force in front of Jackson was Buschbeck's at Dowdall's Tavern. Seeing the rout to the west of them, Buschbeck's men had moved into the shallow trench and were facing westward. But they were extremely frightened by the huge Confederate force descending on them. When a sheet of Rebel fire struck the men in the trench, the survivors vacated the position, many throwing away their arms, and the whole force joined in the chaotic crowd of men, horses, cannons, and wagons rushing down the turnpike toward Chancellorsville.

Hooker did not get word of the disaster until around 6:30 P.M., when one of his aides, Captain Harry Russell, hearing violent noise outside Chancellor house, rushed from the veranda to the road and turned his glass westward. "My God, here they come!" he shouted. Russell thought the fleeing soldiers were part of Sickles's corps, not Howard's. It was only when Hooker and his aides grabbed some of the fleeing men that they discovered the truth.[22]

The scene caused Hooker nearly to panic. He feared that Sickles's entire corps was in jeopardy, and immediately sent word to him to save his command if he could. Hooker thought of retreating and leaving Sickles's 3rd Corps to its fate. Here was solid evidence that, if Colquitt had not stopped, Confederates could have quickly occupied Hazel Grove and Fairview and sealed off the retreat path of the Union corps.[23]

With victory almost in sight, General Rodes, a mile and a half west of Chancellorsville, stopped his advancing division because it was getting disorganized, despite the fact that it was advancing steadily and was no longer facing any real opposition. Here was Clausewitzian friction carried to disastrous lengths. In direct defiance of Jackson's orders, Rodes sent word to bring forward A. P. Hill's division, while he took his division back to Dowdall's Tavern to re-form. Rodes's catastrophic action occurred at precisely the culminating moment in the assault—just before the crossroads at Chancellorsville had been seized, and the just before complete success had been achieved. Darkness was falling, and it was imperative to reach and seize Chandlers crossroads while it could be easily located. Rodes's halt gave the Federals just enough time to take a breath and organize a defense. It took A. P. Hill until nightfall to bring up any troops.

Hooker had two brigades of Hiram Berry's division in the vicinity of Chancellor house and ordered them to move westward at once to halt Jackson. It was a stern test of the division's discipline, but the brigades advanced through the stream of refugees.

Captain T. W. Osborn, chief of Berry's artillery, wrote afterward: "As we passed General Hooker's headquarters [Chancellor house], a scene burst upon us which God grant may never again be seen in the Federal army of the United States. The 11th Corps had been routed and were fleeing to the river like scared sheep. The men and artillery filled the road, its sides and the skirts of the field, and it appeared that no two or one company could be found together. Aghast and terror-stricken, heads bare and panting for breath, they pleaded like infants at the mother's breast that we should let them pass to the rear unhindered."[24]

Around 8:00 P.M., Berry's brigades began entrenching half a mile west of the Chancellor house and just north of the open elevation of Fairview, where twenty Federal artillery pieces were being unlimbered. Alpheus Williams's division from Slocum's 12th Corps arrived soon after, and extended Berry's line southward in front of Fairview to protect the guns.

Meantime, Sickles's men rushed northward behind Pleasonton's cavalry to occupy Hazel Grove. There Pleasonton drew up a number of artillery pieces and organized a defense. The guns discouraged any effort by the Confederates nearby to seize the elevation, and Pleasonton's defense reconnected Sickles's corps with the rest of the Union army.

A. P. Hill was able to get forward the North Carolina brigade of James Lane, but it was 8:45 P.M. before the brigade was lined up on

SUCH TROOPS AS THESE

either side of the Orange Turnpike a mile west of Chancellorsville. Other elements of the division were coming forward. Stonewall Jackson had now arrived. Although it was dark, the night was clear with a full moon, giving sufficient light to move. Moreover, the Union soldiers were thoroughly demoralized, and could have offered little resistance. Jackson intended first to send Lane's brigade straight east to reconnect with Lee. Thus he told Lane around 9:00 P.M.: "Push right ahead, Lane, right ahead." Jackson planned to send other parts of Hill's division northeast to seize Chandlers crossroads by way of Bullock Road, which ran directly to it from Lane's position.

Shortly thereafter A. P. Hill arrived, and Jackson gave him his orders: "Press them; cut them off from the United States Ford, Hill; press them." Hill responded that he and his staff were unfamiliar with the locale, and Jackson turned to Captain J. Keith Boswell, his chief engineer, who was well acquainted with the roads and paths of the Wilderness. He told Boswell to show Hill the way.[25]

A short time previously, Union General Pleasonton had ordered the 8th Pennsylvania Cavalry to charge the enemy. This was a hopeless undertaking in the tangled Wilderness, and the lead squadron collided with part of Lane's line on the turnpike. A trooper in the charge, John L. Collins, wrote: "We struck it as a wave strikes a stately ship; the ship is staggered, but the wave is dashed into spray; and the ship sails on as before."[26] The major who led the charge, the captain in command of the leading squadron, the adjutant, and a few score of their followers all went down together. The detail sent to recover the bodies after the battle found that the major had thirteen bullets in his body, the adjutant nine, and the others fewer. The attack collapsed, but riderless horses and horseless riders rushed about in the dark woods for some time.

Lane's soldiers were still alert from the cavalry charge when Jackson, with Boswell, Hill, and a couple aides, rode forward through Lane's brigade to search out the road that Hill's troops could take to

Chandlers. The party was only sixty or eighty yards ahead of where Lane's 18th North Carolina was standing. At that moment a single rifle shot rang out. A detachment of Federal infantry, groping through the thickets, had approached Lane's brigade. The rifle shot startled the Rebel soldiers, and Jackson, hearing the shot, turned with his party back to the Confederate lines. An officer of the 18th North Carolina, seeing a group of horsemen riding toward him, thought they were Federals, and gave the order to fire. The volley was fearfully effective. Captain Boswell and an orderly were struck dead. Jackson received three bullets, one in the right hand, and two in the left arm, cutting the main artery and crushing the bone below the shoulder. Jackson managed to reach the turnpike, where Confederate officers grabbed him as he fell off the horse and swiftly applied a tourniquet to the bleeding arm. Jedediah Hotchkiss rushed off to alert Hunter McGuire, and three aides carried Jackson to an ambulance that took him to the field hospital at Dowdall's Tavern. Early on the morning of Sunday, May 3, 1863, McGuire operated on Jackson, amputating his left arm.[27]

A. P. Hill had not been hit by the regiment's volley, and he assumed command of the corps. But riding back to his troops, Hill was wounded by a shell fragment. This was a disastrous turn of events, because Hill was the only general who knew of Jackson's plan to move to Chandlers, and Keith Boswell, who also knew, had been killed. Hill, from a litter, sent a courier to notify Jeb Stuart, at the moment at Ely's Ford on the Rapidan, that he was senior commander and was now in command.

Stuart did not arrive at Chancellorsville until shortly before midnight. He was intensely aware of the confusion caused by the wounding of Jackson and Hill, and he suspended operations until daylight. Stuart may have been aware in general terms of Jackson's intention to seal off the United States Ford, but he had not been informed of the details and he had no one to tell him. Stuart was far and away the best cut-and-thrust cavalry leader in either army, but he knew little of infantry tactics, and less of strategy.

Stuart saw as his first priority reestablishing contact with Lee's forces. In doing so, he abandoned Jackson's primary purpose of cutting off the Union army's retreat. So Jackson's great goal of destroying the largest part of the Union army had irretrievably failed. Lee doubtless knew Jackson's plan, but he abandoned it immediately after getting the shocking news of Jackson's wounding early on May 3. He sent a message to Stuart: "It is all-important that you still continue pressing to the right [toward Lee], turning, if possible, all the fortified points in order that we can unite both wings of the army."[28]

This was surely the right decision. Lee knew that Jeb Stuart was not the officer to carry out a bold movement to seal off United States Ford. The safest course for the Confederate army, after the disaster of Jackson's wounding, was to get it back together again.

Now transpired a sensational example of why generals who can *see* are so immensely important in the conduct of war. One of the primary characteristics of great generals—and this was especially the mark of Stonewall Jackson—is that they achieve tremendous results by the use of brainpower, not shedding their soldiers' blood. Jackson's rolling up of the 11th Corps had cost very few Confederate casualties, and, though the Union corps had collapsed in chaos, very few Union soldiers had died. What now took place was an operation that was the exact opposite of the application of intelligence to battle. This resulted in hideous casualties and the wiping away of many of the brilliant gains that Jackson had just achieved.

The problem Stuart faced was breaking through a long Union defensive line that Hooker had established around Chancellorsville. This line had been hastily but effectively fortified with trenches, banked up earth and tree trucks to form bulletproof parapets, and abatis of trees and heavy branches to stop the advance of attacking forces. All the reasons why frontal attacks were almost bound to fail with terrible losses were concentrated in these works. They were the fruit of nearly two years of intense warfare during which soldiers had learned about the lethality of canister-firing cannons and Minié-ball rifles, and about the immense shielding power of field fortifications.

It was becoming painfully apparent that only direct hits by artillery could damage or break these field fortifications. The fact that Burnside had been unable to bring artillery to bear on the Sunken Road at Fredericksburg on December 13, 1862, accounted for the total failure of his fourteen direct assaults and the loss of thousands of men.

Now Stuart faced a similar problem. He had, however, the assistance of Colonel Porter Alexander, the senior artillery officer on the west and already becoming famous for his knowledge and use of artillery. Before the morning of May 3, 1863, Stuart told Alexander to scout out possible artillery sites in the thickets of the Wilderness. Alexander spotted the importance of Hazel Grove the moment he saw it. He perceived that the elevation could be used by his guns to bombard the Federal artillery that had been massed at Fairview, three-quarters of a mile to the northeast. If these Union guns could be silenced, Hooker's defensive line around Chancellorsville on the west and south would be gravely weakened.

Accordingly, Alexander saw that seizing Hazel Grove was the critical objective of the Confederates. He was astonished, therefore, when he discovered that Hooker had so missed the importance of the elevation that, early on May 3, he withdrew Sickles from Hazel Grove, which he had been holding with two divisions and five artillery batteries. "There has rarely been a more gratuitous gift of a battlefield," Alexander wrote.[29]

The Rebels secured Hazel Grove before 7:00 A.M., and Alexander quickly crowned the plateau with forty cannons. These, plus twenty more he emplaced on the Orange Turnpike, converged their fire on the forty Union guns at Fairview. Although most of the Federal guns were entrenched, the Rebel cannons quickly beat them down. The Rebels were so successful because the Federal guns ran out of ammunition, and Hooker did not order up additional shells.

As this titanic artillery duel was going on, Stuart launched an infantry assault against the entire Federal line on the west. The attacks were some of the bloodiest and most violently contested in the entire Civil War. A few of the Federal entrenchments were shallow but all were much better than men standing exposed. Rebel determination was so great that defending Federals suffered heavily as well. There were few instances in the war where the casualties sustained in so brief a period exceeded those on Stuart's front on May 3, 1863. Stuart lost 30 percent of the men he had engaged, and overall the attacks failed, although the Federals at last withdrew toward United States Ford.[30] Two reasons contributed to why the Federals retreated: Hooker did not reinforce the troops on the line, though he had 30,000 men in reserve, and he did not replenish the soldiers' ammunition, and they ran out of bullets.[31]

On several occasions, veteran Confederate soldiers and officers refused to advance into the maelstrom. Even more remarkable, a number of Federal officers commanding regiments and brigades abandoned their positions and marched their troops off the battlefield without orders. One such commander was court-martialed, but there were so many cases of such conduct that Lincoln revoked the sentence and let the officer retire.[32]

This was exactly the wrong way to break a long line of enemy fortifications. Stuart should not have attacked the whole Union western front at the same time, a guarantee that the Union soldiers could inflict maximum casualties on the Rebels. He should have selected a single point on the south, where Alexander's guns on Hazel Grove were massed, and he should have battered the point with shellfire until it was weakened or destroyed. Then he should have launched a small infantry force against this single weak point. At all the other places on the line, he should have made threats or feint attacks, but not subjected his soldiers to death and mayhem. This would have broken the entire Union line, forced precipitate retreat, and achieved the same results with only a tiny fraction of the casualties Stuart actually sustained.

The principle of concentrating force at a single crucial location was not a new idea. Napoleon Bonaparte had expressed it clearly over a half century previously: "It is the same with strategy as with the siege of a fortress: concentrate your fire against a single point, and once the wall is breached, all of the rest becomes worthless and the fortress is captured."[33] But when officers don't know or don't understand the rules of war, disasters, like those ordered by Stuart, occur.

Union General John Sedgwick finally moved on the morning of May 3. Sedgwick had 24,000 men facing Jubal Early's small division on Prospect Hill. Sedgwick could easily have swung around the hill at Hamilton's Crossing, turned Early's entire position, forced Early to flee or surrender, then struck straight for Lee's rear. But this did not occur to him. Instead, joined by John Gibbon's 6,000-man division that crossed over from Falmouth, he marched up the plain and assaulted frontally the same Sunken Road below Marye's Heights that had ruined Ambrose Burnside's offensive in December 1862.

It was almost unbelievable. John Bigelow Jr., noted historian of the Chancellorsville campaign, wrote: "The result was the singular spectacle of a body of troops practically on the enemy's flank moving to the enemy's front in order to attack him."[34]

Sedgwick now faced only a single Confederate brigade on the Sunken Road, however, William Barksdale's Mississippians. The first Federal assaults failed miserably, the Union forces losing 1,000 men in less than five minutes. Then another example of Clausewitzian friction occurred—Thomas M. Griffin, the commander of one of the regiments in the Sunken Road, the 18th Mississippi, foolishly agreed to a cease-fire to allow the Federals to remove their dead and wounded. The Union officers were able to observe how few Rebels were defending the Sunken Road. The Federals now attacked again in heavy force and either killed or captured all the Confederates in the Sunken Road, then moved onto Marye's Heights and seized the artillery there. Barksdale's few remaining troops fled the field.[35]

Early withdrew down the Telegraph Road toward Richmond to protect the RF&P Railroad. Only Cadmus M. Wilcox's Alabama brigade of Anderson's division, guarding Banks Ford, was in position to challenge Sedgwick. But Sedgwick took so long organizing a strike west on the Orange Plank Road and Turnpike that Wilcox was able to build a strong defensive line six miles east of Chancellorsville at Salem Church.

Porter Alexander wrote: "I have always felt surprise that the enemy retained Sedgwick as a corps commander after that day, for he seems to me to have wasted great opportunities, and come about as near to doing nothing with 30,000 men as it was easily possible to do. He gave his men a rest after taking Marye's Hill, and when he did advance it was so cautiously done that Wilcox's Alabama brigade alone delayed him until about 5 o'clock in getting to Salem Church—about four miles only from Fredericksburg."[36]

McLaws's division came up to help Wilcox. Sedgwick had more than twice as many soldiers as Wilcox and McLaws, but he remained immobile on May 4, giving Lee the opportunity to organize a converging assault that drove Sedgwick across Banks Ford by early evening.

On the night of May 5–6, Hooker took advantage of a huge storm to pull his entire force north of the Rappahannock. He marched his beaten army back to Falmouth, and Lee returned to the heights west of Fredericksburg. The Confederates had won, but their casualties were astronomical. Not only had Stonewall Jackson been lost, but—

because of the insane attacks by Stuart on May 3—they lost as many men in battle as the Federals: 1,683 dead to 1,574 Union dead, and 9,277 wounded to 9,554 Union wounded. The Rebels suffered fewer missing, 2,196, than the Federals, 5,711, but many of these were captured.[37]

Late on May 3, 1863, Stonewall Jackson, revived after Hunter McGuire's operation that amputated his left arm, sent orders to find Lieutenant Joseph Morrison and send him to Richmond to bring Anna, his sister and Jackson's wife, to his side. On Monday, May 4, accompanied by McGuire, Jackson was moved by ambulance to a small office building at Thomas and Mary Chandler's home, just north of Guiney Station on the RF&P Railroad.[38]

Late on Tuesday, May 5, Lieutenant Morrison finally reached his sister, who was staying with friends, Susan Hoge and Elizabeth Brown, at the Moses H. Hoge home adjacent to the Second Presbyterian Church on Fifth Street in central Richmond. Anna made plans to go to Jackson as soon as arrangements could be made.

Early on Thursday, May 7, Jackson awoke with discomfort, and McGuire soon found that he had contracted pneumonia, an extremely dangerous ailment given medical knowledge at the time. Anna reached Jackson at noon, accompanied by Morrison, the baby, and a nurse. McGuire called in all doctors he could reach for advice, but Jackson's condition had greatly worsened by Saturday, May 9, and on Sunday, May 10, with his grieving wife by his side, Jackson slipped into a deep coma. In his last hours Jackson's mind wandered back to battle, and he called out: "Order A.P. Hill to prepare for action! Pass the infantry to the front! Tell Major Hawks—" He became silent for a while, then said quietly and clearly, "Let us cross over the river and rest under the shade of the trees." Stonewall Jackson was dead.

General Lee sent a formal announcement to the secretary of war: "It becomes my melancholy duty to announce to you the death of

General Jackson. He expired at 3:15 P.M. His body will be conveyed to Richmond in the train tomorrow, under charge of Major [Alexander] Pendleton [an aide]. Please direct an escort of honor to meet it at the depot."[39]

The news utterly stunned the South. His passing was a complete tragedy, a personal loss felt by almost the entire population. Women were seen on the streets of Richmond wringing their hands and weeping bitterly. A young Lexington girl stated somberly that Jackson's passing "was the first time it had dawned on us that God would let us be defeated."[40]

On Monday, May 11, a locomotive and a single car carried Jackson's remains, in a simple pine box, with Anna, the baby, the nurse, and a small escort of Jackson's staff officers, to Richmond. There all businesses closed, and a deep silence hung over the capital. The train stopped in the suburbs, and Governor Letcher's wife and some other ladies took Anna, the baby, and the nurse by carriage through quiet backstreets to the governor's mansion. The train continued on down the middle of Broad Street past enormous crowds to the station at Eighth and Broad streets. A hearse carried the body to the nearby governor's mansion, built in 1813 on the northeastern corner of Capitol Square. There the body was embalmed and opened for viewing by distinguished visitors on a flower-draped bier in the governor's reception room.

The next day, Tuesday, May 12, a funeral procession proceeded on a roundabout journey through central Richmond back to the capitol, completed in 1788 and designed by Thomas Jefferson on the model of an ancient Roman temple, the Maison Carrée, at Nîmes in southern France. There the casket was placed in the old Senate chamber. More than 20,000 people filed by the casket. Early the next morning, Wednesday, May 13, the body was moved back to the governor's mansion for a private memorial. There the Reverend Thomas V. Moore of the

First Presbyterian Church in Richmond gave the eulogy. A military guard now escorted the casket, family, and friends, including Governor Letcher and his wife, to the Virginia Central Railroad depot. A train carried the funeral party to Gordonsville, where the cars were shifted to the Orange & Alexandria Railroad, and traveled to Lynchburg. There the town's population waited in grief. An evening service was held at the Lynchburg First Presbyterian Church.

Early Thursday morning, May 14, the final stage of the journey began. On the canal boat *Marshall* the body and the funeral party were pulled by two mules up the James River Canal to Balcony Falls, where the boat turned onto the north fork of the James (now the Maury River) and traveled on to Lexington.

The entire cadet corps of Virginia Military Institute met the boat. With reversed arms and muffled drums, the corps escorted the casket to Jackson's old classroom, where it lay in state all night, guarded by cadets at the head and foot of the coffin. On the morning of Friday, May 15, Jackson's body was placed on a caisson draped in black, and carried to the Lexington Presbyterian Church, where Jackson was a member. A crowd of 4,000 people packed the church and grounds. The pastor, Dr. William S. White, conducted the service.

Emmett McCorkle, a small boy at the time, wrote later: "A whole community in tears with every breast bursting with grief. When the old soldiers emerged from the church bearing the body, men whose cheeks had never blanched in battle were wet with weeping." A daughter of Jackson's friend John Preston, wrote: "We were not in any sense spectators, we were heart-broken mourners, a clan bereft of its chieftain, a country in peril, from whom its defender had been snatched."[41]

Led by the cadet corps, a procession moved up South Main Street to the cemetery. Graveside rites were brief. Jackson was buried beside his first daughter and not far from his first wife, Ellie, and his stillborn son.

Anna Morrison Jackson returned with her baby to her father's home in Lincoln County, north of Charlotte, North Carolina, where, at the age of thirty-one, she created a new life from the ruins of her shattered old one. She became one of the most popular persons in the country, devoting her energies both to motherhood and to patriotic pursuits. She urged her friend Robert Lewis Dabney to write a biography of Jackson, which appeared in 1866, and twenty years later she produced her own book of memoirs. She became an honorary life president of the United Daughters of the Confederacy, and she traveled widely, meeting five United States presidents. She died on March 24, 1915, in Charlotte of pneumonia, and she was buried in Lexington beside her husband.

Julia Jackson, an infant when her father died, had a tragically short life. She married William E. Christian in Richmond at the age of twenty-two, and produced two children, Julia Jackson Christian (1887–1991) and Thomas Jonathan Jackson Christian (1888–1952). Julia herself died of typhoid fever in 1889 when she was twenty-six.

EPILOGUE

———•———

The Cause Lost

Stonewall Jackson had recognized that the way to achieve success in war is to strike where the enemy is *not*. Jackson also recognized that the way to avoid making deadly, futile frontal attacks against an enemy is to induce the enemy to make these attacks, and for the Confederates to remain on the defensive. These two insights were the essence of Jackson's intellectual breakthrough. Jackson had tried four times but had failed to convince the Confederate leadership to follow his first principle of avoiding enemy strength and striking at weakness by invading the North. He had also tried four times to convince Robert E. Lee to place the Confederate army in positions to force the Federal army to attack and be defeated. Three times he had failed to do so. A single time, at Second Manassas, he had maneuvered the Union commander, John Pope, into attacking his virtually insurmountable position and thereby losing badly. But Lee had not exploited this defeat by striking Pope's exposed flank in time, and most of Pope's army had gotten safely away.

At Chancellorsville, the Confederacy faced imminent peril of dissolution by Joe Hooker's unanticipated descent on Lee's left flank with a force greater than the entire Rebel army. In this dire situation Lee at last agreed to follow Jackson's concept of striking all the way around to the enemy's rear and cutting off his means of retreat. This was a way to destroy the vast bulk of the Union army. Jackson's sweep was just at the moment of achieving complete success when he was struck down by a mistaken volley from his own troops. No one else was present to carry out Jackson's plan, and the culminating blow was not delivered. However, the principles Jackson employed there could be applied everywhere: the Confederate army should find an easily defensible site with at least one open flank, and either induce the enemy to attack, or threaten the enemy with attack. If the enemy attacked, the assaults would fail, demoralizing the enemy forces. If the enemy feared an attack, he would keep his main forces in place in a defensive stance. At Second Manassas, Jackson had induced John Pope to attack. At Chancellorsville, he had pushed Joe Hooker back into the Wilderness and aroused his deep fear of attack. In both cases, the enemy flank was exposed and vulnerable. In both cases, the Confederates could swing around on the Union rear and force the Federals to flee in chaos or surrender.

Chancellorsville had taught James Longstreet, slow learner that he was, the validity of this argument. He had seen that Confederate attacks against strongly defended Union positions had led to disaster, and he sought to get Lee's agreement to avoid making such attacks in the future. "Our numbers were less than the Federal forces," Longstreet wrote, "and our resources were limited while theirs were not. The time had come when it was imperative that the skill of generals and the strategy and tactics of war should take the place of muscle against muscle."[1]

Longstreet reminded Lee that at Fredericksburg 5,000 Confederates at Marye's Heights had beaten two-thirds of the entire Federal army. Jackson's concept of defending, not attacking, was now widespread in the Confederate army. Porter Alexander, Longstreet's brilliant artillery chief, remarked: "When all our corps were together, what could successfully attack us?"[2]

Immediately after Chancellorsville, Longstreet approached Lee and asked him to agree not to go on the offensive, and to maintain a defensive posture. Longstreet believed that he had gotten Lee's agreement to follow this policy in the future.[3]

Lee now decided to invade the North and seek a decision in the war. To disguise his intent, he dissembled to Jefferson Davis, saying he wanted to tap the abundant food sources of the North.

Lee reorganized the Army of Northern Virginia, creating three corps, one under Longstreet, another under Richard Ewell, and a third under A. P. Hill. He launched the army northward on June 10, 1863, with Ewell's corps leading the way, and Albert G. Jenkins's 1,600-man cavalry brigade scouting ahead of the army.[4]

Avoiding the Union army guarding Washington, Lee's forces moved into the Cumberland Valley of Maryland and Pennsylvania. Jenkins's cavalry nearly reached the Pennsylvania capital of Harrisburg when Ewell's leading elements seized Carlisle, twenty miles west of Harrisburg, on June 27. Meanwhile, Jubal Early's division pressed through York to Wrightsville on the Susquehanna River, about thirty miles southeast of Harrisburg.

The Army of the Potomac was far to the south, and was in the process of changing leaders. Lincoln ousted Joe Hooker and put George G. Meade in his place on June 28. Because the Federals had been so slow to respond, Lee had achieved a splendid strategic position. He was deep into the North and could move in any direction, while Meade could do little more than react to Lee's actions.

Lee had two especially compelling strategic options. He could

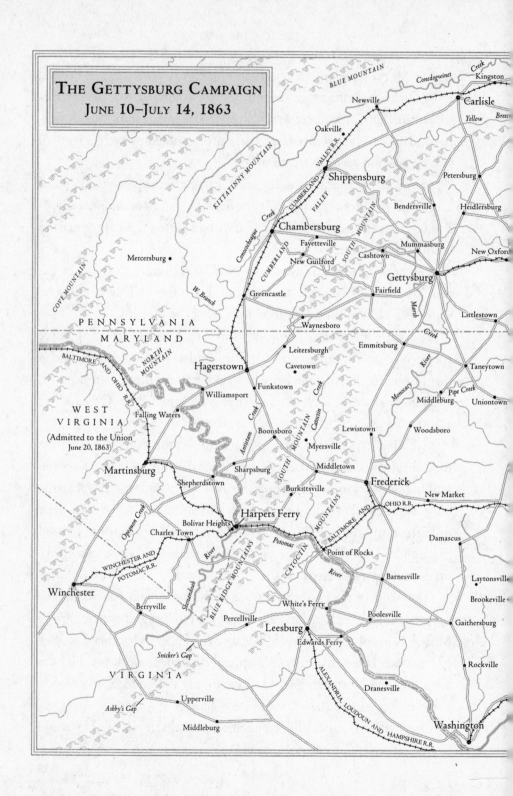

THE GETTYSBURG CAMPAIGN
JUNE 10–JULY 14, 1863

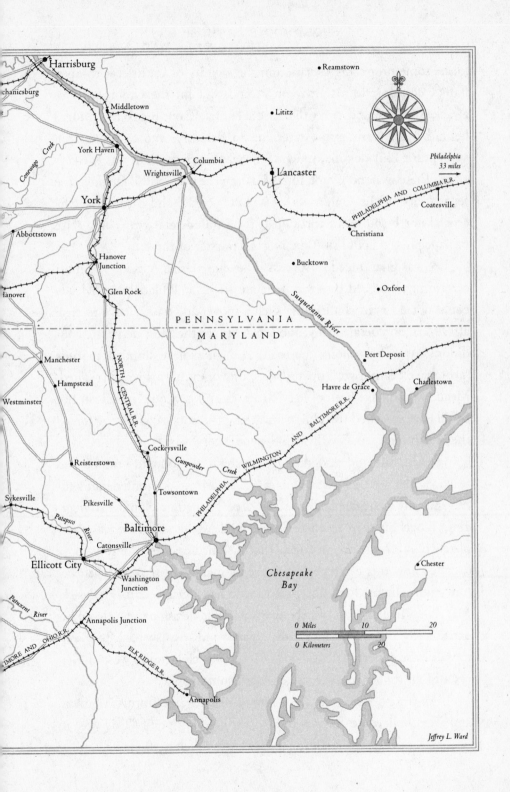

Reamstown

Harrisburg

chanicsburg

Middletown

Lititz

*Philadelphia
33 miles*

York Haven

Columbia

Wrightsville

Lancaster

PHILADELPHIA AND COLUMBIA R.R.

Coatesville

York

Christiana

Abbottstown

Hanover
Junction

Bucktown

Oxford

anover

Glen Rock

PENNSYLVANIA

Susquehanna River

MARYLAND

Manchester

Port Deposit

Hampstead

Havre de Grace

Charlestown

Westminster

NORTH CENTRAL R.R.

WILMINGTON AND BALTIMORE R.R.

Cockeysville

Gunpowder Creek

Reisterstown

Sykesville

Towsontown

PHILADELPHIA,

Pikesville

Patapsco River

Baltimore

Catonsville

Chester

Ellicott City

*Chesapeake
Bay*

Washington
Junction

Patuxent River

Annapolis Junction

IMORE AND OHIO R.R.

ELK RIDGE R.R.

0 Miles   10   20

0 Kilometers   20

Annapolis

Jeffrey L. Ward

locate some promising elevation in the vicinity of Carlisle, with open flanks, concentrate his army on it, and wait for the Union army to attack. Or he could cross the Susquehanna River, break the bridges behind him, turning the river into a defensive moat, and march straight for Philadelphia, to which he was far closer than was Meade's army. There were no Union forces barring the way to Philadelphia, the second city of the Union with 600,000 people, and directly on the crucial north-south rail corridor. If the Confederate army could seize Philadelphia, it could stop the North's pursuit of the war.

Lee was guaranteed of success if he chose either option. The most certain of all would be a Confederate strike at Philadelphia. Meade could not delay in challenging such a move, and would have to rush after the Confederate army, and attack under the most desperate conditions. Anywhere along the road, Lee could have stopped at some favorable elevation with open flanks, drawn up his army, and waited. Meade would have been obliged to attack and he would have lost. Lee could have scattered the Union army, and the South could have forced the North to accept Southern independence.

Yet Lee did not recognize the strategic position his troops had reached. The advances were due to the enterprise of Confederate officers, not any strategic plan devised by Lee. He had no plan, no strategic aim. When his men reached Carlisle and Wrightsville, he was completely blind to the opportunities that they had opened to him.

We know this is true because, the moment he discovered, just before midnight on June 28, that Meade had advanced to Frederick, Maryland, he made almost the worst possible decision: he ordered his entire army to give up its strategic gains and to rush back to Cashtown, at the eastern foot of South Mountain, eight miles west of Gettysburg, in the far southern reaches of Pennsylvania.[5]

Lee's troops were twenty to forty miles distant from Cashtown, and were obliged to force-march to the rallying point. This was an exhausting and disorienting task for the troops, and no one knew what was waiting for them at Cashtown. If, instead, Lee had concentrated at Carlisle, the Union army would have required days to reach the Rebel army, while Lee would have had plenty of time to organize a march on Philadelphia, or select a readily defensible position near Carlisle that Meade could not have assailed successfully.

Instead, Lee marched *toward* the Union army, throwing away the precious advantages of space and time, making the distance separating the armies much shorter, and rendering the approach for the Union soldiers far easier and less strenuous. In other words, Lee abandoned all of his advantages, placed all of the effort and burden on his own soldiers, and handed the initiative to Meade gratis. At least as important, he had no idea what was awaiting him at Cashtown. He didn't even know the lie of the land. It was a plunge into darkness, and it was utterly foolish and totally counterproductive.

Once at Cashtown, Lee allowed the Confederate army to get into a chaotic encounter battle with Federal troops at Gettysburg on July 1, 1863. Lee knew nothing of the conditions at Gettysburg, and nothing of the size and nature of the Union forces arrayed against him.

The moment he realized Union forces were in force at Gettysburg, he should have pulled all his troops back to the heights of South Mountain. There he had a superb defensive position, and would have had ample time to reconnoiter the movements and the strength of the Union army. If Lee had done this, Meade would have been obliged to attack Lee under the most dangerous and unfavorable conditions. He most certainly would have lost.

Instead, Lee, on July 1, abandoned the resolve to remain on the defensive, which Longstreet believed he had agreed to follow, and launched a series of direct frontal assaults against Union forces at Gettysburg. These attacks were extremely costly to Confederate forces in lives lost and men wounded. At the end of the day, he finally drove the

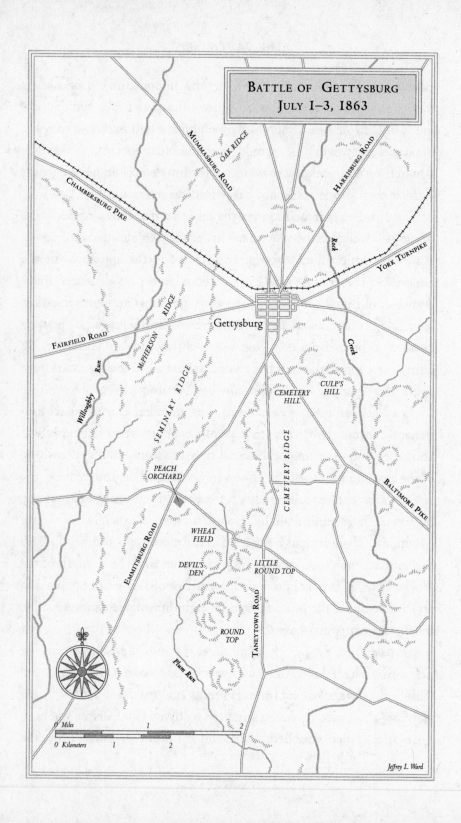

BATTLE OF GETTYSBURG
JULY 1–3, 1863

MUMMASBURG ROAD

OAK RIDGE

HARRISBURG ROAD

CHAMBERSBURG PIKE

YORK TURNPIKE

Rock

McPHERSON RIDGE

Gettysburg

FAIRFIELD ROAD

Willoughby Run

SEMINARY RIDGE

CULP'S HILL

CEMETERY HILL

Creek

CEMETERY RIDGE

BALTIMORE PIKE

PEACH ORCHARD

EMMITSBURG ROAD

WHEAT FIELD

DEVIL'S DEN

LITTLE ROUND TOP

TANEYTOWN ROAD

ROUND TOP

Plum Run

0 Miles   1   2

0 Kilometers   1   2

Jeffrey L. Ward

Federals onto the elevation of Cemetery Hill and Ridge just south of the town.

When Longstreet arrived on the scene as the fighting was ending, he examined the powerful defensive position that Cemetery Hill and Ridge provided for the Union army. He immediately told Lee that the Confederates had a splendid opportunity to pull the Federals off the ridgeline. All they had to do was to move to the south, he said. This would place the Confederate army between the Union army and Washington, something that Abraham Lincoln had specifically forbidden the Federal army to allow. Thus, Meade would be forced to abandon the ridgeline and its exceptional defensive positions, and to attack the Confederates on a battlefield chosen by and favorable to them. Longstreet assured Lee that, when this happened, the Confederates would win.

But Lee absolutely refused. He had learned nothing from Chancellorsville. The option that Longstreet offered was almost identical to the option that Stonewall Jackson had presented at Chancellorsville—to move around the Union army. At Chancellorsville, a Rebel move of this sort would block Union retreat across the only ford available. At Gettysburg, a Rebel move of this sort would block Union access to the national capital. In either case, the Union army would be placed in a despairing position.

But Lee saw none of this. He was determined to attack the Federal army on its formidable positions on Cemetery Ridge. Lee concluded his argument with Longstreet with the following reckless and irresponsible statement: "They are there in position [pointing to Cemetery Hill and Ridge], and I am going to whip them or they are going to whip me."[6]

Lee ordered this headlong assault on the second day of the battle. The Rebels finally pushed Union forces off of a position, the Peach Orchard, just west of the ridgeline at a cost of 4,000 men, but they were unable to capture the ridgeline itself. After this disaster, the only real option left to the Confederate army was to retreat back to Virginia. But again Lee refused, and ordered the climaxing catastrophe on the third day of Gettysburg—the direct assault of 13,500 soldiers in Pickett's Charge against the very center of the Union defenses on Cemetery Ridge. The assault failed completely. Only half of the Rebel soldiers returned to Confederate lines. The other half were killed, wounded, or captured.

Pickett's Charge was actually the end for the Confederacy. The war lasted nearly two more years, but defeat was certain after Gettysburg. The army was commanded by an officer who had demonstrated that he was irresponsible, indifferent to protecting the lives of his soldiers, and incapable of absorbing the most basic rules of warfare. He had learned nothing from Stonewall Jackson. At Gettysburg, he committed the most devastating in a long series of terrible decisions. In doing so, he destroyed the last vestiges of Confederate offensive power.

Many persons have conjectured what would have happened at Gettysburg if Stonewall Jackson had not been wounded and had been present. Jackson had far more influence with Lee than Longstreet, and, so some military historians have speculated, might have talked Lee out of ordering the fatal assaults there. But this is not really the hypothetical question to ask. For if Jackson had been on hand, he would have tried with all of his power to prevent Lee from fighting at Gettysburg in the first place. He would have seen that resourceful Confederate officers, on their own initiative, had achieved spectacular positions at Carlisle and Wrightsville that guaranteed Southern triumph if only they were exploited. Jackson would have used every ounce of his influence to persuade Lee to strike at once for Philadelphia. If he had done this, Meade would have been compelled to set off on a frantic chase to stop him. Jackson knew that the Rebel soldiers would have had ample leisure to prepare a battleground to receive the madly charging Union army. Federal soldiers, not Confederate soldiers, would have been forced to assault impregnable positions. The Federal army, not the Confederate army, would have suffered catastrophic losses. Southern victory would have been certain. If Jackson had been unable to induce Lee to strike for Philadelphia, he would have pressed Lee with all his might to climb on an elevation near Carlisle and wait for the Union army to attack. The actions there would not have been as dramatic as a failed Union attempt to stop a march on Philadelphia, but the results would have been the same.

As G. F. R. Henderson wrote, "The government which commits the charge of its armed forces to any other than the ablest and most experienced soldier the country can produce is but laying the foundation of national disaster."[7] Henderson was referring to Northern leadership, but the advice applied equally well to Southern leadership. The Army of Northern Virginia was one of the most tireless, indomitable, and heroic armies in the history of the world. It possessed in a corps commander one of the supreme military geniuses of all time, Stonewall Jackson. But its senior commander, Robert E. Lee, was a second-rate individual. With this deadweight holding it down, the army was unable to ascend to glory. The cause this army represented was finally lost by Lee at Gettysburg.

SELECTED BIBLIOGRAPHY

Alexander, Bevin. *Lost Victories. The Military Genius of Stonewall Jackson.* New York: Henry Holt and Company, 1992; New York: Hippocrene Books, 2005.

_____. *Robert E. Lee's Civil War.* Holbrook, Mass.: Adams Media Corp., 1998.

_____. *How the South Could Have Won the Civil War. The Fatal Errors That Led to Confederate Defeat.* New York: Crown Publishers, 2007.

_____. *Sun Tzu at Gettysburg. Ancient Military Wisdom in the Modern World.* New York: W. W. Norton & Company, 2011.

Alexander, Edward Porter. *Military Memoirs of a Confederate: A Critical Narrative.* New York: Charles Scribner's Sons, 1907; New York: Da Capo Press, 1993.

_____. *Fighting for the Confederacy: The Personal Recollections of General Edward Porter Alexander.* Chapel Hill: University of North Carolina Press, 1989.

Allan, William. *The Army of Northern Virginia in 1862.* Boston: Houghton Mifflin and Company, 1892; New York: Da Capo Press, 1995.

_____. *History and Campaign of Gen. T. J. (Stonewall) Jackson in the Shenandoah Valley of Virginia.* Philadelphia: J. B. Lippincott, 1880; New York: Da Capo Press, 1995.

Beringer, Richard E., Herman Hattaway, Archer Jones, and William N. Still Jr. *Why the South Lost the Civil War.* Athens: University of Georgia Press, 1986.

Bigelow, John, Jr. *The Campaign of Chancellorsville.* New Haven, Conn.: Yale University Press, 1910.

Chambers, Lenoir. *Stonewall Jackson.* 2 vols. New York: William Morrow, 1959.

Clausewitz, Karl von. *On War.* Hammondsworth, England: Penguin Books, 1968; New York: Dorset Press, 1991.

Connelly, Thomas L., and Archer Jones. *The Politics of Command: Factions and Ideas in Confederate Strategy.* Baton Rouge: Louisiana State University Press, 1973.

Cooke, John Esten. *Stonewall Jackson: A Military Biography.* New York: D. Appleton and Company, 1876.

Dabney, Robert Lewis. *Life and Campaigns of Lieut.-Gen. Thomas J. (Stonewall) Jackson.* New York: Blelock and Company, 1866; Harrisonburg, Va.: Sprinkle Publications, 1985.

Davis, William C. *Battle at Bull Run*. Baton Rouge: Louisiana State University Press, 1977.

Dodge, Theodore Ayrault. *A Bird's-eye View of Our Civil War*. Boston: Houghton, Mifflin and Company, 1883, 1997.

Doubleday, Abner. *Chancellorsville and Gettysburg*. New York: Charles Scribner's Sons, 1882.

Douglas, Henry Kyd. *I Rode with Stonewall*. Chapel Hill: University of North Carolina Press, 1940, 1968.

Freeman, Douglas Southall. *R. E. Lee, A Biography*. 4 vols. New York and London: Charles Scribner's Sons, 1934–35.

_____. *Lee's Lieutenants: A Study in Command*. 3 vols. New York: Scribner's, 1942–46.

Fremantle, Arthur James Lyon. *The Fremantle Diary*. Edited by Walter Lord. Boston: Little, Brown and Company, 1954.

Fuller, J. F. C. *The Generalship of Ulysses S. Grant*. New York: Dodd, Mead, 1929; Bloomington: Indiana University Press, 1957.

_____. *Grant and Lee: A Study in Personality and Generalship*. London: Eyre & Spottiswoode, 1933; Bloomington: Indiana University Press, 1957.

Gallagher, Gary W., ed. *Lee the Soldier*. Lincoln: University of Nebraska Press, 1996.

_____. *The Confederate War: How Popular Will, Nationalism, and Military Strategy Could Not Stave Off Defeat*. Cambridge, Mass.: Harvard University Press, 1997.

Goodwin, Doris Kearns. *Team of Rivals. The Political Genius of Abraham Lincoln*. New York: Simon & Schuster, 2005.

Hattaway, Herman, and Archer Jones. *How the North Won*. Urbana: University of Illinois Press, 1991.

Henderson, Colonel G. F. R. *Stonewall Jackson and the American Civil War*. 2 vols. New York: Longmans, Green and Company, 1898; 1 vol., New York: Longmans, Green and Company, 1936, 1937, 1943, 1949; 2 vols., New York: Konecky & Konecky, 1993.

Hicks, John D. *The Federal Union. A History of the United States to 1865*. Boston: Houghton Mifflin Company, 1937.

Hood, John Bell. *Advance and Retreat: Personal Experiences in the United States and Confederate Armies*. New Orleans, 1880; Bloomington: University of Indiana Press, 1959.

Jackson, Mary Anna. *Memoirs of Stonewall Jackson*. Louisville, Ky.: Prentice Press, 1895.

Johnson, Robert U., and C. C. Buel, eds. *Battles and Leaders of the Civil War*. 4 vols. New York: Century Magazine, 1887–88; reprint, Secaucus, N.J.: Castle, n.d.

Johnston, Joseph E. *A Narrative of Military Operations*. Bloomington: Indiana University Press, 1959; New York: Kraus, 1969.

Jones, Archer. *Civil War Command and Strategy: The Process of Victory and Defeat*. New York: Free Press, 1992.

Lee, Robert E. *Lee's Dispatches. Unpublished Letters of General Robert E. Lee., C.S.A., to Jefferson Davis and the War Department of the Confederate States of America, 1862–65*.

Edited by Douglas Southall Freeman. New York: G. P. Putnam's Sons, 1957 (originally published in a limited edition, 1915); Baton Rouge: Louisiana State University Press, 1994.

Liddell Hart, Sir Basil H. *Strategy.* New York: Praeger, 1954.

Long, A. L. *Memoirs of Robert E. Lee.* Charlottesville, Va., 1880; Secaucus, N.J.: The Blue and Grey Press, 1983.

Longstreet, James. *From Manassas to Appomattox.* Philadelphia: J. B. Lippincott, 1903.

Luvaas, Jay. *The Military Legacy of the Civil War. The European Inheritance.* Chicago: University of Chicago Press, 1959; Lawrence: University Press of Kansas, 1988.

_____. *Napoleon on the Art of War.* New York: Touchstone, 1999.

Marshall, Charles. *An Aide-de-Camp of Lee.* Edited by Sir Frederick Maurice. Boston: Little, Brown and Company, 1927.

Maurice, Major General Sir Frederick. *Robert E. Lee the Soldier.* New York: Houghton Mifflin Company, 1925; New York: Bonanza Books, n.d.

McKenzie, John D. *Uncertain Glory: Lee's Generalship Re-examined.* New York: Hippocrene Books, 1997.

Nolan, Alan T. *Lee Considered: General Robert E. Lee and Civil War History.* Chapel Hill: University of North Carolina Press, 1991.

Palfrey, Francis Winthrop. *The Antietam and Fredericksburg.* New York: Charles Scribner's Sons, 1882.

Paret, Peter, ed. *Makers of Modern Strategy.* Princeton, N.J.: Princeton University Press, 1986.

Robertson, James I., Jr. *Stonewall Jackson: The Man, the Soldier, the Legend.* New York: Macmillan Publishing USA, 1997.

Ropes, John C. *The Army Under Pope.* New York: Charles Scribner's Son, 1881.

Sears, Stephen D. *Landscape Turned Red. The Battle of Antietam.* New York: Ticknor & Fields, 1983.

_____. *To the Gates of Richmond. The Peninsula Campaign.* New York: Ticknor & Fields, 1992.

Selby, John. *Stonewall Jackson as Military Commander.* London: B. T. Batsford Ltd., n.d.; Princeton, N.J.: D. Van Nostrand Company, 1968.

Southern Historical Society Papers. 50 vols. Richmond, Va.: 1876–1953.

Taylor, Richard. *Destruction and Reconstruction. Personal Experiences in the Late War.* New York: D. Appleton and Company, 1879; Nashville, Tenn.: J. S. Sanders and Company, 1998.

Thomas, Emory M. *Robert E. Lee: A Biography.* New York: W. W. Norton & Company, 1995.

Tucker, Glenn. *High Tide at Gettysburg.* Boston: Bobbs-Merrill Company, 1958; New York: Smithmark Publishers, 1995.

Vandiver, F. E. *The Mighty Stonewall.* New York: McGraw-Hill Book Company, 1957.

The War of the Rebellion: A Compilaton of the Official Records of the Union and Confederate Armies. 128 parts in 70 vols, and atlas. Washington, D.C.: Government Printing

Office, 1880–1901. Available online at Cornell University Library Digital Library Server, Making of America Collection, htty://cdl.library.cornell.edu.

Weigley, Russell F. *The American Way of War: A History of United States Military Strategy and Policy.* New York: Macmillan, 1973.

Whan, Vorin E., Jr. *Fiasco at Fredericksburg.* State College, Pa.: Pennsylvania State University Press, 1961.

Wiley, Bell Irvin. *The Life of Johnny Reb.* Baton Rouge: Louisiana State University Press, 1952, 1978, 1995.

_____. *The Life of Billy Yank.* Baton Rouge: Louisiana State University Press, 1952, 1978, 1995.

Wolseley, Field Marshal Viscount Garnet Joseph. *The American Civil War: An English View.* Charlottesville: University Press of Virginia, 1964.

Woodworth, Steven E. *Davis and Lee at War.* Lawrence: University of Kansas Press, 1995.

NOTES

In these notes, some references give only the last name of the author or editor or the last name and a short title. These works are cited in full in the Selected Bibliography. References not listed in the bibliography are cited in full the first time they appear in the notes of each chapter, and then are cited by author and short title afterward. Numbers in the notes refer to the pages.

Introduction: Jackson's Recipes for Victory

1 Field Marshal Viscount Garnet Joseph Wolseley, who became commander in chief of the British army, conferred with Davis during a visit to Virginia in 1862 and knew his actions well. He called Jefferson Davis "a third rate man, and a most unfortunate selection for the office of president." Wolseley wrote that Davis was puffed up with a belief in his superior wisdom, and rejected the urgings of his military advisers to adopt a policy of concentration. This policy, Wolseley wrote, had lost the war by 1862. "It is the old, old story over again, of civil rulers who blunder, and, failing to foresee events, sacrifice everything to a momentary popularity, in order to divert popular wrath from themselves to the unfortunate soldiers who have been their victims." See Wolseley, xxxii, 76–77. John D. Hicks, in his monumental history of the United States, seconds Wolseley's appraisal of Davis. "He had an exaggerated idea of his military ability," Hicks writes, "and often gravely handicapped his generals by dictating to them, or interfering with their plans. He was not a good judge of men, and surrounded himself with mediocre subordinates when he could have had the best talent in the South for the asking. He was proud to the point of arrogance, and his overbearing attitude toward those who held opinions at variance from his own often cost him dear." See Hicks, 608.

2 Bevin Alexander, *Sun Tzu at Gettysburg* (New York: W. W. Norton & Co., 2011), xiv, 92.

3 Lawrence H. Keeley, *War Before Civilization: The Myth of the Peaceful Savage* (Oxford, England: Oxford University Press, 1996). Keeley gives meticulous archaeological evidence of Stone Age warfare.

4 Bevin Alexander, *Sun Tzu at Gettysburg*, 13, 250 note 22.

5 Hicks, 494.

6 Claudia Goldin and Frank Lewis, "The Post-bellum Recovery of the South and the Cost of the Civil War, Comment," *Journal of Economic History* 38: 2 (June 1978), 487–92.

7 Mary Boykin Chesnut, *A Diary from Dixie* (Cambridge, Mass.: Harvard University Press, 1980), 265.

Chapter 1: The Making of a Soldier

1 The narrative on Jackson's youth, education, service in the United States Army, and career at Virginia Military Institute is drawn largely from the vast, comprehensive, and incisive biography of Jackson by James I. Robertson Jr. See Robertson, 1–188.

2 Robertson, 16.

3 For example, Napoleon Bonaparte based his campaigns on meticulous study of all possible aspects of every problem, and what the solutions might be. Before every operation, he meditated deeply about what might happen if one approach was tried, and what might happen if another was tried. But he never began by asking, "What can the enemy do?" He first sought to place his own army in the best position and then asked, "What then can the enemy do?" See Theodore A. Dodge, *Great Captains* (Boston: Houghton Mifflin, 1889; Whitefish, Mont.: Kessinger Publishing, n.d.), 197.

4 Johnson and Buel, vol. 2, 297.

5 Robertson, 118.

6 Ibid., 120. Jackson was hobbled intellectually by what is called the "military mind," or an excessive reliance on authority and order in how a person with this affliction thinks and how he behaves. For example, he once asked a cadet: "What are the three simple machines?" The cadet answered, "The inclined plane, the lever, and the wheel." "No sir," Jackson replied, "the lever, the wheel, and the inclined plane." They were listed in that order in the textbook, and that was how they were supposed to be identified. In response to examples like this, many at VMI shared the appraisal of one of his students, James T. Murfee, who wrote: "Not only did we not understand him, but I think that no one at the time understood him, for genius is incomprehensible until displayed in action." See ibid., 121, 132.

7 Ibid., 149.

8 Ibid., 191.

9 Ibid., 690–91.

Chapter 2: "There Stands Jackson Like a Stone Wall"

1 Robertson, 213.

2 Goodwin, 349–50.

3 Bevin Alexander, *Lee's Civil War*, 4–5.

4 Robertson, 219.

5 Ibid., 233–34.

6 Ibid., 239.

7 McDowell, forty-two years old, was an Ohio West Pointer (class of 1838) who had served with distinction in the Mexican War, but had been satisfied with a staff appointment to Winfield Scott, chief of the army.

8 Beauregard had been part of the same West Point class as McDowell. He also distinguished himself in the Mexican War. He was briefly superintendent of West Point in 1861 before his Southern sympathies led to his removal.

9 Anna Jackson, 176.

10 To get away from the war, McLean moved to Appomattox, Virginia, and bought a house near the county courthouse. By strange coincidence, this was the very house in which Robert E. Lee and Ulysses S. Grant met on April 9, 1865, to arrange the surrender of the Army of Northern Virginia and end the war.

11 Porter Alexander, *Military Memoirs,* 30.

12 Ibid., 33, 38.

13 All members of the Henry household except Judith Henry had vacated the house, but she, aged and bedridden, remained. She was killed in her bed, struck by a cannon shot and several bullets.

14 Davis, 187.

15 Johnson and Buel, vol. 1, 234–35.

16 Robertson, 263.

17 Freeman, *Lee's Lieutenants,* vol. 1, 81–83, 733–34; Davis, 197–98; Robertson, 263–64.

18 George B. McClellan, *McClellan's Own Story* (New York: Charles I. Webster and Company, 1887), 66–67. See also Henderson, vol. 1, 155.

19 Jefferson Davis was an 1828 graduate of West Point, and had distinguished service in the Mexican War. He served as a chairman of the military affair committee of the U.S. Senate and as secretary of war in President Franklin Pierce's cabinet. Davis considered himself a military expert. But in fact his strategic vision was extremely limited.

20 Robertson, 276–77.

Chapter 3: Jackson Shows a Way to Victory

1 The maximum *effective* range of rifled cannons was about 2,500 yards and of smoothbores about 1,500, though many could not reach that distance. Cannons fired solid shot from 350 yards out, shrapnel from 500 to 1,000 yards, and canister from 500 yards in. The best rifled pieces were twenty-pounder Parrotts with a maximum range of 4,500 yards, ten-pounder Parrotts with a maximum range of 6,200 yards, and three-inch ordnance guns with a range of 4,180 yards. The Army of the Potomac also used twelve-pounder smoothbores with a range of 1,660 yards. Both sides used the light twelve-pounder Napoleon with a range of

1,300 yards. But the Napoleon, loaded with canister, was increasingly employed up close to defenders' lines to assist riflemen in fending off attacks. In these situations, Napoleons usually fired at ranges of 300 to 500 yards. The Confederates used a large number of six-pounder guns and twelve-pounder howitzers, discarded by the Federals as too light. "Pounder" referred to the weight of the projectile or charge fired, "inch" to the diameter of the bore. See Porter Alexander, *Military Memoirs,* 280; Bigelow, 22–23, 27–28; Ian V. Hogg, *Illustrated Encyclopedia of Artillery* (Secaucus, N.J.: Chartwell Books, 1988), 92, 194, 248–49; Diagram Group, *Weapons, an International Encyclopedia* (New York: St. Martin's Press, 1990), 171, 174–5, 179.

2 Johnson and Buel, vol. 1, 233.

3 Geoffrey Wawro, *The Austro-Prussian War* (Cambridge: Cambridge University Press, 1996), 22–23. A French officer observing Prussian army maneuvers in 1861 sneered that the Prussian use of the needle-gun was "compromising the military profession."

4 There was no solution until an entirely new method of attack was developed. For the rest of the nineteenth century and beyond, commanders wrestled with the problem. At the same time, even more powerful offensive weapons were developed, including Alfred Nobel's dynamite in 1866, the repeating magazine bolt-action rifle with a range well over 1,000 yards, Hiram Maxim's machine gun in 1884, far more accurate fuses for far longer-range artillery, and a system of hydraulics that permitted cannons to absorb the recoil of firing shells and to remain in the same place without having to be rolled back into position. In the Boer War of 1899 to 1902, British soldiers still tried to advance in formation, albeit in extended order, not shoulder to shoulder. But Boers, sitting on hills and firing the German Mauser Model 98 bolt-action magazine rifle, easily picked them off at ranges of a thousand yards. This was clearly not the answer, and soldiers went into World War I in 1914 advancing in formation. Killings were so stupendous, however, that a solution had to be found. It came in 1915 from a German captain, Willy Martin Rohr, who developed "infiltration" or "storm troop" tactics. One small group of soldiers held down an enemy trench position or strong point with heavy directed fire by automatic weapons, mortars, and sometimes light cannons, while one or more well-trained teams of eight to twelve "storm troopers," working in conjunction, infiltrated the trench line or sneaked up on the strong point, and "rolled it up" with grenades, small-arms fire, and sometimes flamethrowers. Soldiers were in no formation at all and each man had a particular task. This fire-and-maneuver system overcame enemy guns and fortifications, returned movement to the battlefield, and became the fundamental method of tactical engagements to this day. See Bevin Alexander, *How Wars Are Won* (New York: Crown, 2002), 19, 253, 361 n. 15.

5 For example, Union General Henry W. Halleck, advancing on Corinth, Mississippi, after the battle of Shiloh in spring 1862, ordered his men to throw up embankments and dig foxholes, or "ditches" as they called them, even for a night's stop. And Union General Jacob D. Cox said, "One rifle in the trench is worth five in front of it." See Paddy Griffith, *Battle Tactics of the Civil War* (New Haven: Yale University Press, 1989), 129–30.

6 Bevin Alexander, *How the South Could Have Won,* 38; J. F. C. Fuller, *Military History of the Western World* (New York: Funk & Wagnalls Company, 1954; New York: Da Capo Press, n.d.), 3 vols., vol. 2, 416 (Da Capo edition).

7 Porter Alexander, *Fighting for the Confederacy*, 408–9, describes these fortifications at the battle of Cold Harbor in June 1864, when they were reaching near perfection. He includes a sketch of how parapets were constructed: a trench two feet deep was edged by a mound two and a half feet high of dirt, rocks, and logs. Even artillery fire could not breach such defenses.

8 The source of this proposal by Jackson is a personal letter written by General Smith to G. F. R. Henderson and printed in Henderson, vol. 1, 173–76.

9 John D. Hicks has a map in his superb volume, *The Federal Union*, which shows plainly the heavy concentration of industry along the Eastern Corridor in 1860. See Hicks, 557.

10 During the winter of 1862, Jackson tried to recover parts of northwestern Virginia beyond the Allegheny Mountains. Beginning on January 1, 1862, he foiled a projected offensive by Union Major General William S. Rosecrans to seize Winchester and threaten the western side of the main Confederate position at Manassas. Jackson drove his small army through snow and rain, attacked Federal garrisons, temporarily broke the Baltimore & Ohio Railroad along the Potomac River, and seized Romney, thirty-five miles northwest of Winchester. This highly successful campaign threatened Federal rail communications with the Midwest and regained a large part of West Virginia at little cost. Officers of Jackson's chief subordinate, Brigadier General W. W. Loring, became angry with the conditions they faced in Romney. Eleven officers complained to the Confederate secretary of war Judah P. Benjamin. And Colonel William Taliaferro complained personally to President Jefferson Davis. Davis committed a gross error in military protocol in listening to the complaints of a colonel about his commanding general. According to James I. Robertson Jr., President Davis told Secretary Benjamin to send a directive to Jackson to bring the Romney garrison back to Winchester immediately. See Robertson, 316–17. Jackson complied but sent his resignation at once. "With such interference in my command, I cannot expect to be of much service in the field," he wrote. The abrupt response shook General Johnston, who recognized Jackson's ability. By his pleadings and those of Alexander S. Boteler, a close friend of Jackson's, as well as the intervention of Governor John Letcher, Jackson withdrew his resignation. And the secretary of war never again tried to second-guess Jackson. The War Department transferred Loring and part of his troops elsewhere.

11 Robertson, 299–300.

12 Ibid., 330.

13 Ibid., 325 quotes James Robert Graham, "Some Reminiscences of Stonewall Jackson" in *Things and Thoughts* (1901), 126.

14 Henderson, vol. 2, 391.

15 Ibid.

16 Ibid.

17 Since the Shenandoah Valley drains northward, forces moving south in it go up, not down.

18 From Frederick the Great's *Instructions to His Generals* written toward the end of his reign. See Henderson, vol. 1, 173.

19 For a full analysis of the *Monitor* and the *Merrimac*, see Johnson and Buel, vol. 1, 692–750.

20 Henderson, vol. 1, 244.

21 Johnson and Buel, vol. 2, 307. The officer was Colonel E. H. C. Cavins of the 14th Indiana.

22 Henderson, vol. 1, 260–61.

23 Although Jackson preferred charges against Garnett, he was never court-martialed. He did, however, remain under a cloud. He was nevertheless able to gain command of another brigade, which formed part of Pickett's force that charged Cemetery Ridge on the third day of Gettysburg, July 3, 1863. Garnett died in this charge.

24 Allan, *History of the Campaign*, 85.

25 Goodwin, 432.

Chapter 4: The Shenandoah Valley Campaign

1 More than twenty years after the end of the war, Joseph Johnston wrote in an article in the "Battles and Leaders" series in *Century* magazine about the April 14, 1862, meeting. In the article he said nothing about a strike into the North, and devoted the entire argument to the need to bring all forces together and to attack McClellan at Richmond. See Johnson and Buel, vol. 2, 203.

2 Henderson, vol. 1, 289. Field Marshal Viscount Garnet Joseph Wolseley, commander in chief of the British army, was a great admirer of Stonewall Jackson and was responsible for getting Henderson to write his classic on Jackson, which appeared in 1898. Wolseley was impressed with an article Henderson had written after touring the Virginia battlefields in 1883–84. He had Henderson assigned to Sandhurst, the British military academy, and encouraged him to write *Stonewall Jackson and the American Civil War*. At Henderson's request Wolseley wrote the introduction to the second edition. See Wolseley, xxxi.

3 Robertson, 358.

4 Ibid., 357 quotes Wilder Dwight, *Life and Letters of Wilder Dwight* (Boston: 1868), 236.

5 Some observers have remarked that, if Banks had been bold, he could have marched at once to Conrad's Store, seized the bridge over the South Fork there, and bottled up Jackson's whole force in Elk Run Valley. This, however, was not a feasible choice for Banks. If he had marched on Conrad's Store, Jackson could easily have left Turner Ashby's cavalry to guard the bridge there while he set his infantry and guns on a fast march down Luray Valley, then over Massanutten to seize New Market. Ashby's troopers could have held the bridge as long as possible, then burned it, leaving Banks isolated deep in enemy country with his supply line on the Valley Pike cut. Jackson explained this concept himself in *The War of the Rebellion*, vol. 12, part 3, 848. See also Henderson, vol. 1, 276.

6 Jackson's first choice in dealing with the situation facing the Confederacy provided a dazzling glimpse into the depth and scope of his strategic thinking. He proposed to Lee on April 29, 1862, that, if he could get 5,000 reinforcements to send to Edward Johnson to contain Frémont temporarily, he would march his army northward to Luray, cross at Thornton Gap (present-day U.S. Route 211) to Sperryville on the eastern slope of the Blue Ridge, and from there turn north, leaving the enemy to doubt as to whether he was aiming at Front Royal to the northwest or at Warrenton to the northeast, only twenty-five miles from Centreville and the main Federal positions protecting Washington. This march along a single line would

immobilize the Washington garrison, keep Irvin McDowell's 38,000-man corps from marching to aid McClellan, and force Banks into retreat (since his line of supply would be threatened)—all with practically no casualties. Lee could not promise the 5,000 reinforcements, however, and Jackson was forced to abandon the concept. But this plan demonstrated in very practical terms how he could implement his admonition to General Imboden always "to mystify, mislead, and surprise the enemy." Jackson's letter is recorded in *The War of the Rebellion,* vol. 12, part 3, 372, and in Allan, *Campaign of Gen. T. J. (Stonewall) Jackson,* 68n.

7   Up to this time, Jackson had been hampered by orders from Joe Johnston to remain close to the railway in the event that his forces had to be withdrawn quickly to help protect Richmond, if McClellan broke the lines at Yorktown. But Robert E. Lee freed Jackson from this obligation by wiring him on April 21: "If you can use General Ewell's division in an attack on Banks, it will prove a great relief to the pressure on Fredericksburg [where Lincoln, no longer anxious about Jackson, had allowed McDowell to move preparatory to a march on Richmond]." See *The War of the Rebellion,* vol. 12, part 3, 859. See also Bevin Alexander, *Lost Victories,* 59, note 16.

8   Henderson, vol. 1, 288.

9   To ensure that Frémont remained bottled up in the mountains, Jackson dispatched his topographical engineer, Captain Jedediah Hotchkiss, with a few cavalry to block all of the passes through the Alleghenies to the east by means of felled trees and burned bridges. See Henderson, vol. 1, 303. Jackson also ordered John D. Imboden, recruiting troops at Staunton, to seal off any routes by which Frémont might reach Harrisonburg. Imboden knew of a spot four miles east of Franklin on the road to Harrisonburg (present-day U.S. Route 33). "There was a narrow defile hemmed in on both sides by nearly perpendicular cliffs, over 500 feet high," Imboden wrote. "I sent about fifty men, well armed with long-range guns, to occupy these cliffs, and defend the passage to the last extremity." On May 25, Frémont, under orders from Stanton to cut off Jackson's retreat up the valley, sent his cavalry to feel out passage to Harrisonburg. "The men I had sent to the cliffs let the head of the column get well into the defile, when, from a position of perfect safety, they poured a deadly volley into the close column." The Federal troopers halted in confusion. "Another volley and the 'rebel yell' from the cliffs turned them back, never to appear again." Frémont abandoned the effort to reach Harrisonburg, went to Moorefield, and emerged into the Shenandoah Valley far to the north at Strasburg. See Johnson and Buel, vol. 2, 290–91.

10   Robertson, 384.

11   *The War of the Rebellion,* vol. 12, part 3, 896–97.

12   Ibid., 896–98. There is no record of Lee's response, but he probably got President Davis's approval. See Bevin Alexander, *Lost Victories,* 76, note 7.

13   Richard Taylor, 49–50.

14   Henderson, vol. 2, 395; Bevin Alexander, *Lost Victories,* 65.

15   Robertson, 408, 412.

16   Henderson, vol. 2, 393.

17   Hicks, 608.

18   Wolseley, xiv, xxxii, 76–77; Davis, 608.

19 All of Jackson's proposals to Colonel Boteler are recorded in a narrative by A. R. Boteler in *Southern Historical Society Papers*, Richmond, Va., vol. 40, 165, 172–74. See also Robertson, 416; *Philadelphia Weekly Times*, February 11, 1882.

20 Robertson, 511–12, 517, 522; Robertson cites Susan Leigh Blackford, comp., *Letters from Lee's Army* (New York: 1947), 86.

21 Robertson, 418.

22 Dabney, 397; Robertson, 424.

23 Robertson, 423.

24 Ibid., 451–52.

25 Ibid., 454, cites the *Philadelphia Weekly Times*, February 11, 1882.

26 Jackson told Boteler to inform Lee that if he could get a total of 40,000 soldiers, he would cross east of the Blue Ridge and proceed northward until he found a gap that would put him on the rear of General Nathaniel Banks's army, which had been partially reconstituted and was moving south up the Shenandoah Valley. This would also place Jackson behind John C. Frémont and the divisions of James Shields and James B. Ricketts, who was following Shields. Once these forces were disposed of, Jackson wrote, he would invade western Maryland and Pennsylvania. By marching east of the Blue Ridge, Jackson would prevent forces protecting Washington from moving for fear he would strike directly at the capital. Likewise, the forces in the Shenandoah Valley could not move for fear he would descend on their rear. Advancing northward on this single line, in other words, would hold all forces in the valley and around Washington in place. And he could defeat any single Union element that might venture against him. Once he had crossed the Potomac, there were no substantial Union forces to oppose him. This is similar to the proposal Jackson made April 29, 1862, to Lee, when he asked for 5,000 troops to help Edward Johnson stop Frémont temporarily. Since these reinforcements were not forthcoming, Jackson abandoned the plan. See *War of the Rebellion*, vol. 12, part 3, 372; Allan, *Campaign of Gen. T. J. (Stonewall) Jackson*, 68n.

27 *Southern Historical Society Papers*, Richmond, Va., vol. 40, 173–74; Robertson, 454. Davis's endorsement of Lee's letter is shown in MS in *The Centennial Exhibit of the Duke University Library* (Durham, N.C.: Duke University, 1939), 15–16.

28 Johnson and Buel, vol. 2, 297.

29 Wolseley, 116.

30 Theodore A, Dodge, *Alexander* (New York: Houghton Mifflin, 1890; London: Greenhill, 1991), 657.

Chapter 5: The Disaster of the Seven Days

1 Major Thomas R. Phillips, ed., *Roots of Strategy* (Harrisburg, Pa.: Military Service Publishing Company, 1941), 407–11; Jay Luvaas, *Napoleon on the Art of War* (New York: Touchstone, 1999), 130.

2 Johnson and Buel, vol. 2, 361.

3 Ibid., 337.

4 Johnson and Buel, vol. 2, 394.

5 Ibid., 417; Freeman, *R. E. Lee,* vol. 2, 211–15.

6 Cooke, 234.

7 General William W. Averell in Johnson and Buel, vol. 2, 432.

Chapter 6: Finding a Different Way to Win

1 Dabney, 486–87; Henderson, vol. 2, 76–78; *Southern Historical Society Papers,* vol. 40, 180–82. Porter Alexander shared Jackson's view. Lee could not wait idly at Richmond for the enemy slowly to make up his mind what to do, he says. See Porter Alexander, *Military Memoirs,* 179.

2 Robertson, 60–61.

3 Jackson also developed an alternative method of achieving victory that involved an *offensive* rather than a defensive posture. He saw that he could achieve the same goal by attacking an advancing Union force and throwing it back on the defensive. If the Union commander feared that the Confederates were about to assault his new defensive position, he would keep his main forces in place in a defensive stance. In this case, as well, his flank and rear would be exposed and vulnerable, and the Confederates could swing around the Union position and force the Federals to flee. Jackson found no opportunity to employ this alternative method of victory until Chancellorsville in May 1863. But his application of the principle there produced the greatest Confederate victory in the war. See Chapter 10 and the Epilogue.

4 Because of his extreme reticence to express his mind, it is very difficult to document how Jackson came to his new theory of battle. His first expression of the subject was most indirect, and occurred five months later at the battle of Fredericksburg. Heros von Borcke, a Prussian officer on Jeb Stuart's staff, wondered aloud whether the Rebels could stop an assault by the vast Federal army arrayed in front of them. Jackson replied: "Major, my men have sometimes failed to take a position, but to defend one, never!" After the battle of Chancellorsville in the spring of 1863, Jackson said much the same thing to his medical officer, Hunter McGuire: "We sometimes fail to drive them from position; they always fail to drive us." We can conclude from these statements that, since Rebels in strong positions could always defeat attacks by Union soldiers, the Confederates should avoid direct attacks themselves, and instead induce the enemy to attack. The Confederates could then win by moving swiftly on the open flank of the defeated Union force. The only record we have of Jackson discussing this concept comes from Hunter McGuire. After Jackson was wounded at the battle of Chancellorsville, he told McGuire "he intended, after breaking into [the Federal commander Joe] Hooker's rear, to take and fortify a suitable position, cutting him off from the [Rappahannock] river and so hold him until, between himself and General Lee, the great Federal host should be broken to pieces." See *Southern Historical Society Papers,* vol. 25, 110, 119; Heros von Borcke, *Memoirs of the Confederate War for Independence* (New York: Peter Smith, 1938), vol. 2, 117; Bigelow, 340n. Jackson's close associate, Robert Lewis Dabney, expressed some of the same ideas in somewhat different words. See Dabney, 699–700.

5 Pope was the most ridiculed and vilified of the Union generals who faced the Army of Northern Virginia. His reputation was scarcely better in the Federal army. Pope made the mistake of issuing a bombastic order to his troops on July 14, 1862, from his "headquarters in the saddle." In it he said: "I come to you from the West where we have always seen the backs of our enemies; from an army whose business it has been to seek the adversary and beat him when he was found, whose policy has been attack and not defense. . . . I presume I have been called here to pursue the same system and to lead you against the enemy. . . . Meantime I desire to dismiss from your minds certain phrases, which I am sorry to find so much in vogue amongst you. I heard constantly of 'taking strong positions and holding them'; of 'lines of retreat' and of 'base of supplies.' Let us discard such ideas. . . . Let us study the possible lines of retreat of our opponents and leave our own to take care of themselves. . . . Success and glory are in the advance. Disaster and shame lurk in the rear." See *The War of the Rebellion,* vol. 12, part 3, 474; Porter Alexander, *Military Memoirs,* 176–77; Allan, *Army of Northern Virginia,* 156–58; Freeman, *R. E. Lee,* vol. l2, 263–64.

6 John Pope brought a new level of horror to the war by instructing his army to live off the country and reimburse only citizens loyal to the United States, and to hold local citizens hostage for actions of guerrillas, without distinguishing between partisans and ordinary Confederate cavalry. He went so far as to treat a mother who wrote her soldier son as a traitor, subject to being shot as a spy. Pope's orders so incensed Lee that he wrote twice that Pope must be suppressed. With the approval of President Davis, Lee notified Halleck that the Confederacy would be compelled to retaliate if Pope's orders were enforced. Halleck modified Pope's orders materially, but did not renounce them entirely. See Cooke, 252–54; Henderson, vol. 2, 81–82.

7 Goodwin, 468.

8 Lincoln appointed Pope on June 27, 1862, to take command of forces of Frémont (who had resigned and had been succeeded by Franz Sigel), Banks, and McDowell, totaling 50,000 men, plus 12,000 garrisoning Washington, as well as Brigadier General Jacob D. Cox, with 11,000 men, coming from Lewisburg, West Virginia. See Johnson and Buel, vol. 2, 281, 449–51; Allan, *Army of Northern Virginia,* 154; Porter Alexander, *Military Memoirs,* 177.

9 Henderson, vol. 2, 83.

10 Freeman, *Lee's Lieutenants,* vol. 2, 20; Allan, *Army of Northern Virginia,* 167, 169.

11 Henderson, vol. 2, 113.

12 Lee, 56–58; Freeman, *R. E. Lee,* vol. 2, 259, 328–29.

13 George H. Gordon, *The Army of Virginia* (Boston: Houghton, Osgood and Co., 1880), 9; Henderson, vol. 2, 115; Dabney, 511.

Chapter 7: Second Manassas

1 Douglas, 133–34.

2 Hunter McGuire, Jackson's surgeon, believed that Jackson originated the idea for the movement on Pope's rear (Henderson, vol. 2, 123–24). But it is evident that the concept came from Lee. See Freeman, *R. E. Lee,* vol. 2, 300–1; Freeman, *Lee's Lieutenants,* vol. 2, 82–83;

The War of the Rebellion, vol. 12, part 2, 553–54 and 642–43; and Porter Alexander, *Military Memoirs*, 191–92.

3 Lee's report reads as follows: "In pursuance of the plans of operation determined upon, Jackson was directed on the 25th [of August 1862] to cross above Waterloo and move around the enemy's right, so as to strike the Orange & Alexandria Railroad in the rear." Jackson's report, on the other hand, reads as follows: "Pursuing the instructions of the commanding general, I left Jeffersonton on the morning of the 25th to throw my command between Washington City and the army of General Pope and to break up his railroad communication with the Federal capital." See *The War of the Rebellion*, vol. 12, part 2, 553–54 and 642–43.

4 Robertson, 548.

5 Dabney, 517; Henderson, vol. 2, 126–27.

6 Henderson, vol. 2, 373.

7 Ibid.

8 Ibid., 343.

9 Ibid., 344.

10 Allan, *Army of Northern Virginia*, 211; Johnson and Buel, vol. 2, 461, 463, 517; *The War of the Rebellion*, vol. 12, part 3, 672, 675, 684; Henderson, vol. 2, 138. Pope asked Halleck that William B. Franklin's 10,000-man corps of McClellan's army, being directed to Alexandria rather than Aquia Creek, be sent to Gainesville. He also asked that another division, either Jacob D. Cox's from West Virginia or Samuel D. Sturgis's from Washington, be moved to Manassas Junction. Halleck sent none of these forces forward, however.

11 Johnson and Buel, vol. 2, 461n.; Allan, *Army of Northern Virginia*, 214.

12 Fuller, *Grant and Lee*, 165.

13 Johnson and Buel, vol. 2, 517.

14 *The War of the Rebellion*, vol. 12, part 2, 71–72; Allan, *Army of Northern Virginia*, 21–23.

15 *The War of the Rebellion*, vol. 12, part 2, 383–84, 564; Allan, *Army of Northern Virginia*, 225, 228; Porter Alexander, *Military Memoirs*, 262.

16 Johnson and Buel, vol. 2, 469–72; *The War of the Rebellion*, vol. 12, part 2, 37–38, 75; Allan, *Army of Northern Virginia*, 240; Freeman, *Lee's Lieutenants*, vol. 2, 110.

17 Johnson and Buel, vol. 2, 477n.

18 Maurice, 142–43.

19 *The War of the Rebellion*, vol. 19, part 2, 590; Allan, *Army of Northern Virginia*, 323; Woodworth, 185.

20 Bevin Alexander, *How the South Could Have Won*, 133.

21 Porter Alexander, *Fighting for the Confederacy*, 251.

22 Lee, 56–58; Freeman, *R. E. Lee*, vol. 2, 259, 328–29.

23 Henderson, vol. 2, 173.

24 *The War of the Rebellion*, vol. 12, part 2, 666–67; Freeman, *R. E. Lee*, vol. 2, 331.

25 Allan, *Army of Northern Virginia*, 283n.

26 Porter Alexander, *Military Memoirs,* 214.

27 Bevin Alexander, *Lost Victories,* 202.

Chapter 8: Calamity in Maryland

1 *The War of the Rebellion,* vol. 19, part 2, 600; Freeman, *R. E. Lee,* vol. 2, 358.

2 Mary Boykin Chesnut, *A Diary from Dixie* (Cambridge, Mass.: Harvard University Press, 1980), 265.

3 Wolseley, 35–37. This pattern of oppression and destruction was applied wherever Union forces were present. Two recent studies give details of Northern depredations in northern Alabama from early 1862 onward and in Atlanta, Georgia, in 1864. They are Joseph W. Danielson, *War's Desolating Scourge: The Union's Occupation of North Alabama* (Lawrence: University Press of Kansas, 2012), and Stephen Davis, *What the Yankees Did to Us: Sherman's Bombardment and Wreckage of Atlanta* (Macon, Ga.: Mercer University Press, 2012). Danielson describes how in north Alabama, Confederates were arrested, abused, and occasionally executed, houses and personal belongings were destroyed, crops were confiscated, and slaves were set free. Davis describes the devastation of a major American city. After shelling Atlanta for a month, beginning July 20, 1864, William T. Sherman made a concerted effort to dismantle and deplete a Southern population center. The railroad, government buildings, and civilian dwellings were ripped apart and burned. As Clay Mountcastle of the University of Washington, Seattle, writes in a July 2013 review in *The Journal of Military History,* Davis's book "serves as a powerful reminder that the American Civil War was not at all confined to the conventional battlefields; its violence carried into villages, towns, and major cities throughout the South." He adds: "The destruction of the South . . . did not occur by happenstance or by unintended consequence. Davis more than succeeds in showing it as a deliberate, orchestrated part of the Union war effort that it was." See also Mark Grimsley, *The Hard Hand of War: Union Military Policy Towards Southern Civilians 1861–1865* (Cambridge: Cambridge University Press, 1995).

4 Henderson, vol. 2, 205–6.

5 Ibid., 201.

6 Ibid., 604–5.

7 Freeman, *Lee's Lieutenants,* vol. 2, 721; Allan, *Army of Northern Virginia,* 440–41.

8 Johnson and Buel, vol. 2, 621.

9 Dabney, 548–49; Henderson, vol. 2, 212. William Allan (Allan, *Army of Northern Virginia,* 331) gives a somewhat more detailed explanation of Lee's reasoning. He says that Lee intended to draw McClellan away from "his base of supplies and his supports" at Washington. "Lee designed to give battle where, in case of success, the distance of the Federal army from Washington and Baltimore would be too great to admit of its reaching speedy shelter." Lee's aim, Allan says, was "to damage or defeat" McClellan's army, "and for this purpose he desired to draw it as far as possible from Washington." See also *The War of the Rebellion,* vol. 19, part 1, 144–45, and part 2, 590–92; Long, 204; Freeman, *R. E. Lee,* vol. 2, 352–53, and *Lee's Lieutenants,* vol. 2, 168.

10 Dabney, 549.

11 *The War of the Rebellion,* vol. 19, part 1, 65.

12 Dabney, 549.

13 Johnson and Buel, vol. 2, 621n.

14 Ibid., 687–88.

15 Leighton Parks, *Century* magazine 70:2, 255ff.; Freeman, *R. E. Lee,* vol. 2, 355.

16 Henderson, vol. 2, 214; Douglas, 152.

17 Dabney, 551; Johnson and Buel, vol. 2, 623.

18 Johnson and Buel, vol. 2, 603; Bevin Alexander, *How the South Could Have Won,* 150–51; Henderson, vol. 2, 217.

19 Porter Alexander, *Fighting for the Confederacy,* 141; *Southern Historical Society Papers,* vol. 13, 420–21.

20 Peter Paret, ed., *Makers of Modern Strategy* (Princeton, N.J.: Princeton University Press, 1980), 202–3.

21 *The War of the Rebellion,* vol. 19, part 1, 951.

22 Freeman, *R. E. Lee,* vol. 2, 411; Freeman, *Lee's Lieutenants,* vol. 3, 225. Garnet Wolseley, later commander of the British army, reported that Lee told him in October 1862 that he had no more than 35,000 men at Antietam. See Wolseley, 21. In an interview with William Allan at Lexington, Virginia, on February 15, 1868 (Freeman, *Lee's Lieutenants,* vol. 2, 721), Lee said he had about 35,000 men in the battle. See also Porter Alexander, *Military Memoirs,* 244–45. For an analysis of the figures in the battle, see Allan, *Army of Northern Virginia,* 379, 397–98; *The War of the Rebellion,* vol. 19, part 1, 67; Henderson, vol. 2, 242–43. Johnson and Buel, vol. 2, 693, give total Federal strength as 87,164 and Confederate as "less than 40,000." The Army of the Potomac actually counted 94,000 men, but this figure included cooks, teamsters, and other detailed men. In addition, a 6,000-man division of Porter's corps was at Frederick, and marching hard to the battlefield.

23 James Longstreet (Johnson and Buel, vol. 2, 666–67) says that Lee should have retired from Sharpsburg the day he learned that Jackson had captured Harpers Ferry. He adds: "The moral effect of our move into Maryland had been lost by our discomfiture at South Mountain and it was then evident we could not hope to concentrate in time to do more than make a respectable retreat, whereas by retiring before the battle we could have claimed a very successful campaign." Porter Alexander (*Fighting for the Confederacy,* 145–46) calls the decision to stand at Antietam "the greatest military blunder that General Lee ever made." A drawn battle was the best possible outcome one could hope for, he writes. See also Porter Alexander, *Military Memoirs,* 242–49. Major General Sir Frederick Maurice (Maurice, 152) says: "Of all Lee's actions in the war this seems to me to be the most open to criticism. He was only justified in giving battle if retreat was impossible without fighting or if he had a good prospect, not merely of repulsing attacks, but of beating his enemy soundly. . . . The ground he chose for battle, while admirably suited for defense, left him no opportunity for such a counterstroke as Longstreet had delivered at the second battle of Manassas. He could at best hope to beat off the Federals. But at the end of a battle he would be no better off than he was on the morning of 15th [of September]. The

Antietam, the most desperately fought struggle of the war, must be numbered among the unnecessary battles." Major General J. F. C. Fuller (Fuller, *Grant and Lee,* 169) calls Antietam "a totally unnecessary battle," caused, he says, because Lee's "personal pride could not stomach the idea that such an enemy [as McClellan] could drive him out of Maryland."

24 Henderson, vol. 2, 338; Bevin Alexander, *How the South Could Have Won,* 157.

25 Henderson, vol. 2, 338.

26 In a Clausewitzian case of friction in warfare, General McLaws failed to guard a road around the western side of Maryland Heights. This allowed a thousand Union cavalrymen to escape during the night of September 14, 1862. The troopers crossed the pontoon bridge into Maryland and moved northwest, fleeing into Pennsylvania, and capturing forty-five wagons of Longstreet's ordnance train on the way. Colonel Miles could have evacuated a large number of the Union infantry by this same unguarded road if he had shown any initiative. McLaws's failure to post guards on this road illustrates how the mistake of a subordinate can jeopardize even the best-laid plans of an army commander. Lee never gave McLaws any wider responsibilities after this blunder. See Sears, 151; Porter Alexander, *Fighting for the Confederacy,* 144.

27 Stonewall Jackson originally approved Lee's decision to fight at Antietam, but, before the end of the day of the battle, September 17, 1862, he regretted it. His initial approval came when he arrived at Sharpsburg on the morning of September 16, and Lee told him he intended to fend off McClellan's attacks, and Jackson could then swing around the northern flank of the Union army and throw it into retreat. We know this is true because Lee called on Jackson to execute the turning movement before the end of the day of battle. Jackson was unable to carry it out because Lee had selected a battlefield that—because of the course of the Potomac River—offered an open space less than a mile wide between the river and heavily defended Federal positions on the northern or right flank of the Union army. Jackson told General John G. Walker at the end of the day that he was surprised because he supposed the river to be much farther away. "It is a great pity," he told Walker. "We should have driven McClellan into the Potomac." See Johnson and Buel, vol. 2, 679–80. The decision did not represent an acceptance of Jackson's new plan demonstrated at Second Manassas because it was the only time Lee proposed such a flanking attack, and he had not selected the battlefield with this intent in mind. Later in the year he specifically refused a proposal by Jackson to fight a defensive battle on the North Anna River, using the same defend-then-attack tactics of Second Manassas, but on a battlefield specifically selected for this purpose. Lee endorsed a flank attack at Antietam only after he was forced onto the defensive there, not from any conviction that it was a way to win the war. The whole matter is discussed in detail, with confirming references, in Bevin Alexander, *How the South Could Have Won,* 160–61; 298n8.

28 Byron Farwell, *Stonewall: A Biography of General Thomas J. Jackson* (New York: W. W. Norton, 1992), 447.

29 Full details about the conduct of the battle are given in Bevin Alexander, *How the South Could Have Won,* 164–67, *Lost Victories,* 230–54, and *Lee's Civil War,* 93–114.

NOTES

Chapter 9: Hollow Victory

1 Roy P. Basler, *The Collected Works of Abraham Lincoln* (New Brunswick, N.J.: Rutgers University Press, 1953–55), vol. 5, 537; John Hope Franklin, *The Emancipation Proclamation* (Garden City, N.Y.: Doubleday, 1963), 61–62, 66–67.

2 Porter Alexander, *Military Memoirs*, 277; Allan, *Army of Northern Virginia*, 45–52; Sears, 325.

3 Johnson and Buel, vol. 3, 105–6n.

4 Freeman, *R.E. Lee*, vol. 2, 415–17; Porter Alexander, *Military Memoirs*, 278–81; *The War of the Rebellion*, vol. 19, part 2, 625, 629, 640, 656–57, 660, 674, 679, 713, 722.

5 Henderson, vol. 2, 390, quotes Lawley in the June 12, 1863, issue of *The Times* of London.

6 Ibid., 390.

7 Wolseley, 34–36.

8 Ibid., 39–40.

9 Henderson, vol. 2, 283–84.

10 While the course of the Rappahannock River is generally from west to east, the river runs approximately in a southerly direction at Fredericksburg. Therefore, the hills occupied by the Confederates lie along a roughly north-south axis, and they are more or less *west* of the river and the plain lying alongside the river. For clarity, therefore, the actions in this narrative describe the elevations as running north-south and the plain and river as being east of the elevations. Thus Franklin's far left flank facing Stuart's cavalry was on the south, and Sumner's assaults on Marye's Heights were made in a westerly direction.

11 The left and right banks of a river are defined by the direction of the river's flow. In a river flowing in a generally eastward direction, for example, the left bank is on the north and the right bank is on the south.

12 Johnson and Buel, vol. 3, 71.

13 Robertson, 645; Henderson, vol. 2, 384. A day or two later, a letter arrived at Jackson's headquarters, written in the hand of Harriet Irwin: "My own dear father,—As my mother's letter has been cut short by my arrival, I think it but justice that I should continue it. I know that you are rejoiced to hear of my coming, and I hope that God has sent me to radiate your pathway through life. I am a very tiny little thing. I weigh only eight and a half pounds, and Aunt Harriet says I am the express image of my darling papa, and so does our kind friend, Mrs. Osborne, and this greatly delights my mother. My aunts both say I am a little beauty. My hair is dark and long, my eyes are blue, my nose straight just like papa's and my complexion not all red like most young ladies of my age, but a beautiful blending of the lily and the rose. . . . My mother is very comfortable this morning. She is anxious to have my name decided upon, and hopes you will write and give me a name, with your blessing. . . . I was born on Sunday [November 23, 1862], just after the morning services at church. . . . My friends, who are about me like guardian angels, hope for me a long life of happiness and holiness and a futurity of endless bliss." See Robertson, 645.

14 Dabney, 596.

15 Robertson, 649.

16 Dabney, 595; James Longstreet in Johnson and Buel, vol. 3, 71–72; Henderson, vol. 2, 304–5; Porter Alexander, *Military Memoirs*, 287–88.

17 This was by no means some arcane theory. It was a well-known concept. It was precisely what Napoleon Bonaparte intended to do with the Duke of Wellington's British army after the French Marshal Michel Ney stopped the British at Quatre Bras in Belgium on June 16, 1815, during the Waterloo campaign. Wellington was forced to retreat back toward his supplies at Brussels, twenty miles away, on June 17, and Napoleon directed Ney to launch French cavalry to stop this retreat and hold the British until French infantry and guns could come up and force the British to stand. Napoleon expected to destroy Wellington's army in this fashion. But Ney did not send out his cavalry on the morning of June 17, as ordered, and left his infantry and artillery in bivouac until 1:00 P.M. when Napoleon discovered the blunder and set Ney's wing in pursuit. The British thus had a long head start and a violent thunderstorm impeded French movements. This allowed Wellington time to pull up on Mont St. Jean at Waterloo and organize his army for defense, with his supply line back to Brussels secure. This is where the battle of Waterloo was fought on June 18, 1815, resulting in a British and Prussian victory. See Bevin Alexander, *Sun Tzu at Gettysburg* (New York: W. W. Norton, 2011), 54–57.

18 Henderson, vol. 2, 330. Henderson wrote that the position an army occupies to gain a decisive victory has four requirements: (1) it should not be too strong, or the enemy will not attack it; (2) it should give cover to the troops both from view and fire from artillery, and have a good field of fire; (3) it should afford facilities for a counterstroke; and (4) it should offer facilities for pursuit. Henderson said Fredericksburg offered only the first two requirements, whereas the North Anna offered all four. See ibid., 330.

19 Johnson and Buel, vol. 3, 130.

20 Franklin's left grand division on December 13, 1862, actually consisted of 6th Corps with 24,000 men, 1st Corps with 18,500 men, two divisions (David B. Birney's and Daniel E. Sickles's) of 3rd Corps of Hooker's center grand division totaling 10,000 men, one division (William W. Burns's) from 9th Corps of Sumner's right grand division totaling 4,000 men, and George W. Bayard's cavalry brigade, 4,500 men. Sumner had about 27,000 men, comprising his own grand division, less Burns's division from 9th Corps. Hooker's command was about 26,000 men, two divisions of George Stoneman's 3rd Corps having reported to General Franklin. These numbers aggregated 114,000. See Johnson and Buel, vol. 3, 145–46.

21 E. Porter Alexander, *Southern Historical Society Papers*, vol. 10, 384; Whan, 61.

22 Henderson, vol. 2, 309, has a diagram that shows the relative positioning of Lane and Archer, as well as the positions of adjacent Confederate forces and Jackson's artillery.

23 Dabney, 610; Freeman, *Lee's Lieutenants*, vol. 2, 343, 347; *The War of the Rebellion*, vol. 21, 631–33; Allan, *Army of Northern Virginia*, 478–79. In his report on the battle, Jackson drew attention to Hill's blunder.

24 Palfrey, 152–53, 160; Porter Alexander, *Military Memoirs*, 294; Freeman, *R. E. Lee*, vol. 2, 457–60; *The War of the Rebellion*, vol. 21, 70, 90–91; Whan, 54–55, 62.

25 Heros von Borcke, *Memoirs of the Confederate War for Independence* (New York: Peter Smith, 1938), vol. 2, 117.

26 Johnson and Buel, vol. 3, 79.

27 Ibid., 113.

28 Ibid., 81n.

29 Porter Alexander, *Military Memoirs,* 309.

30 Robertson, 663; Henderson, vol. 2, 326.

31 Johnson and Buel, vol. 3, 82.

32 Goodwin, 486.

33 Freeman, *R. E. Lee,* vol. 2, 477.

34 Henderson, vol. 2, 336–37.

35 Goodwin, 514; Johnson and Buel, vol. 3, 216–17, 239–40; Porter Alexander, *Military Memoirs,* 373.

36 Ibid., 332.

Chapter 10: The Fatal Blow

1 Robertson, 675.

2 Ibid., 694–95.

3 Ibid., 695.

4 Abraham Lincoln was more concerned with opposition at home than he was in finding a more suitable commander. The Emancipation Proclamation turned the war into a crusade to free the slaves. This virtually stopped volunteering for the army. Lincoln responded by pushing through Congress a conscription act, which he signed into law on March 3, 1863. The administration used the law to suppress dissent as well. Whenever army provost marshals encountered opposition, they jailed the disaffected person and denied him trial. This caused immense opposition and chilled Democrats who had previously supported the war effort. Democratic Party leadership fell into the hands of persons opposed to Lincoln, especially "Peace Democrats" such as Fernando Wood, a former mayor of New York City, and "Copperheads," especially in the Midwest, who were weary of the bloodshed and ready to end the war by compromise.

5 Henderson, vol. 2, 344–45.

6 Freeman, *R. E. Lee,* vol. 2, 477.

7 Thomas, 272.

8 Freeman, *R. E. Lee,* vol. 2, 478–79, 499–501; Bigelow, 114–19; *The War of the Rebellion,* vol. 21, 1096–97. In March 1863, serious illness struck General Lee. He called it a severe cold, but the symptoms included an elevated pulse rate and pain in his chest, back, and arms. After two weeks in bed, he still felt weak and unsteady, and he never completely recovered. His ailment may have been angina pectoris, caused by atherosclerosis, or gradual constriction of the blood flow through the arteries. The attack was the signal for the onset of cardiovascular problems that resulted in his death from a stroke in 1870.

9 The Orange Plank Road and Orange Turnpike ran as a single road out of Fredericksburg for about five miles to a point just east of Zoan Church, about four and a half miles east of

Chancellorsville. At Zoan the Plank Road arched southwest but rejoined the turnpike at Chancellorsville. The two roads ran together for about two miles to Dowdall's Tavern (also the location of Wilderness Church), where the Plank Road again diverged south and pursued a more southerly course to Orange Court House. Present-day Virginia Route 3 pursues the course of the old turnpike to Wilderness Tavern (two and a half miles west of Dowdall's Tavern), where it becomes Virginia Route 20 and turns southwest to Orange. Virginia Route 610 traces the southerly route of the Plank Road from Zoan to Chancellorsville, and Virginia Route 621 the southerly course of the Plank Road west from Dowdall's Tavern. It rejoins Virginia Route 20 at Verdiersville.

10 Doubleday, 4–5.

11 Porter Alexander, *Fighting for the Confederacy,* 195.

12 Bevin Alexander, *How Wars Are Won* (New York: Crown, 2002), 329–38.

13 Accounts also listed this church as Zion and Zoar. The church was on the turnpike about a mile and a quarter west of the junction of the turnpike and the Orange Plank Road and was immediately west of the entrenchments Anderson and McLaws were constructing on the morning of May 1, 1863. This position also was known as Tabernacle Church, named for the house of worship on the Mine Road, three-quarters of a mile southwest of the turnpike–Plank Road junction. The Mine Road cut across the Plank Road and joined the turnpike a third of a mile east of Zoan Church. The intersection of all three of these roads collectively was known as Zoan Church or Tabernacle Church. They are carried here as Zoan Church.

14 Henderson, vol. 2, 417; Bigelow, 223.

15 Porter Alexander, *Fighting for the Confederacy,* 216.

16 Porter Alexander, *Military Memoirs,* 327; Bigelow, 250–51, *The War of the Rebellion,* vol. 25, part 2, 326, 328.

17 Johnson and Buel, vol. 3, 161; Bigelow, 259.

18 *Southern Historical Society Papers,* vol. 34, 16–17; Freeman, *R. E. Lee,* vol. 2, 521; *Lee's Lieutenants,* vol. 2, 541; Henderson, vol. 2, 429–32. English Major General Sir Frederick Maurice, editor of the papers of Colonel Charles Marshall, an aide-de-camp of Lee, maintains that Lee, not Jackson, came up with the idea of a march around Hooker (see Marshall, 163–70). This is almost certainly incorrect, because the conference between Lee and Jackson was not about *whether* to attack around Hooker's southern flank but about *how* to carry it out. The Confederates had no other option except retreat. It is most probable that Lee's original idea was for a simple flanking movement to dislodge Hooker and force him to retreat. Jackson extended the concept to an assault fully on Hooker's rear, with the intention of destroying his army.

19 Sources for the entire account of the decision on the route of Jackson's march as well as the decision to make it are as follows. Henderson, vol. 2, 429–32 (Henderson's source is a personal letter from Hotchkiss); Dabney, 675–77; Bigelow, 272; Freeman, *Lee's Lieutenants,* vol. 2, 546–47; *R. E. Lee,* vol. 2, 523–24

20 *Southern Historical Society Papers,* vol. 25, 110; Bigelow, 340n. Robert Lewis Dabney writes that Jackson, speaking afterward, "said if he had had an hour more of daylight or had not been wounded, he should have occupied outlets toward Ely's and United States Fords, as

well as those on the west. . . . If he had been able to do so dispersion or capture of Hooker's army would have been certain." See Dabney, 699–700.

21 Johnson and Buel, vol. 3, 198.

22 Henderson, vol. 2, 445–46; Bigelow, 301.

23 Doubleday, 38–39.

24 *The War of the Rebellion,* vol. 25, part 1, 483; Bigelow, 311.

25 Henderson, vol. 2, 449–50; Bigelow, 316.

26 Johnson and Buel, vol. 3, 183.

27 Henderson, vol. 2, 450–54; Dabney, 693–96.

28 Freeman, *R. E. Lee,* vol. 2, 533–35; Bigelow, 342; *The War of the Rebellion,* vol. 25, part 2, 769.

29 Porter Alexander, *Military Memoirs,* 345.

30 Ibid., 359; Dabney, 703.

31 Johnson and Buel, vol. 3, 165–66.

32 Bigelow, 349–51, 354, 355, 361; *The War of the Rebellion,* vol. 25, part 1, 433, 442, 445, 452, 460, 462, 690, 1006.

33 Jay Luvaas, *Napoleon on the Art of War* (New York: Touchstone, 1999), 80. One of Napoleon's most successful and characteristic practices was to concentrate artillery at one point to destroy a part of the enemy front to make a gap for a decisive penetration. He got the idea from the Comte de Guibert's 1772 *Essai général de tactique* and from Chevalier du Teil's 1779 *L'Usage de l'artillerie nouvelle dans la guerre de campagne.* See B. H. Liddell Hart, *The Ghost of Napoleon* (New Haven, Conn.: Yale University Press, 1933), 77.

34 Bigelow, 338.

35 Porter Alexander, *Military Memoirs,* 351–52. Alexander reported that no Federal account mentions this cease-fire. "The flag was probably sent by only a brigade commander," Alexander wrote. "Without referring to his brigade commander, Griffin granted the request, and, still more thoughtlessly, allowed his own men to show themselves while the wounded were being delivered. The enemy, to their great surprise, discovered what a small force was in their front. They lost little time in taking advantage of the information. The action was reopened, and now a charge was made with rush, and the enemy swarmed over our works." Johnson and Buel, vol. 3, 226, contains a graphic picture of the Sunken Road immediately after the Federals seized it. It shows dead Rebels and abandoned rifles and equipment in the trench, and shows clearly the strength of the wall that had stopped Ambrose E. Burnside's attacks on December 13, 1862.

36 Porter Alexander, *Fighting for the Confederacy,* 212–13.

37 Porter Alexander, *Military Memoirs,* 361–62.

38 The narrative of Jackson's sickness, death, and burial is largely drawn from the thorough, detailed account by James I. Robertson Jr. See Robertson, 728–62.

39 Ibid., 754.

40 Ibid., 755.

41 Ibid., 761.

NOTES

Epilogue: The Cause Lost

1 Johnson and Buel, vol. 3, 246–47.

2 Porter Alexander, *Fighting for the Confederacy*, 230.

3 Johnson and Buel, vol. 3, 247. Longstreet wrote: "Our purpose should have been to impair the *morale* of the Federal army and shake Northern confidence in the Federal leaders. We talked on that line from day to day, and General Lee, accepting it as a good military view, adopted it as the keynote of the campaign."

4 The full story of the Gettysburg campaign is given in Bevin Alexander, *R. E. Lee's Civil War,* 169–235; *How the South Could Have Won,* 209–48; *Sun Tzu at Gettysburg,* 108–25.

5 Porter Alexander, *Military Memoirs,* 379–80.

6 Johnson and Buel, vol. 3, 340.

7 Henderson, vol. 2, 344.

INDEX

Page numbers in *italics* indicate maps.

INDEX